CRIME OF PASSION

CRIME OF PASSION

Leo Janos

G. P. Putnam's Sons
New York

Copyright © 1983 by Leo Janos
All rights reserved. This book, or parts thereof,
must not be reproduced in any form without permission.
Published simultaneously in Canada by
General Publishing Co. Limited, Toronto.

Library of Congress Cataloging in Publication Data

Janos, Leo.
  Crime of passion.

  1. Murder—California. 2. King, Geoffrey. 3. Juvenile
delinquents—California—Biography. 4. Narcotic addicts
—California—Biography. 5. Rehabilitation of juvenile
delinquents—California. I. Title.
HV6533.C2J36 1983   364.1'523'0924 [B]   82-21469
ISBN 0-399-12780-1

Printed in the United States of America

7041701

Acknowledgments

Many people contributed to the making of this book. I am particularly grateful to family members and friends who willingly relived recollections that were often painful, and to various staff members of both Atascadero and Camarillo state hospitals, the Los Angeles public defender's office and the office of the district attorney, as well as police and other officials of several departments and jurisdictions involved in this case. I am further indebted to Irv Schwartz and Joy Harris of the Lantz Office, and to Pat Anderson, Jess and Karen Cook, Steve Gelman, Roberta Ashley, Betty Spence, Francis and Joan Delaney, and my editor Ellis Amburn and his able assistant, Roger Scholl, whose various contributions are contained in the pages of this book.

To Bonnie

This is a true account of the first twenty-one years of a young man who killed his mother and grandmother. In several instances, names and identities have been altered at the request of the individuals involved. Reconstructing real human beings is at best an approximation of their unique complexities; but fortunately, Geoffrey King's recollections of his family and childhood experiences were uncommonly vivid, including a startling ability to recall whole conversations and an unusually perceptive insight into the personas of his family. In those very few instances where circumstances make it impossible for there to be any witnesses to conversations, I created them from the best judgments of those who intimately knew the participants. Despite sharp, painful memories, there was never a discrepancy between Geoffrey's version of events and those of others, so that while this book is based largely on his perceptions and point of view, the author is satisfied that it is a faithful rendering of the life of a troubled boy and his equally troubled family.

If youth did not matter so much to itself,
it would never have the heart to go on.
—Willa Cather

I

Tears wept on enemy graves are
often peculiarly sincere; we weep
our now homeless energy.
    —John Fowles,
     The Aristos

Prologue

The Day the World Ended

Geoffrey King ran for his life, knowing he was finished, one way or another, in a footrace he must lose. Ahead in the darkness loomed a thicket of trees—his escape from a furious pursuer. He was stoned out of his mind, but the chase was real. Kicking off his shoes, Geoffrey ran blindly, his white socks pounding on the asphalt of the deserted parking lot. There was no noise except his own motion, yet he knew the football player was right behind him. Geoffrey could picture him running, head down, his arms and legs pumping like powerful pistons, struggling to reach him before those trees and hurl himself in a desperation tackle to stop him.

Twenty yards to go. Suddenly Geoffrey leaped into a tangle of brush and was swallowed by a greater darkness. Terror owns its own clock, and Geoffrey quickly lost track of time or distance as he thrashed through the dry brush of the Pasadena hillside. He was running now, not sprinting, still gripped by fear, sensing invisible tree trunks, his shoulders scraping against their rough bark. The idea that he was safe never dawned until he heard a distant bellowing shout.

"Keys!" Then he knew. He grinned at the football player's frustrated outrage and became aware of small metal teeth biting into his clenched fist. Keys! For a moment he thought he was clutching his own, but then he remembered why he was running. He must have passed out in the front seat while the guy was driving him to his car, because when he awoke . . . "You're in no shape to drive home, friend," the football player had observed, slipping his arm around Geoffrey's shoulder, locking him into a vise as he began to nuzzle him. Geoffrey's elbow speared into his face, knocking the football player backward with a gasp so that he lunged too late to keep his keys in the ignition and his prisoner in the parked Ford, ripping Geoffrey's silk shirt as Geoffrey leaped from the car.

"Kiss my ass," Geoffrey shouted into the darkness, and hurled the football player's keys far in front of himself. Then he began to run again. When next aware of where he was, he was loping in steady strides across an open field. He breathed rhythmically through his nose, feeling strong, determined to keep on running beyond this lifetime into another. Salt burned his eyes and he shook his head to ease a painful crick, but otherwise he felt exhilarated; because he was so stoned, he credited his irresoluble strength to bursts of cosmic energy. He was uncatchable, unstoppable. Free.

It was reckless to leave his own car at the first party and drive off with a group he didn't know to another party on the other side of Pasadena. Without his car he was trapped, at the mercy of others. He knew better, but this particular night he didn't give a damn. His friend had warned him against the LSD stored in an ice tray. "I've tried some and it's very peculiar," he was told. "I should've flushed it down the john." Geoffrey was in no mood to listen. He swallowed it on the spot and then sped off in his VW Beetle to party in Pasadena, some fifty miles away. Actually, he didn't want to party at all: he wanted to see his close friend Bud, get stoned, and disgorge some of his problems. "Bud, I'm at the end of my rope. I got fired today. I'm finished. At seventeen, I've hit the bottom. I'm drowning, Bud." But Bud wanted to party, and Geoffrey, sulking, tagged along, stoking up on a pint of bourbon and chain-smoking endless joints of marijuana, until the bad acid chain-reacted and, for the first time ever, he experienced frightening hallucinations: the other teenagers began to melt in front of his overly bright eyes, and he staggered outside onto the patio to get away from the rock music and noisy chatter. The football player followed him out, saw he was unwell, and offered to drive him to his car. "I want Bud to drive me," Geoffrey mumbled, but Bud was already too high to drive safely. The football player was in training.

Geoffrey King crossed a field and saw a high-security chain-link fence blocking his path. What more can happen? he wondered. There was no retreat from this night. The security fence irritated him; he was in no mood to be stopped. He began hoisting himself up, surprised at his agility. On top, the fence was laced with strands of barbed wire, which he gripped indifferently even as he tore his jeans. He shimmied down the other side and dropped the remaining few feet into the glare of floodlights. Blinded, for a moment he hesitated. Then he laughed aloud in surprise and ran across the tarmac, a bare-chested, dazed trespasser, covered with sweat and drying blood from dozens of scratches, resembling a savage from the bush. He grinned as he approached the gleaming machine. He touched it admiringly and climbed the rungs up its cold, smooth side, thinking: I'll put it down right in my own backyard. All he had to do was follow the freeways home to Palos Verdes. He chuckled, visualizing his mother's reaction, as he opened the Plexiglas hatch and climbed into the cockpit of a Bell helicopter.

1

Ruth King returned home around midnight and heated the teakettle. She had just started a new job as hostess in a chic French restaurant. The house was quiet, and on the blackboard next to the refrigerator her mother had scrawled a message: "G called at 6. Won't be home this weekend." The message was strange because her son seldom informed her when he would or would not be coming home—a fact that heightened the household's tension. If they knew when to expect him, they could brace themselves for the onslaught. This current crisis with Geoffrey was now in its sixth week. He was often incoherent, tipped off balance by an internal mechanism clearly out of control. Geoffrey had always been unpredictable and melodramatic, and Ruth had a long history of problems with her brilliant, excessive son. He seemed desperate, running wild, erupting often without provocation to the edge of violence. She pleaded with him to sit down to talk to her, but he closed her out. Sometimes he locked himself in his room, throwing things at the door when she knocked. She tried to placate him and grew angry whenever Eleanor, her mother— who, despite her own alarm, could not keep her mouth shut— tried to lecture him into rationality.

"Geoffrey, what do you plan to do with your life?"

"Dunno. You think about it and let me know."

Ruth often greeted him at the door with a drink and served him a candlelit dinner when he came home from his job with Laurence Harvey. She even gave him money they could ill-afford to decorate the duplex when they moved in. But her son was beyond such appeasement, even though decorating was his passionate vocation and her compliments were genuine.

"Well, it doesn't look lovely to me," he responded. "I don't want to live here."

The squall began over the issue of his moving out, shortly before the lease expired on the large house which his mother had rented the year before. He wanted to move into Beverly Hills and be closer to his two-hundred-a-week job and friends. The daily commute was an hour each way. "You're too young," Ruth insisted. "Maybe next year. Drop the subject, because that's that, Geoffrey."

In the end, he surrendered, as they both knew he would—but she began to suspect that somehow he equated this defeat with a flaw or weakness in himself. The battle was fierce, draining them both. At one point Ruth had actually begged him on her knees to stay.

"I need you," she sobbed. "Don't you care how alone I am?"

He knelt beside her and began to cry too.

"I know, Mother, I know. But you've got to understand that my only chance is to get out of here and be on my own. Can't you see that? I love you, Mother, but I can't let you pull me down."

Ruth, slouching under seventy pounds of excess weight, was often mistaken for his grandmother. Her appearance embarrassed him. But shortly after his father's death, when she declared her intention of uprooting him from Santa Monica and moving forty miles down the coast to Palos Verdes, an affluent coastal community, her son cheered the idea. Several close friends lived in retirement in Palos Verdes, and his mother had paid her dues being married thirty-three years to Robert Luther King.

Geoffrey would never understand the mysterious pullings and tuggings that had existed between his unhappy parents. All he ever wanted from them was affection, a sense of security, but theirs was a household without a single compelling idea of why they lived together. His parents coexisted as if punching a factory time clock, showing no curiosity about each other or their son. Bob King used his family as a tool toward economic advancement. Each had assigned roles to play: Ruth was the charming, unflappable hostess; Geoffrey, the polite, well-mannered young adult—quality possessions like a Gucci briefcase. Over the years they entertained an army of strangers in a succession of homes that kept pace with King's rising career. It was a life of pretense, but only Geoffrey rebelled. His parents labeled him a problem child. Then everything fell apart.

From the moment of his father's death, Geoffrey lived mostly outside the house, doing as he pleased. Ruth felt that being unfettered was the cure for her son's simmering hostility. On the day that Bob King died, she released Geoffrey from a psychiatric hospital, where he had been living as if in a transient hotel—the doctors insisting he was better off there than at home, in constant battle with his father. He actually matriculated from the ward to his freshman class at Santa Monica High School, and his first request to his mother upon his father's death was that she allow him to drop out of school for a while—he needed time to catch his breath. Ruth agreed reluctantly; she was apprehensive about her unstable son running loose at the height of the sixties, a time that turned L.A.'s beaches and parks, and particularly the Sunset Strip, into a promenade of half-naked kids and drug users.

Often Geoffrey stayed out all night and was uncommunicative about where he had been, but she saw his life in revealing bits and pieces and was alternately shocked and bemused. In Santa Monica, he and other teenage friends used the house as a staging area to paint themselves and dye their hair, emerging like bangled savages to go dancing or to rock concerts. At one point he had Ruth sign a release form, because he was a minor, to enable him to be hired as a fashion model in magazine ads. But shortly after the move to Palos Verdes, he seemed to settle down. He got a job that thrilled him, working for actor Laurence Harvey in his antique shop. Reports reaching her indicated that Geoffrey was now part of the actor's entourage, driving around Beverly Hills in one of his Bentleys, attending film screenings at his mansion, where he met other famous stars. With his dark eyes and strong white teeth, her son was stunningly handsome and used most of his salary to buy expensive mod clothes.

But from the moment they moved into the duplex, Geoffrey

seemed dazed, as if sideswiped by a wayward truck. He complained about the pressures of living half a dozen different lives simultaneously. "I'm fed up with this fucking life and this fucking house," he shouted. He was drinking openly and heavily at home, an awful mixture of bourbon and Coca-Cola. His hands shook holding the glass. On one of the worst nights, he returned home with a group of Palos Verdes kids, all of them obviously high on drugs, and when Ruth told them to quiet down, her son cursed at her so vilely that even his friends were embarrassed. Then in the midst of a minor argument about taking out the garbage, Geoffrey slapped her hard. He ran from the house and later returned in tears. "Mother, I'm going insane and I don't have the strength to fight it. I'm so confused . . . I'm drowning." She put him to bed and sat with him until he fell asleep. Clearly he was out of control; her mother was so terrified that she locked the bedroom door. A few nights later, Ruth began locking her door, too.

During the last week in August he announced that he had quit his job with Laurence Harvey. "I can't handle it," he sighed, and left the house. He was gone three days, and when he returned, he seemed pale and wasted, as if bled dry, stumbled into bed, and slept seventy-two hours. "We've got to do something," her mother warned her. "That boy is a ticking bomb."

With her brother Raymond, Ruth sought the guidance of Municipal Court Judge Tom Hemmings, her occasional Palos Verdes bridge partner. She listened on the patio while Ray did most of the talking. "My nephew," Ray Lowe said, "is obviously on drugs and dangerously out of control. My sister can't handle it: she's scared to death of him and we've reached a point where her safety and my mother's are at stake."

Judge Hemmings sighed. He knew the family's financial plight and the high cost of decent private care. "If you knew for certain that he was addicted to drugs, we could perhaps place him in some sort of rehabilitation program," the judge said. "Otherwise, if you seek to have him committed for his own safety and yours, you face a sanity hearing before juvenile authorities. I'm not even certain the state would take him unless he did something to warrant incarceration, because, face it, these institutions are very overcrowded. Are you certain, Ruth, that you want to go through the ordeal of a sanity hearing?"

Ruth broke down and wept. She knew that if Geoffrey were forced into a mental hospital for the second time in his young life he would be lost to her forever. Yet it was agonizing to live with a son she now feared. She needed time to think.

Ruth poured herself a steaming cup of tea, spooned cottage cheese into a dish, and carried a tray upstairs to her bedroom, determined to confront Geoffrey on his drug use the moment he returned home on Monday or whenever. If drugs were the problem, she would put a stop to it somehow.

Two weeks earlier, Ruth had finally picked herself up and taken a job at a restaurant. "Penury" was her explanation; they were practically broke. They were living off King's modest estate, and when they had moved to Palos Verdes a year ago, Geoffrey tried to dissuade her from signing a lease on a two-thousand-dollar-a-month rental, but she insisted because the pool was especially lovely. "I'm going to get myself into shape," she promised. "Do a lot of swimming, play a lot of bridge, and just catch my breath. Then I'm going to go out and find myself a good job." And she also insisted on inviting her mother to move in with them. Geoffrey was opposed. He had especially loved Gram from childhood, but she was now a cantankerous, disruptive invalid—more than either of them could handle. Ruth was adamant: "Your Uncle Ray has had her for years, and now that he's having hard times, it's my turn."

Soon, however, Ruth King acknowledged the futility of her hopes by collapsing like an eroded sea cliff. She sat alone drinking endless rounds of bourbon, ignoring her mother's scoldings, trying to recall who she had once been, inconsolable at her losses. Life with Robert King had ruined her. Geoffrey spent the year nursing and cajoling her. The only friends she saw were those he called and invited over, after forcing her to wash her hair and put on a dress. He also used shock: resenting how she sat most days, staring dully at TV game shows with a drink in her hand, he drew back the drapes and shouted, "Look, Mother, the sun is still shining and another day has passed you by." The only time she used the pool was when he shoved her in one day in her clothes. "You said you wanted to swim. Well, swim."

Well, Ruth felt she was finally swimming. Having a job for the first time since she was a teenager invigorated her with a new sense of pride. Her year-long depression was definitely over, and her principal resolves were to shape up herself by losing at least fifty pounds and be uncompromising in shaping up Geoffrey by eliminating his use of drugs. Before going to bed this night she would thoroughly search her son's room for suspicious pills or tablets. "Drugs are out," she planned to tell Geoffrey. "No arguments."

Ruth had barely kicked off her shoes and settled onto the bed when the phone rang. The caller was a desk sergeant from the Pasadena police, and she listened to him disbelievingly, as if she had tuned to a police melodrama on TV. He was curt reporting the facts, but she heard an insinuation of blame in his voice, a gruff edge accusing her of neglect and permissiveness that caused kids like her son to run wild. "I'll have to call you back," Ruth told the officer, because she felt dizzy with shock and dismay. She hung up and began to dial her brother's house, but sat numbed, trying to remember the number, and was finally forced to look it up. She was crying when Raymond answered. She told him that Geoffrey was under arrest in a Pasadena jail. What he had done was so far beyond belief that even Raymond was speechless for several moments. Geoffrey had climbed a security fence onto the grounds of the Jet Propulsion Laboratories in Pasadena and attempted to steal a government helicopter. He had actually started the engines before he was discovered. Apparently he could not get the chopper to lift off, and instead stole the pickup truck of a worker who had spotted him and ran to get help. Geoffrey smashed the truck through a gate barrier and roared down the freeway, overturning the truck at an off-ramp. He was dazed but uninjured. Incoherent on drugs. The police officer had used the word "deranged" to describe his condition.

"Well, Ruthie, this is it," her brother sighed. "I think he's burned his final bridge. We have what we need to put him away, and we'll just let him stay in jail until there's a court hearing on the case. He's obviously over the edge. Now, listen, you've got to stay strong. This is our chance."

"Ray," she sobbed, "I can't."

2

The Kings were childless nearly into middle age because Ruth suffered from an ovarian-tube blockage that doctors did not discover how to repair until after the war. But not long after moving from Indianapolis to Kansas City, their marriage began to dip, as was so often the case whenever Bob was dissatisfied with work. He was the personnel man for Kansas City Power and Light, and claimed that a jealous cabal was keeping him from becoming a vice-president. He relapsed into cold indifference at home, whereas Ruth, remembering how proud and appreciative he was during their courtship and his compliments about her glowing beauty, followed instructions about how to improve the chances for conception. She became pregnant—but there was no magic. His ambivalence at the news was obvious. Her pregnancy added fifty pounds to her figure and caused her ankles to swell, giving her incessant backaches, constant nausea, a sluggish, crabby disposition, and forcing her to spend most of a hot summer in bed. Her face became puffed, and mysterious red and purple blotches appeared, and Geoffrey's restlessness inside her kept her awake, depriving her husband of a usually patient wife. Bob King began going to dinner parties without his wife, using the excuse that Ruth was under the weather, although she knew he was ashamed of how she looked. They stopped entertaining, their home unusually quiet and empty, as if a sign had been posted: CLOSED FOR PARTURITION. King disappeared on long business trips, causing fresh tensions. Long before the baby's due date, Ruth was muttering, "Who needed this?" At birth the doctors on duty were almost forced to choose between Geoffrey's life and his mother's, until Robert King arrived and set them straight. "Save my wife," he demanded.

Ruth was hemorrhaging and vomiting. Her blood pressure plummeted and she was rushed to surgery, where the doctor had to perform a cesarean. And so, two weeks early, Geoffrey King was born—a six-pound, two-ounce boy with flailing, tiny fists.

"Happy birthday, dear," Ruth whispered to her husband. Bob King was thirty-nine this day. "Is she pretty?" she asked.

The baby was nestled in her arms, but King was so determined to have an adorable girl that in Ruth's postoperative confusion it never occurred to her that she could have failed to deliver what he wanted. Especially on his birthday.

It was months before Ruth was back on her feet in a household that had become uncharacteristically topsy-turvy. By then King was so disgusted that he barely looked at his son.

"My son brought us grief from the day he was born," King would often complain in later years. He was not a man to shed a grudge easily, and he meant what he said whenever he complained that having a child was Ruth's idea and that he never, ever had wanted a son.

3

SEPTEMBER 6, 1969

The hallucination was frighteningly real. No film could compete with the blinding lights, the trumpets and seraphim in his jail cell—a kitsch Technicolor extravaganza, transforming the steel and concrete into a giant chessboard suspended between heaven and hell. First, Geoffrey, still hallucinating from the LSD, had been assailed by the most unwelcome visitor imaginable—his dead father—whose voice, chillingly vivid, set in motion all that was to follow. King was still doing personnel work, this time for the Ultimate Chairman of the Board, searching for a human hero to contest Lucifer for the soul of mankind.

"Where are you?" Geoffrey had whispered.

"In heaven," King replied.

"Like hell," his son muttered.

But the proof followed as radiant light blazed through the thick walls and the Lord of Hosts Himself explained the ground rules for the struggle between the youthful contestant and the wily Evil One. The contest would be waged as a dance, and here God demonstrated sublime sagacity because Geoffrey was a spectacular dancer, so good that he and a group of friends often appeared as the floor show at rock-'n'-roll dance clubs on the Sunset Strip. But this dance was as precise and defined as the Ten Commandments, and if Geoffrey lapsed or lost concentration, important points would be lost. God ordered him to begin by standing on one foot and holding his breath (he did so until he collapsed), and then to begin dancing in ways that may have seemed inexplicable, but actually were highly significant despite the jerking moves and gestures. He needed to concentrate all of his powers while the devil's imps heckled and harassed him, causing him to make errors and lose vital points. Only God knew how long he danced, although sometime during that long night he saw his mother's face appear in the thick glass window of the steel cell door, and he danced carefully toward her.

"Mother," he shouted in panic, "something very terrible is happening to the world right now."

For most of her life, Eleanor Lowe had been an unusually handsome woman, buxom and forceful, who spoke her mind in simple declarative sentences. She had lived long and seen much. An aristocratic dowager by temperament, she had been forced by her late husband's meager estate to spend the past fifteen years living with her children, usually six months at a time. But after a number of years the situation in the King household had so deteriorated that Eleanor decided to stay with Ray and his wife in New York. Now Ray had decided to move to L.A. so his actress wife could be closer to her work. He was in worse financial shape, if possible, than Ruth, and had moved into a tiny North Hollywood apartment with no extra bedroom. Eleanor, as a result, moved back in with Ruth and her son Geoffrey in the summer of 1969.

Eleanor was dismayed and appalled at the lack of resilience in both Ray (her favorite) and Ruth, who chipped and cracked at life's rough handling like delicate Wedgwood. She thought she had raised them to be made of sterner stuff, but their failed courage broke her heart, already crippled by advanced arteriosclerosis. Enduring constant angina attacks, Eleanor sat silently beneath a lap robe with the shriveled, dried-apple look of a failing invalid, little more than a helpless spectator to her family's ordeals. "Old age is not for sissies," she wrote to her younger sister in Cleveland. "I have no more strength, no more tears, no more words. God's curse is that my eyes can still see."

Both of her children had failed her. Ray, whose career as an advertising executive was once as bright as a freshly minted coin, had lost his job and was now unemployed. Ruth, always weak and cloaked in despair, had lived a self-fulfilling prophecy of failure. She had botched everything, this sweet, gifted girl, by attaching herself to a husband who dragged her into the pits. Over the years, Eleanor devoted her energies to trying to salvage her grandson from the family wreckage. That King (the Lowe family called Bob by his last name—a twit to his egotism, which Ruth's husband enjoyed nevertheless) would be a terrible father didn't surprise her; but that Ruth would be such a vacillating, often indifferent mother choked Eleanor with indignation. Ruth was the product of a home crowned with love and devotion by parents who placed their children's welfare ahead of their own. How could Ruth turn her back on these implanted values—the Lowe legacy of love and pride?

"Don't you understand, Ruthie," Eleanor had argued, "if you fail to raise Geoffrey properly, you've failed in your life. Your child is the measure of your own worth as a human being. Ruth, he's your mission on earth."

"Oh, Mother, stop it!" Ruth invariably replied to such scoldings. "What do you want from me? Can't you see I've got my hands full? What does everyone want from me? My God!"

Eleanor watched her grandson evolve from a bright, promising child into one of those incurable brats, simultaneously spoiled and neglected. He was so sensitive, so hurt . . . so hungry for affection and attention that she became his tireless ombudsman to his parents, particularly his father, who deeply resented her intrusions. "I can assure you," King snapped, "that my son is not Oliver Twist." Geoffrey's problem, he claimed, was his mother's lack of supervision and discipline. "Ruth lets him have his way so much that he doesn't know what he wants. Believe me, he's already received a thousand times more of everything than I ever got."

Desperate children are neither pleasant nor easy to be around, yet Eleanor never lost her pity for Geoffrey, even as she frequently lost her temper. She was as hurt and bewildered over his neglect as he was. But the Kings insisted on living as if they were childless, caught up in King's grandiose designs for success.

"What has become of your basic values?" Eleanor chided them, but her voice was lost in the endless rooms in a succession of big luxurious houses King leased over the years.

Oh, she had seen plenty! The worst, perhaps, was when Ruth finally separated from King after enduring a nightmare of abuse, only to rush back to him, leaving Eleanor in charge of her hysterical son, who loathed and feared his father beyond the parameters of sanity. Geoffrey took out his hostility on his grandmother, and from that point, the Geoffrey Eleanor loved and sought to protect ceased to exist.

Yet she treasured her memories of what Geoffrey might have become, if given a chance. Her favorite anecdote concerned a summer visit by her grandson when he was twelve. King was then still seemingly in control of a lucrative career and Geoffrey was groomed to act as a young scion. He arrived in Manhattan with a busload of California teenagers touring the country, and for a night on the town with Eleanor, he rented a limousine, used his father's broker for front-row-center tickets to a Broadway show, then treated his Gram to a late-night supper at a famous New York restaurant. He was tanned, tailored, and charming, but their reservations weren't honored, and after a long wait they were seated at a humiliating table next to the washrooms. The waiter was insolent; Geoffrey's *filet de boeuf braisé Prince Albert* was dry as treated hide; Eleanor's Dover sole retained the chill of the North Atlantic. Geoffrey fumed, and when the check was deposited ceremoniously on a silver tray, he turned deathly pale. Suddenly Eleanor saw her grandson stand up and tap a knife against his water glass for attention. The noisy restaurant became silent as the maître d' ran to their table.

"You have taken advantage of me all evening," Geoffrey declared calmly but firmly. "My grandmother and I were forced to wait forty minutes for a miserable table even though our reservations were made weeks ago. The food was terrible, the service even worse. Now I've been handed a bill for one hundred and sixty dollars. I will not pay it. My grandmother will not pay it. You can call my father in California, but I'm sure he won't pay it either."

Then Geoffrey placed Eleanor's blue fox stole around her shoulders, took her arm in his, and they marched out in regal dignity that brought them an admiring round of applause from the stunned diners.

But now she was deathly afraid of this boy. As much as she pitied him, she feared him more; the idea of being alone with him in the apartment caused ominous constrictions in her chest. Ruth was maddeningly myopic to her son's hateful stares and incapable of forceful action, so Eleanor turned to her son, Raymond, for help and begged him to intervene. But he, too, lacked courage to be decisive, so she was trapped there, not wanting to live with Ruth at all, but with nowhere else to go. She cried her fears in front of family friends; they sympathized. Her own doctor tried to humor her when she told him she would not survive another month of such tension, even if her lunatic grandson didn't murder her in her sleep. She was furious at everyone who refused to become involved in what she and they saw so clearly.

"There's going to be a tragedy here one of these days," she warned. The men looked away and changed the subject.

Now, seated stoically in front of the TV set in the living room, Eleanor awaited Geoffrey's arrival home from his night in jail. She begged Ruth, pleaded with her to leave him there, because if Ruth stood firm, Geoffrey could be sent away to get needed help. But Ruth wouldn't hear of it, even though she had returned home without him after a predawn trip to Pasadena. Ruth didn't say much, but Eleanor could tell that what she had seen out there had been terrible. By noon the police called again, this time to report that Geoffrey was quiet and could be picked up anytime. He was a juvenile and could not be held for stealing a truck if his mother wanted him to come home.

"What are you going to do with him when you get him back?" Eleanor demanded to know.

"He needs my help and my love," Ruth replied.

"My God, Ruth, that child is beyond mothering. Can't you see that? Face the truth for once."

Ruth flushed with anger. "Mother," she replied, "you should know better than anyone why I can't do what you want. That boy has suffered enough at the hands of doctors. I'm going to get him off those damned drugs and clean him up. I feel stronger now and I know I can do it. You'll see. I won't have it any other way, Mother, and that's that."

Eleanor reported this conversation by phone to her son and urged Raymond to talk some sense into his sister; but in the end, he became so disgusted with Ruth's stubbornness that he refused her request to accompany her to Pasadena and fetch Geoffrey home. Instead, she dragooned a stocky civil engineer named Mike Phillips, who lived nearby.

"Geoffrey needs my help and he's going to have it," Ruth repeated as she departed for Pasadena. Eleanor was so despondent that she just closed her eyes and turned away.

4

Geoffrey locked his bedroom door and sat down wearily on his big brass bed, his proudest possession, purchased at a bargain price from a decorator friend. The day was thick and hot; but inside the duplex, the drapes were drawn and it was dark and cool. Alone in the backseat, he hadn't said much during the long drive home. Mother's friend was so nervous having Geoffrey in the car that he missed the freeway entrance. Geoffrey didn't blame the guy: he knew how he looked and acted.

"The worst night of my life," he had told Ruth, "but those bastard cops just let me suffer. Why didn't they give me some Thorazine?"

"What's that?" Ruth asked, but Geoffrey didn't answer; instead, he gazed fixedly at the rolling, sun-baked hills of late summer, realizing suddenly that this parched deadness was a certain indication that he had lost the battle with Lucifer. He began to tremble so violently that his mother had to light his endless succession of half-smoked cigarettes. The LSD was still dancing in his skull.

But, locked in his own room, he thought that maybe he would be safe from harm. He was filthy; he stank. His jeans were torn and ripped, his shoes, shirt, and socks long gone. His hands were cut from the barbed wire, his arms and body torn from dozens of scratches during his dash through the woods. He was beyond exhaustion, but tense and highly wired, his mind swirling with the memories of the previous night's vivid adventures, although clouded with an uncertainty about whether or not he had hallucinated everything. He remembered his overwhelming elation when he flipped a switch causing the helicopter's rotor blades to whir directly above his head. He recalled the look of terror on the face of the worker who drove up in his truck and dashed to a phone to call for help—and his own terror at stealing the man's truck and blasting it through a guard barrier in escape. Climbing out of the overturned truck, he remembered wondering if he wasn't actually dead and hadn't become his ghostly, troubled soul departing his crushed body.

A couple had stopped, only because he had darted directly in front of their Oldsmobile and begged them to take him to a police station. The grim driver reluctantly agreed, but then turned angrily on his wife, who seemed genuinely concerned and sympathetic. "Leave him be," the man shouted; "he's all right." He remembered the kindly police officer who told him: "Just do what you're told and everything will be fine." It was so exactly what he wanted to hear said that he began to cry in gratitude, until they locked him alone in that dark, frightening cell. He pounded on the steel door, begging not to be left alone, but he was ignored. The hallucinations were a torment, but so real, so vivid, so encompassing, that nobody would ever be able to convince him that everything he had seen, suffered, and experienced had not actually happened. It was all there, every significant moment of it, right beneath the conscious surface of his mind, like a secret he could not share, a secret that transformed his life forever.

Mike Phillips knocked on Geoffrey's bedroom door. "Everything okay in there?" he called out. "Are you hungry? Why don't you come downstairs for a while?"

Son of a bitch! Lucifer was still on the prowl! Another ploy meant to catch Geoffrey off-guard because both combatants knew what would happen if he foolishly dared to open his door.

He was too frightened to reply.

It was after five when Ruth called her brother to report that Geoffrey was safe at home, now upstairs and probably asleep, and that she was going to take Phillips home. "I'm going to fix a light supper and then go to bed myself," she said. "I've called the restaurant and they've given me the night off. Mother and I are simply exhausted. Why don't you plan on coming to dinner tomorrow, and then we can talk things over?"

"Maybe," Raymond Lowe said. He was annoyed by the triumphant note in his sister's voice, the I-told-you-so chord vibrating as she described her contented, sleeping lamb of a son.

Ruth knocked quietly at Geoffrey's door and whispered his name; when he heard his mother's voice, Geoffrey sprang from his bed and unlocked the door, cautiously peeking out.

"I'm going to drive Mike Phillips home," Ruth said. "Why don't you go downstairs and keep Gram company?"

Staring into her soft eyes, he saw her register curiosity, pity, and then a hardening resolve.

"Do you need anything?" she asked.

He shook his head, though there was something; but he forgot what it was even as she turned away and left. He closed the door and returned to his bed before noticing the unlit cigarette in his hand. That was it! He wanted Ruth to light his cigarette because Lucifer was sabotaging Geoffrey's desires—he couldn't get his lighter to work.

"Well, don't dawdle," he heard his grandmother call out just as the front door closed downstairs.

Eleanor was very nervous when Ruth left, and decided to delay making herself a cup of tea until her daughter returned. She sat quietly on the living-room sofa, a sweater draped over her shoulders, her fingers playing with the edges of the warm afghan blanket tucked around her waist. She didn't turn when

33

she heard Geoffrey clomping down the staircase.

Her bare-chested, barefoot grandson came to her solemnly with an unlit cigarette in his hand. Eleanor forced a smile, looking up at him, and agreed to his request, as much as she detested smoking. She took the cigarette from his shaking hand, placed it to her lips, and with her own trembling hand ignited the lighter, blew smoke from her mouth, and handed the cigarette back to him, fanning the air in front of her face. Geoffrey began pacing while inhaling deeply.

"Are you all right?" she asked him.

His nostrils flared. "Do I look all right?" he countered.

"What happened?"

He shrugged and threw himself into a chair.

"Well, whatever happened, just know that we love you."

"Who cares anymore whether you do or you don't?" he replied, and sat down near her. "There's not much left for me to care about, is there? I mean, you still have eyes in your head. You can see that I've had it. I'm finished. It's all over."

His free hand fanned across his eyes as he sat slumped dejectedly in a high-backed chair he had recently had reupholstered. He seemed close to tears.

"Don't get upset," Eleanor said softly.

"Oh, of course not," he said sarcastically, and bouncing out of the chair, began pacing again in a parody of distress, when he suddenly paused and flopped down in his chair and rubbed his eyes wearily.

"I was arrested," he said. "I stole a truck or something. I'm in terrible trouble. I think they're going to send me to jail for this. I've no future at all. Nothing to look forward to, and I'm only seventeen. How did this happen to me? I've been pushed into this crazy corner from the day I was born. Oh, Gram, you used to be my best friend. Why did you let them do this to me?"

His eyes filled with tears as his grandmother patted the soft cushion next to her with the palm of her hand. "Come," she said. "Sit down next to me."

He ignored her. "They systematically destroyed me, didn't they? But why? I'll never understand why. I was the only one in this family who really cared, the only one who wanted us to be a real family."

"True," Eleanor agreed.

"They accused me of wanting the moon and stars, but that was plain bullshit, Gram, absolute fucking bullshit. All I ever wanted from them was love. Was that asking so much? I just wanted my parents to love me. My God, how different it would've been around here if only . . . If only, if only, if only. We came so close at times, but lost by a hundred miles, and it's all too late. Look what I've become. Just look at me. The only thing left for me is a padded cell."

Suddenly he bolted out of his chair and ran toward the window, parting the drapes cautiously.

"What's the matter?" Eleanor asked, trying to hide her alarm.

"You hear that?" he said, cocking his head in perplexity. "The bastards! They're sucking the air from this room. Can't you feel it? Don't you hear their vacuum machine?"

"I'm sure they're not," his grandmother said kindly. "You're just exhausted. Please, sit down and rest for a while."

"The point is," he said, "none of you ever wanted to deal with me except on your own terms. I was expected to be the perfect young man, and none of you cared who I really was. Dammit, I'm a human being, not some goddamn puppet on a string!"

One moment he stood before her blazing in anger; in the next, he seemed to shudder, turned wearily, and ran off in the direction of the kitchen.

Now what? Eleanor wondered and sat erect. Then she heard the engine of Ruth's car as it entered the garage outside the kitchen door.

But Geoffrey heard something different: a commotion, a murmuring angry horde headed for the house in an ultimate showdown that would test his courage.

Ruth King, wearing a green-and-orange dress and orange shoes, hesitated a moment in the kitchen doorway while she dropped her keys into her straw purse. Then she looked up. "Oh, no," she exclaimed, half to herself, as if she had locked herself out without a key.

Geoffrey, framed in the doorway less than three feet away, was bare-chested and trembling violently, his face a dead mask lost to her. Ruth saw him wielding a twelve-inch bread knife— the blade pointing at her from above his head. Both hands were squeezed around the brown wooden handle. The knife was

part of an eight-piece cutlery set friends had given her last
Christmas, which she kept on the counter next to the sink. Ruth
King stared at her son disbelievingly. Then she turned to flee.

Geoffrey grabbed her by the shoulder and pulled her toward
him as if meaning to embrace her. His strength surprised her;
his right hand above her still gripped the bread knife. Too
frightened to speak, Ruth desperately sought eye contact, hoping to bring her son to his senses, but his glazed pupils appeared unfocused. With his free arm he pulled her forward
until their bodies met. It was hopeless to try to wriggle from his
embrace. Her son felt the heat of her body as he plunged the
knife into his mother's back.

Ruth slumped, but Geoffrey held her fast, and in wild ferocity plunged the knife repeatedly until her weight began pushing him backward and he finally yielded to her insistence to be
free of him. He stepped away and let her fall.

In defending himself against the overwhelming danger surrounding him, Geoffrey had reacted with righteous anger. He
had seen, felt, heard nothing—neither sound, nor scream, nor
struggle. When he finally noticed a stout woman lying in the
doorway, steeped in her own blood, he stared down indifferently, as if glancing at an unimaginative piece of abstract
sculpture.

The killing of his mother had taken less than twenty seconds.

Eleanor Lowe heard an unsettling noise in the kitchen—a
thud, or perhaps a moan. She threw off her afghan and painfully stood up while lowering her head—a trick her doctor
had taught her to keep her from becoming dizzy. She was stiff
and tired, and pressed both hands to the small of her back as
she turned the corner by the alcove toward the kitchen and
bumped into Geoffrey. They stared at each other for a brief
moment, and he saw her startled look and then pity for him
shining in her eyes. For a fraction of a second the hint of a
smile of resignation creased the corners of her mouth, even as
she put up one hand, perhaps as a reflex, to defend herself—a
feeble and useless gesture against a steel blade. She grunted
and fell, landing heavily across two cardboard boxes near the
entryway. Even as it happened, Geoffrey blanked it from his
mind.

Standing alone at the bottom of the stairway in the silent apartment, Geoffrey felt peaceful and contented, having accomplished all that was expected of him in his mighty confrontation. He was fulfilled. Somehow, the late-afternoon sun was shining through the opaque walls of the duplex, a glowing orange wash of color that seemed to him a heavenly sign of deliverance. He, who was meant to be the Evil One's victim, had courageously turned the tables, and there was only one remaining item on the unfinished agenda. He pointed the knife at his own naked chest and felt a twinge of fear. But then he remembered a divine promise that he would feel no pain. Nevertheless, his hands shook in apprehension. "Oh, big deal!" he said aloud. "What if it does hurt?" But it didn't. Not on the first thrust into the center of his chest . . . not on the second . . . the fourth . . . the eighth . . . not on the tenth or the twelfth or the thirteenth, either.

Geoffrey threw aside the knife and smiled at the pleasant idea of spending his final moments in the warmth of the summer sun. He staggered to the front door and somehow found the strength to open it, then lurched onto the front steps in the dazzling golden light of late afternoon. The world was lush and brilliant as he raised his arms triumphantly toward heaven.

5

How I Spent My Easter Vacation

Geoffrey King   April 16, 1962
English, Mrs. Silbert

My dad took me with him on a business trip. We went first to New York City. It was my first visit there. We stayed at the Carlyle Hotel, where President Kennedy stays, and my dad showed me the presidential seal outside the door of the president's suite. Our suite was two floors below his. The president was not there when we were. There was a fireplace in my bedroom, but it was too warm to use. I loved New York, and at night when we walked back to the hotel, the steam from the manholes in the street reminded me of a great engine cooling off after a busy day. We went to shows and favorite restaurants like the Four Seasons and the 21 Club. The food was great. My grandmother lives in Manhattan, and we visited her too. It was a wonderful trip.

Then we went to Chicago and stayed two days. The weather was terrible there, and after N.Y. the city was dull to me, although Dad took me to the Art Institute and I liked that very much. When my dad finished business there I thought we were going back to L.A., but he surprised me instead at the airport and said we would fly to Ohio and see the town where he was born. We flew to Toledo and rented a car. Then we drove to a pretty town called Radollia with neat, lovely streets and old Victorian houses. I saw the house where he was born and visited his relatives. We also went to the cemetery where his families lie. My favorite memory is visiting the drugstore where my dad worked as a young boy. It is a Rexall drugstore, and now my Dad is a vice-president of Rexall.

It was a great vacation.

There was a brief moment after King turned off the ignition and his son caught him glancing at himself in the rear-view mirror, his face softening as he adjusted his felt hat, when Geoffrey sensed all of his father's pride and satisfaction. They were both wearing camel's hair coats and their shoes had been shined to a glossy polish in the Chicago Hilton's barbershop the day before. They looked spiffy, and King winked at his ten-year-old son seated next to him in the rented Buick. Geoffrey smiled, seeing that his father was pleased. King's big hand brushed at the soft collar of his son's coat, then quickly skimmed across the top of his burred head. "They could've taken off a little more around the ears," his father said to him. "But you look fine. Come on, let's give the local yokels their thrill for the day." Geoffrey followed his dad inside the small Rexall drugstore.

Radollia was exactly as King had described it on the plane: four blocks of stores on Main Street that sloped down to the

railroad tracks and the big red-brick engine roundhouse beyond the marshaling yard. A quiet, kind of sad little Midwestern town that time had bypassed, with no earthly reason
for still existing except that farmers had to shop somewhere;
the railroad business was dead. Geoffrey could picture his dad
as a very young boy jerking sodas for the rowdy switchmen and
brakemen on muggy summer afternoons from behind this
same ornate marble soda fountain. He could see his father as a
tall, gangly boy, his broad forehead laced with beads of sweat,
wiping his hands on his white apron, rinsing out the soda
glasses, and smiling politely at the small talk directed at him by
the noisy, beefy men perched on six stools. He saw that scene
clearly even as he watched his big, broad-shouldered dad having his hand pumped by Mr. Milburn, the owner, who wore a
bow tie and a hearing aid and grinned in surprise. "Bobbie
King! My Lord, if it isn't Bobbie King! And who's this, Bobbie?
Why, that must be your boy! Geoffrey, is it? Well, hello there,
Geoffrey. Now, do you know that your dad worked for me
after school—what was it, Bobbie, most of the way through
junior and senior high, I recollect?—and that was only day
before yesterday, it seems, and now, here he is back here after
all these years, and *I'm* working for *him*. He's my boss now. Oh,
we heard all about you, Bobbie. My vest is bustin' buttons. From
jerkin' sodas to running Rexall's show. Well, your dad was always serious and ambitious even way back then. A fine boy, the
most dependable who ever worked for me, and neat as a pin,
too. Kept that counter shining. My God, Bobbie, if I don't
remember the day you went away to college! Your dad brought
you in here, and you were wearing a new blue suit—a real
string bean you were, carrying that heavy suitcase—and Charlie said to me, 'George, one root beer for the road. My boy's off
to Cleveland to get his degree.' You remember? Off you went
on the two-oh-eight. You haven't missed a thing, Bobbie—this
town's dead as hell. By God, I guess the last time I saw you was
at Richie's funeral. Twenty years ago! That's right! You was just
in the navy."

The excited old man called to a fat, pimply young girl behind
the soda fountain: "Maureen, fix up this young man with a
chocolate frosted. Use plenty of syrup and put in three scoops."

Geoffrey was led to an empty stool at his father's soda fountain, smiling as he watched that mysterious stranger whom he loved, his father, flush with pleasure at the fuss being made over his unexpected appearance, and thinking that he finally understood the source of his father's stubborn ambition to become a powerful, important man. Yes, he was witnessing Dad's payoff for all those years of unrelenting struggle to get ahead— so that he could walk into this place being who he was and show them all what he was made of. That's why they made this detour on the way back home. En route to the drugstore, they had passed a small Esso station on the corner where three or four loafers were seated on a bench next to an ice chest holding soda pop, and King had remarked: "See that third fellow from the end? That's Billy Short. I went to grade school with him. I'd guess most of the people I grew up with are still here." But not Bob King.

He felt such pride being his father's son that he had to resist an impulse to hug him.

They spent the night with Dad's elderly Aunt Gladys, who lived alone with her cats and dogs. Geoffrey was fascinated, because his father never talked about his boyhood and seldom mentioned his family.

"You ought to give Patsy a call," Aunt Gladys remarked to King during dinner. His father looked startled.

"Is Patsy still around here?" he asked, remembering his sister-in-law.

"Lord, yes," his aunt replied. "She hasn't changed a jot, either. Been divorced at least twice since Richie died, and in and out of those places to dry out, which don't do her a bit of good as far as I can see." After dinner, King called Patsy and drove off to see her, leaving Geoffrey alone with his aunt, which pleased Geoffrey, who was eager to ask questions about the Kings, something he couldn't do if his father was present. He was desperate for clues to explain his secretive father: who his father really was was a measure of who Geoffrey was; yet, somehow, this vital information was kept from him. His mother had told him: "Dad doesn't like to be questioned about his childhood because it was very unhappy. I know next to nothing about it myself." Aunt Gladys showed him a photo album, including snaps of her brother—his grandfather—Charles King, a postal inspector, who rode the mail cars to Dayton, Akron, and Cleveland; they sorted letters en route. He was a stout, balding man with gentle eyes. "Everyone liked Charlie," the old lady said sadly.

"When did my grandfather die?"

"Oh, Lord, in the thirties. Yes. I'm not even sure your parents were married. I think they were just engaged. He just dropped dead in the street on the way to work."

Looking at unsmiling photos of his grandmother, Geoffrey discovered that his father and he himself had received her ample Roman nose. She appeared petty and mean, a strong-willed woman dissatisfied with her lot in life. Aunt Gladys leaned toward him confidentially and muttered, "Your grandma was something else. She gave your Dad fits with piano practicing. Made him come straight home from school and practice till dinner. Poor child never could play with friends. But your dad did play beautiful, and she thought he could make something of it. 'That's your only hope,' she told him. Imagine saying that to a child! Well, your grandma was a little peculiar, I must say. And, oh my, was she ever strict! She kept a ledger in the kitchen and everyone in that family—Charlie included—had to write down every cent they spent that day. Let's see. Rose died just before you were born. Tell you the truth, not too many folks around here shed tears."

"Who's this?" Geoffrey asked, pointing to a photo of his father as a teenager standing next to another boy who seemed to be a slightly more mature version of King himself.

The old lady looked startled. "Why, that's your Uncle Richie, Bobbie's older brother." Geoffrey was amazed; he didn't know that King had a brother. "He's dead too?" he asked. The old lady bit her lip and nodded. "Poor thing had a stroke," she said. "He was way too fat. Just huge. Six-foot-five and about three hundred pounds."

"What did he do?"

"Smart as a whip, that one. He was a lawyer, but to tell the truth, he wasn't too interested in that. He had a million-dollar vocabulary and loved to show it off, using words nobody understood. He was a character. Loved the railroad. Just drifted around the country as a brakeman for weeks and months. I think maybe he wanted to get away from your grandma's nagging and your Aunt Patsy, too."

41

He was fascinated to discover the existence of these relatives. He wanted to pepper the old lady with endless questions about them, but he was afraid his father would find out that he had been nosy, so reluctantly he helped his elderly aunt tune in the TV so she could watch Liberace. "He plays so beautiful," she sighed. "And he's such a gentleman." Before long, Geoffrey fell asleep.

"Oh, Bob, he's your spitting image," a woman's voice whispered. Geoffrey slowly opened one eye and saw his father and a surprisingly attractive blond woman looking down at him on the sofa, where he had fallen asleep. It was very late. He pretended to still be asleep to hear what his father might say, but King remained silent and led the blond woman toward the front door. Geoffrey was shocked to see his father kiss her on the lips. "I'm so glad you called," she said, and she hugged him. Dad walked her out to her car; Geoffrey realized she was his aunt.

They left Radollia the next morning, a cold, gray day periodically spitting icy drizzle, but not before they drove past Dad's boyhood home, a modest framed house on a hill overlooking the railroad tracks far below. "My mother gave this place to the damned Lutherans," King said. "I guess the minister lives there now." They parked next to a small cemetery less than a block away. "I used to play in here as a kid," King remarked as they entered through a rusty iron gate. "Watch out for dog doo," Dad said, walking among the weeds and faded tombstones, the collar of his camel's hair coat turned up against the chill. "Ohio spring," he said and grimaced, kicking aside some weeds and stones with the tip of his shoe. Three brass plates in the earth—his family's remains. King stood silently, his son at his side, staring down with a vacant, lonely look his son had never seen before.

"I wish I had known your family," Geoffrey said.

"They weren't much to brag about," his father replied, but was it the wind causing his eyes to tear?

"That's my brother," he said, pointing to Richard King's brass plate with the toe of his black wing-tipped shoe. Geoffrey pretended to be surprised. "He was three years older than I," his dad remarked, "and I loved him very much."

"How did he die?" Geoffrey asked.

"He was the town drunk," his father said sadly. "What a waste. Brilliant. All the makings of a great man. Staying in this town just destroyed him."

Geoffrey followed his father back to the car. "You wouldn't ever be like your brother, would you Dad?"

King turned back. "What do you mean?"

"Be a drunk."

"My God, of course not," Dad said, holding on to his hat against a biting wind.

They drove in silence back through town and over the bridge, passing the welcoming sign erected by the Rotarians, and onto the rolling Ohio countryside, heading for the highway to Toledo and the airport.

"Thanks for bringing me here, Dad," Geoffrey said.

"Well, so much for nostalgia," King replied, and Geoffrey understood that he had been granted a brief glance inside the forbidden book of his father's past, but that this book was now closed. "But I did want you to see all of the advantages you have that I never even knew existed," his dad added.

Years later, Geoffrey would recall being overwhelmed at the time with the special destiny of being the son of such a man. He sat watching King drive in that familiar leaning posture with both arms slumped across the top of the steering wheel, a skilled driver who knew his roads and negotiated them with relaxed confidence. Geoffrey felt fortunate that fate had selected, from among millions and millions of random possibilities, this particular man to be his father. Yet he often felt guilt and frustration for having failed somehow to win King's acceptance and love. Being alone with King, like intimacy with God, revealed only the distance one had yet to travel to comprehend unfathomable mysteries. But Geoffrey would remember this particular trip as if floating contentedly like a puff in a summer's breeze. He wished they would drive on forever, just the two of them, sharing their lives together on the open road. He often felt that way during trips with Dad and suspected that his father did, too.

Unfortunately, these pleasurable trips occurred infrequently and their moments of intimacy were large stones stored in a small pocket. At certain points on these trips together, basking in an alpenglow of warm feelings, Geoffrey felt an urge to blurt thoughts and feelings stored in his heart that he only partly understood and probably could not clearly articulate, nevertheless yearning to share them with his father, to cement an intimacy. But he just couldn't find it in him to reveal those inner thoughts. Amid the relaxed silences and comfortable small talk, he sometimes sensed his father resisting a similar impulse of his own to blurt things he was aching to say. And why not? Blood of blood . . . flesh of flesh . . . father-son was a holy alliance. Geoffrey believed that—even during the worst of times, when father and son could not be alone together in the same room.

6

Lying spread-eagled on the cool grass in front of the duplex, Geoffrey was aware of God's existence in the scent of the soil and the loveliness of His late-afternoon sky, shimmering overhead with silver streamers from paradise. Death's grip was feathery, a light and gentle touch; and emptied of himself, he floated effortlessly as if on a languid pond sheltered from the wind. A shriek of horror jolted him back to consciousness in time to see the retreating figure of the middle-aged building manager, an overweight widow in polyester slacks. She had just turned the corner with two prospective tenants to show them the empty duplex across the street—her amiable patter extolling the virtues of a quiet residential neighborhood—when she came upon Geoffrey King in his front yard bleeding to death. Somehow Geoffrey picked himself up and staggered back inside through the open front door. Defying probability, he crawled up sixteen stairs to the second floor. When the police arrived, they found him lying in his bed with his face to the wall. By then he had no more blood to offer his sheets, and his face was the color of granite. He was wrapped in shrouds of blissful tranquillity when he heard a rude army charging up the stairs. Slowly he turned to confront a pistol pointing at him.

"What's happened here? Who did this? Who are you?"

The questions multiplied as his bedroom filled with unwelcome visitors. At first they treated him gently, thinking he was a victim like the other two downstairs; but he was so desperate to be rid of them so that he could die in peace that he told them, "I did it," a confession he hoped would cause them to lose interest in him and leave his bedroom.

"I did it," he repeated. He couldn't believe he wasn't dead yet, and his words chilled his visitors and evaporated their gentleness. They peppered him with questions, ignoring his request to be propped up on pillows because he couldn't breathe.

"No pillows until you answer some questions: who are those women downstairs?"

He refused to talk; he couldn't. Finally, gruff hands yanked him upright and stuffed pillows beneath his back.

"My mother and grandmother," he gasped.

"Why did you do it?"

"If you look into my heart through the holes in my chest, you'll see and know everything God told me."

The ambulance attendants could not negotiate the gurney up the curving staircase, so he was lifted onto his feet and half-carried down.

"I can't," he moaned as they tried to make him walk.

"You got yourself up here, so you'll get yourself back down," they told him, and held him under his arms from behind to avoid his splattering blood.

He dimly recalled the ambulance siren and then lying on a cold stainless-steel table surrounded by a group of doctors and nurses working over him in feverish haste as if he were the final case before they could go home and start their weekend. They cut off his pants, and the sticky denim stung as it was torn away from his thighs. He lay helplessly, naked and cold, growing resentful at being prodded, pulled, and jerked around by strong, purposeful hands. No gentleness here.

"Hey, he's going into cardiac arrest," he heard a doctor exclaim, using a tone of voice that reminded him of his dead father chiding him as a child: "Watch what you're doing!"

The overheard remark made it official: he was finally dying. About time, he thought. The crew in the emergency room saw him smile with his last breath.

The hospital was called "Little Company of Mary," and the fire-department rescue ambulance had raced to its door only because it was closest to the scene of the crime and the murderer was rapidly dying from his self-inflicted wounds. But the trauma team that received him raced him into surgery even as he began to sink into cardiac arrest. Three times during the four-hour operation, the patient's heart stopped, and three times, heroic measures saved him. Most fateful of all, a leading thoracic surgeon happened to be visiting the hospital at the moment Geoffrey arrived, and was immediately called upon to head the damage-repair team. Three knife wounds had penetrated into the chambers of a strong seventeen-year-old heart; but the wounds were punctures rather than slashes, and more easily reparable. Three transfusions were required because the patient arrived virtually drained dry. Despite deep shock and trauma and multiple serious wounds, the strength of youth was keeping him alive—in extremely critical condition, but alive nevertheless. If he could survive the next forty-eight hours without serious complications, he might live—though much the worse for the damage he had wrought. Probably a chronic cardiac case for the remainder of his life.

When Geoffrey next opened his eyes, he was so overwhelmed by grief that he ripped out the tubes in his nose and throat and began to scream. They tied his hands to the bed and plugged him back into the various tubes and monitoring devices of the life-support system in intensive care. A sheriff's deputy sat nearby, guarding him around the clock.

7

SEPTEMBER 7, 1969

If Raymond Lowe had his way, Geoffrey, like his father before him, would not be buried by his family. King was buried by a few old cronies in an unmarked grave in Ivy Lawn Cemetery; and on this muggy Sunday morning, Lowe decided that even a boot-hill square in the middle of the Mojave was too decent a place for his nephew. Ray sat huddled in misery, an address book in his robed lap, placing excruciating phone calls to friends and family. News of the tragedy was on the front page of the Metro section of the Los Angeles *Times*, the two-column headline declaring "JET LAB TRUCK THEFT LINKED TO BIZARRE DOUBLE MURDER." The story reported the police theory that the killings were the result of a family quarrel over the youth's arrest the night before. Ray learned what happened from two grim-faced detectives who appeared at his door at eight in the evening; on the eleven-o'clock Saturday-night news, brief footage of his mother being wheeled out of his sister's duplex had almost torn his heart, even though he was already under sedation. Early Sunday morning, a sad-voiced detective from the juvenile division in Pasadena had called to express condolences.

"We've been doing a lot of soul-searching over what happened," the detective admitted. "It was a judgment call, letting that kid go home, and we guessed wrong. But with juveniles, our hands are tied if a parent wants to take him home."

"I know," Ray sobbed. "I begged her not to do it."

"If we felt he didn't have a solid home, or caring parents, or posed a danger, we could've gotten a detain petition from the juvenile probation department for admittance into Juvenile Hall. But he seemed calm and sufficiently rational when we released him. He was a mess Friday night, though, drunk and out of his mind on drugs."

"He was a mess all of his life," Lowe declared bitterly. "He was diagnosed as a paranoid schizophrenic."

The detective sighed. "Well, you see, if we had only known *that*."

The worst call he was forced to make this day was to his Aunt Jessica, his mother's seventy-two-year-old sister, back in Ohio. In the end, he just couldn't do it and called her son-in-law, a minister, and left the chore to him.

Later that evening Lowe, hoarse and exhausted, refused a plate of scrambled eggs offered by his wife, Nora, and instead uncapped a fresh bottle of Canadian whiskey. He had been drinking since morning. Once again the phone rang and he weaved his way back into the living room to answer it on the fourth or fifth ring. That phone call was like a blow at the end of this tragic day.

"This is Dr. Brennan at the intensive-care unit of Little Company of Mary. I'm calling about your nephew, Geoffrey King. He's in very critical condition."

"You mean he's still alive?" Ray shouted incredulously.

"Well, it's touch and go for the next—"

"Why was he sent to you people?"

"I suppose because we were closest to the home. He's lucky, I'd say. He wouldn't have survived another five minutes."

"Lucky? Do you know what that kid did?"

"I've been told, yes. He also did terrible damage to himself, but—"

"You people played God. That's what you did. Are you telling me that you saved him?"

"If he makes it through the next seventy-two hours, he has at least a fifty-fifty chance, I'd say."

"God almighty, why couldn't you bastards let him go?" Ray Lowe sobbed.

Nora heard a crash and ran into the living room. She found her husband passed out on the floor, an open bottle of whiskey forming a puddle around his bare feet.

8

SEPTEMBER 9, 1969

The Westwood chapel was packed. One of the sadder sights at the King funeral was the late arrival of the ailing, elderly actor Charlie Ruggles, a family friend now desperately ill, being helped into a front-row pew. "Nothing could keep me from saying good-bye to those two angels," he said. Raymond Lowe sat slumped in his seat, looking diminished in his dark suit. His wife, Nora, had created her own privacy beneath a wide-brimmed hat with a heavy, protective veil. There was no organ music and no caskets. The deceased were represented by two slender glass vases, each holding a single perfect rose. The bodies had been cremated, Ruth's ashes scattered to the winds, her mother's urn shipped back east to be buried next to her husband. The young, bearded minister seemed genuinely moved by the occasion, even though he didn't know the family. Yet it was clear to the well-tailored middle-aged mourners that he had done his homework, for he chose texts and poetic stanzas that exquisitely personified mother and daughter. And when he learned that Ruth King had considered herself an aspiring poetess earlier in her life, he asked to borrow her notebooks and read aloud from one of them:

> I am not afraid when death shall come,
>   to follow him to an unknown place.
> For I shall know that all my life
> I have waited for its embrace.
>
> I cannot fear death's peaceful bed,
>   whose quietness and rest
>   is reward enough
>   for all the pain and dread.

The sentiment was so plainly Ruth's that many mourners wondered if the poem had been written in the past few days or weeks; the young minister, perhaps diplomatically, failed to mention that it was written for her high-school English class when she was only sixteen. Hearing these words, the audience wept their leave-taking. There was nothing else to do. "Give us the strength, O Lord," the minister prayed, "to withstand the shock and sorrow of a grievous tragedy and find within ourselves the love, strength, and compassion exemplified by these two dear friends taken from their earthly home into your merciful kingdom, peace without end."

Nick Hopps, the Kings' lawyer, was seated in a back row. He hadn't been listening, mostly because he was too drained and upset. Nick was a bald, lean man with a ruddy complexion and intense, piercing eyes that missed nothing. He had known the Kings most of his adult life, and loved them as if they were his own kin. He was Robert Luther King's closest friend, and there was no other companion that Nick would've chosen ahead of Bob for long hikes through the woods, stalking solitude and campfire camaraderie, or passing a flask on the banks of a quiet stream. In the woods, the two friends became country boys again, scooped out of the same vat, discovering they shared the same pride and prejudices.

In the woods, Nick thought he was on the verge of understanding his eccentric, enigmatic friend. King had been the most decisive man Nick knew, and he watched him rise from obscurity and impressively accomplish his career goals. Nick was betting on him from the start, yet he was not surprised when King finally crashed. When the two were alone together, King abandoned his arrogance to allow his uncertainty and rage to flicker to the surface—unable either to acknowledge or to explain his own internal destructiveness, which he may have sensed would someday strip him bare. Nick was the only friend who ever saw King weep. By then Bob's life was beyond repair; and for a brief moment he faced the certainty of who was responsible.

Nick bled for him. He bled for the entire family. King's wife and child were his possessions to use, abuse, discard, or neglect as he saw fit. In exchange for feeding and clothing them, he demanded obedience and order—at the cost of any real intimacy, showing more affection to his dogs than to Ruth and the boy. Like many ambitious men, King lived most ardently outside his front door. Home was a mere extension of the impression he sought to make; his family was treated no better or worse than his own employees, who found him quick to punish but eager to reward. He strove to avoid confrontation, but dealt forcefully with rebellion. It was a futile, empty life-style, demanding continual achievement on his part and the continual subservience of Ruth and Geoffrey. Toward the end, when he fell and reached out in need for sharing and affection, his victims became his victimizers. All of their stored hurts and resentments exploded.

Nick Hopps stood with the congregation in a final silent prayer, feeling angry and frustrated. These deaths should never have occurred; Geoffrey should've been stopped. Nick had witnessed several of the clashes between King and his son in the last years of Bob's life and knew there could be no survivors in such a brutal battle of wills. He tried to intervene and talk sense to both combatants, and against his better judgment, even sought to prod Ruth into assertive action, detecting her secret satisfaction in the mayhem surrounding the challenge to her husband's iron authority. It was sick and pathetic stuff, and he felt ashamed for all of them. He saw his friends as their own worst enemies, but also as vulnerable victims of society's complex pressures. Hopelessly befuddled by the vanities, wealth, and status dangled at the upper echelons of the corporate structure, they became dazzled and corrupted. He watched Bob crack and Ruth blunder, she in particular leaning on Nick for advice which she never took. In disgust, he had thrown up his hands; but goddammit, her friends should've forced her to do what was right! She would have been alive this day if they had, and Geoffrey's life would've been saved as well.

"Nick, you're my parents' lawyer," Geoffrey had often said. "You see what's going on here. Can't you talk to them? What right do they have to do these terrible things to me and to themselves? Don't you get angry? Why do you always lecture me? I'm not the one who's destroying us."

Geoffrey was right. Painfully right, and Nick, who valued honesty and integrity, was forced to admit that if Geoffrey had only been more likable, he and other family intimates might have been tempted to form a posse to march on Bob and Ruth and order them to cease and desist or face having their son removed from their guardianship by court order. To Nick, Geoffrey was as emotional as a woman: his feelings quivering on the surface of his skin; his impulsiveness and "intuitions" as alien as his propensity to blurt all of his feelings, even though he was unusually insightful about his family's failings and justified in most of his complaints. Geoffrey loved Ruth; but after Bob's death, she was in no shape to raise her son alone—and something should have been done about that right then and there. Allowing that boy to run loose was an invitation to disaster.

Nick had no idea of what could have been done to intervene in the Kings' problems. He only knew that Ray Lowe and a host of others would have made a difference if all had not followed paths of least resistance. Becoming intimately involved in the lives of others demanded courage and commitment that were all too rare nowadays, and Hopps knew this was so the moment he entered the duplex and surveyed the evidence of recent carnage. At the request of Raymond Lowe, Nick had gone to the duplex to itemize the family's possessions and sort through silver, jewelry, paintings, and other valuables before they were packed into storage. Spots of Ruth's blood remained on the kitchen walls and ceiling; Geoffrey's still stained the downstairs carpets. Nick steeled himself entering Eleanor Lowe's bedroom and confronting her lavender scent, and in Geoffrey's room he discovered in a cardboard box back in his closet a smug magazine for gays which featured on its cover the naked torso of Ruth King's son, a man-child smiling seductively with his pelvis thrust forward.

But entering Ruth's room, dominated by the big bed she shared with King for decades, was for Nick the most disconsolate moment of all. He remembered Ruth as she was years before, a languidly sensual woman with lively eyes and a voice husky from smoking too much. She loved her booze even then, but she was bright and witty, the brightest, best-informed person Nick had met in a long time, with sprightly opinions on everything from theater to politics. King was no match for her and seemed to take pride admitting that fact. But how could such a woman willingly suspend all of her critical faculties to follow compliantly in her husband's meandering footsteps? She lived her life exactly as she signed her checks: Mrs. Robert L. King.

"Ruth, you brought all of this down on yourself," Nick declared aloud in her empty bedroom, "and I'll be damned if I can figure out why." Pondering the fate of his dead friends, Nick convinced himself that Geoffrey's mother had known her life would end in a Greek tragedy. She had been expecting it for a long time.

Nick Hopps joined the other mourners in the warm sunshine on the circular driveway outside the chapel. He wondered what he should say to the Lowe family. Geoffrey's name was not mentioned by any of the friends or relatives, but his presence was palpable in the way men stared into the bright sun and the women pursed their lips.

"They were two angels," Charlie Ruggles repeated, "two angels dead for no reason."

Family friends equated the murders with the massacre in Benedict Canyon by the Charles Manson family that had occurred two weeks earlier. No question, the barbarians were pulling down the gates; kids and drugs, drugs and kids—tragedy had struck home. "When is it all going to end?" an elderly Lowe cousin asked. "This country—all of us—we can't take much more."

Nick looked down on the pale familiar face set in a death mask.

"Geoffrey," he called softly, and the boy seemed to stir. His eyes fluttered open and he stared at Nick with recognition. Hopps was the only member of the family circle that Geoffrey feared and grudgingly respected. He was the toughest man he knew. "Son, when I say no I don't mean yes" was all Nick had to say to end an argument when Geoffrey was small, and not much more than that when he was older.

"I'm going back to Arizona and I thought I'd stop by," the lawyer explained.

"Nick, you always come when the family needs you. I'm trying hard to die, but my body won't do it. Are they both dead?"

"Yes, I've just been to their funeral."

"Nick, I didn't want to hurt anyone. I was crazy. Oh, Nick, I can't believe this. I really killed them! I just want to die, but they won't let me."

"I wish I could help you. I mean it."

"Nick, I was like an animal. Nothing could've stopped me."

"Geoffrey, I just wish to God I had been there, because I would've stopped you cold."

Geoffrey closed his eyes, and when he opened them next, it may have been hours or days later. Nick was gone, and although the faithful family lawyer would never again see him, Hopps would one day affect his future.

9

Raymond Lowe kept his nephew's conservative suit—wool, dark blue—in a hall closet. Geoffrey would either be buried in it or wear it at his trial. At Little Company of Mary Hospital he was The Boy Who Wouldn't Die, a miracle of perseverance; there was no rational explanation for anyone, no matter how young, surviving thirteen serious stab wounds, and his doctors agreed that normally a single knife thrust into the heart proved fatal. He was a controversial patient: a minor, a murderer, probably deranged, requiring both around-the-clock nurses and police guards. But he was too weak to be moved to larger downtown facilities, and each day brought a fresh crisis. He had already developed pleurisy, and the doctors now worried about hepatitis from the blood transfusions or pneumonia from the chest injuries. Among the monitoring devices in intensive care there was no apparatus to measure a patient's will to live. Had there been, Geoffrey's would have registered a flat, dead line.

He was in agony over what he had done, but there was no morphine for his conscience. Powerless with his hands tied to the bedrails, he tried to stop breathing with sheer willpower, but his weakened condition was no match for the body's stronger, independent impulse to exhale. The sisters hovered over him busily, and the doctors probed and checked his life signs. He understood that their efforts to keep him alive were impersonally professional. He wanted to die. He begged to be left alone, crying while awake and moaning in his sleep—a restless, miserable boy at the mercy of stubborn strangers. No family or friends visited him, prayed for his recovery, or sent messages or flowers; and only gradually did he become aware of the daily presence of a plump, kindly middle-aged woman in a gray uniform who sat at his bedside several hours each day— a soothing maternal figure who could have been his own mother—feeding him ice shavings from a paper cup and hold-

54

ing one of his tied hands. She was a volunteer Gray Lady, and to her he confessed his crime:

"I killed the only two people in the world that I really loved. I just can't live with this. Please, please, tell them to turn off all their machines and go away. Can't you understand? I've got to be allowed to die. It's my right."

"No," she replied. "Only God decides when."

She sat with him when they changed his dressings, but had to turn away. From his collarbone to his navel, he was cross-stitched with livid scars like a baseball. At times he cried like a child or hurled deprecations at those tending to his needs, and finally began to beg for tranquilizers to ease his mental anguish. The Gray Lady tried to intercede with the head nurse in his behalf, but was told that the patient faced a sanity hearing for his crime and was not permitted any mood-altering drugs beforehand. So he wept and moaned, and at times, the Gray Lady wept with him.

He found himself hauling in a succession of nightmarish monsters from the deep pool of memory, images that gave him no peace. Reliving his crime moment by moment, frame by frame, his mental movie screen filled with scenes of the murders. Over and over again he saw himself reaching out for his mother in the doorway and stabbing her repeatedly. Often the images blurred, and Ruth unexpectedly became Eleanor; he relived bumping into his Gram as she turned a corner in the hallway, and once again he peered into her weary eyes and saw her small smile the moment before she died. These images flooded his thoughts, independent of his will, forcing his scrutiny. The merciless camera operator torturing him was himself, but he simply had to know what had really happened, know it with absolute certainty, and determine beyond any doubt whether or not he knew what he was doing when he killed his mother and his grandmother. But each rerun brought a different conclusion. He did; he didn't. He didn't; he did.

He knew that the triggering event that led to the murders occurred while he was pacing in the living room, flashing so rapidly between reality and LSD hallucination that he could no longer tell which was which. Suddenly he had heard a noise, and became convinced that he was in mortal danger from a mob of Lucifer-agents approaching the kitchen door. He had dashed to the kitchen and grabbed a bread knife, his knees shaking, his teeth sticking to his dry lips, to make a last stand at the back door. He knew that once he raised the knife above his head, no power—earthly or otherwise—could stop him from thrusting it in self-defense. He was wrapped in a cloak of terror, but he couldn't say he didn't see Ruth King, instead of a phantom demon, confronting him. He saw his mother; he knew she was his mother; he recognized her immediately. But yet, he didn't. He was operating simultaneously on two levels of awareness. But reality was overwhelmed by the emotional grip of his drugged illusion. He saw her transposed into a threatening alien phantom and then saw nothing and became lost in terror and fury as he lashed out. (The police would find all the jets on the kitchen stove turned to full flame, and when he was later asked about this, Geoffrey could offer no explanation nor remember doing it.)

But he killed his mother. He saw what he had done, saw her lying halfway through the doorway, knew that she was dead. Ergo, he thought, he murdered his mother, knowing it was she. Was that the truth? Was that the complete, terrifying truth? Yes! his guilt and remorse told him. No! the rational part of his mind rebelled. He was crazy, drugged out of his mind on bad acid. There was no way he could ever bring himself to harm those two women without the LSD. Was *that* truth? Yes! *No!* The acid was a courage-booster, an excuse, yet another internal voice insisted.

And so Geoffrey went—around and around—in an exquisite Chinese water torture of his own invention, switching his certainties a dozen times an hour, one moment a cunning, cold-blooded killer, the next a helpless victim of drug paranoia. In his role of grand inquisitor, he applied pincers in all the most sensitive places, more brutal than any police interrogator, trying to wring the truth from himself. But with each replay, the sickening recognition grew that he might never know.

Somehow, however, these murders had purged him of the madness that had festered within him for so long. It was as if the blood transfusions he had received removed a vile, feverish blood, replacing it with something very different. There was a new kind of madness in his soul—dark, anguished, guilt-stricken. But rage had been washed clean, and for the first time in his life he successfully blocked out his angry memories of his parents, leaving only himself to hate.

Late one afternoon as the sisters were changing shifts, he hoisted himself on one elbow and demanded to see a psychiatrist, causing such a commotion that one was finally summoned, only to inform him that the law prohibited a patient facing a sanity hearing from talking to any psychiatrist not court-appointed. Geoffrey became abusive and an orderly had to forcefully remove his clenched fists from the doctor's jacket lapels. The small hospital had had enough, and early the next morning they surprised him. He was gently lifted out of bed onto a gurney and rolled to a waiting ambulance. The sisters patted him on the shoulder and wished him well.

No one had the heart to tell him where he was going.

10

AUGUST 1952

There is a series of dated snapshots found loosely inserted in the King-family album, taken by neighbor Nick Hopps, who had rented the guest cottage next door to the King house. Ruth is shown seated on a blanket in a sloping meadow, holding her infant son while her husband's ubiquitous Great Danes sniff at her bare feet. Ruth is wearing a wide-brimmed hat against the sun; her features seem thick, her breasts massive. Her heavy arms are those of a farm wife who churns her own butter and licks her fingers often. All of these changes are obviously the result of her difficult pregnancy and delivery, because on a preceding page in the album, a photo taken a year earlier shows her appearing at least thirty pounds trimmer and ten years younger. Plump Geoffrey, wearing only diapers, has both arms around his mother's shoulders and appears to be trying to hoist himself up by her left breast. "The baby is healthy, thank God," Ruth wrote to a girlfriend that summer. "But he is fiercely demanding of my time, clinging to me at every opportunity, and wailing the moment I put him down." In another picture, standing to one side is Ruth's elegant, handsome mother, Eleanor Lowe. She's shielding her eyes with one hand, her soft white hair swept backward by the breeze. Eleanor is wearing a white print dress, holding a beaded handbag, and standing amid meadow flowers in pointed high heels: a New York matron transplanted into the country. Ruth seems to be staring out to sea.

The final snap reveals King holding his son firmly around the waist while the child seems intent on scrambling out of a rubber inner tube floating on a pond. On the back of the snap is an inscription in Ruth's small, neat hand: "A daddy contented." She often mistook moments of tranquillity for contentment. "Oh, why can't we always be as contented as we are right now?" she would remark in the midst of a lovely day of family relaxation. "I wish we could seal this moment in amber." But contentment was precisely the missing ingredient: no one was content under King's roof.

JULY 1956

The Kings lived twelve miles outside Kansas City in the tiny hamlet of Parkville, Missouri, where stray dogs slept in the center of the main street. They lived in a beautiful house on a high bluff overlooking the Missouri River. Their house had a red gabled rooftop, garden terraces, a stone fireplace, and a brick patio shielded by a striped awning on which copperhead snakes occasionally were discovered sunning themselves.

Ruth resented the isolation and complained about staying alone—several miles from the nearest neighbor—with King so often away on business. As a result, the guest house was rented and the Hoppses became neighbors. Ruth raced to the city for luncheons and shopping the moment that the maid arrived, which left four-year-old Geoffrey bearing the brunt of the isolation. Left alone all day with only Claudene, the housemaid, for company, he never saw anybody or heard anything except the wind sweeping across the meadows and the chimes of a small college chapel across the valley. In bad weather he was allowed to stay indoors, and Claudene let him ride on her vac-

uum cleaner and help her dust. But she scolded him when he
sulked: "Pep up, boy, you ain't got no reason for mopin' that I
can tell. You a blessed child in every way, and I know what I'm
sayin'."

He didn't. His only companion was Ruth. When she was at
home, he followed in her wake like a hungry gull at the stern of
a shrimper. He lived for special moments in a daily ritual, especially moments alone with Mother. On weekdays, after the
others had left for the day, she took her morning bath and he
sat on her bed, waiting patiently, thumbing through her fashion magazines, enjoying the opulent silky gloss of the pages and
the sensuous colors of the models. These fashion pictures became embedded in his childhood memories the way that Ernest
Shepard's *Winnie-the-Pooh* illustrations became glowing re-
membrances for generations of other children. But no one
read to Geoffrey. There just wasn't time. So he entertained
himself until Ruth emerged from the bathroom wrapped in her
robe, looking pink and beautiful, to stand in contemplation in
front of her burgeoning closet.

"What dress should I wear today?" she asked. "It's ladies' day
at the Kansas City Club—veddy swank, you know." Mulling,
she swished aside hangers until he shouted, "That one! That
one!"

"The black linen? Hm, maybe so. Good choice, dear."

He would beam with pleasure and then help her get dressed,
zipping up her back, fixing the clasp to her pearls, avidly watching as she applied face powder and dabbed on lipstick. He
wanted her to do so much more—her dressing table was
crowded with lotions and bottles of all sorts—but she seldom
bothered. He experimented with these beauty aids after she left
the house, and often played inside her closet, surrounded by
her scent, caressed by her silks, prolonging an intimacy with
her long after she abandoned him.

To keep Ruth at home, he tried to intimidate her with tears
and pleading; but seeing only annoyance, he turned to wild
tantrums, kicking and screaming on the floor, more to work out
his pent feelings than as a tactic against her.

Ruth's kitchen was a marvel of gleaming copper pots and
pans suspended from overhead racks, a butcher's block within
reach of an array of cutlery that would have dazed a Civil War

surgeon. She taught him to be her vegetable man, shelling peas or stringing beans grown in their own garden, while she put up the roast. She hugged him while stirring the soup on the stove.

"I'm lonely," he whined. She sighed sympathetically and pulled him to her. Her hug signaled understanding of his dilemma. "This is a lonely place," she agreed. "But next year you'll start nursery school, and then you won't be lonely anymore."

"But I'm lonely *now!*" he insisted.

She looked down at him with an expression of real grief, a look he had seen before in her unguarded moments, which always made him feel guilty, wondering what he had done or said to make his mother so sad.

"Are you sad, Mommy?"

"Of course not," she replied to his question. "Why should I be sad? Mother is just tired."

"Then go to bed," he told her. But she couldn't. Dad was bringing guests home for dinner.

"Why?" he asked. Guests, always guests.

"Because that's part of his job."

His father always seemed happiest in the evening, after he had showered and changed his clothes and stood impatiently on the patio, a drink in one hand and the other jingling the change in his pocket as he waited for the guests to arrive. Different faces all the time, strangers mostly, or so Geoffrey gathered from the way his parents fussed over them. His parents drummed into him the phrase: "May I serve you these?"— usually a dish of nuts or candy, though he didn't get to serve real trays of food. But he liked these parties because the house was crowded and noisy and the guests fussed over him, called him adorable, and pinched his cheeks. His parents did not allow showing off—he'd be sent packing to bed for that—but he managed to charm and delight nevertheless.

Geoffrey was told he was too young to sit at the table with the grown-ups, which made him angry. *"When* is up to you," his father said when they ate together as a family. "The way you gulp your milk . . . and you hold your fork as if it were a sword. I'm telling you for your own good and ours, too—people judge all of us by your manners."

Eating was suddenly a grim business and he struggled to get

it right. He had no way of knowing that every other four-year-old in the world wasn't living exactly as he was, lonely and frustrated and starved for attention, because he had never played with another child. He was absolutely alone on a rural hilltop; and perhaps because there were no other diversions, his isolation emphasized his neglect and exacerbated his obsession to be at the center of his family's life. He was intimidated by a six-foot-two-inch father with a booming voice and purposeful stride: overwhelmed, terrified by his wrath, and anxious for his love and approval. King was not just the center of their lives—he was their entire life. When King was relaxed and happy, so were they; when he was moody, they walked on eggs. It was that way with everybody—not just his family. King hired and fired everyone who worked for Kansas City Power and Light. Geoffrey saw guests struggling to please his father as much as he did. His father was mean, at times very mean, and when he lost control of his temper, his hands trembling, even the dogs scattered, although King never used his hands—thank God, because he could probably splinter a fence post. No, his most terrifying quality, Geoffrey realized, was his unpredictability: he knew all of his son's ticklish spots and might explore them with delight on a rainy afternoon, then suddenly lose interest and turn his back on Geoffrey for the rest of that day and many days to come. Yet he always seemed to sense Geoffrey's secret disappointment when he returned home from a business trip—the house was so much lighter and more carefree while he was gone—and more to prove the point of his indispensability than to make amends, he had only to lift his son into his strong arms and carry him to the tractor for Geoffrey to experience the purest joy he had ever known. King rode him across the meadows, showing him how to steer and shift gears, letting him try. Seated on King's lap, straining to hear his shouted instructions above the engine—feeling his father's chest convulse in a laugh of approval when he got it right—Geoffrey glowed with a sense of well-being; the privilege of being his father's son belied all of his resentments and left him feeling ungrateful. His father was a god. And gods were not easy to live with. Nobody had to tell him that.

Nick Hopps and King had taken to each other like brothers

from the day they met, and the older King was uncommonly generous to the young attorney, not only directing clients his way but also insisting that Nick and his wife, Marion, attend the Kings' almost nightly dinner parties to make important contacts. He had a fairly important job as the power company's personnel man, in charge of industrial relations, but acted as if he was chairman of the board. The Hoppses were surprised by the older couple's stamina. They found these nightly soirees exhausting, the volume of alcohol consumed breathtaking, although the two hosts never appeared drunk. By seven the following morning, King was awakening his young neighbors by playing a medley of Cole Porter on his rosewood Chickering piano, his morning ritual. Hopps believed that, most of all, King was a man's man, the kind of friend another man values no matter his faults. Geoffrey, he felt, was a handful, a pest. High-strung, endlessly curious, restless, he hung around their cottage much too much, bored and neglected. Not an easy child to raise, but adorable and affectionate. He was flamboyant, slightly reckless to gain attention, the kind of child you might find hanging upside down from a telephone pole. Very bright. Very sensitive. And very angry when his temper was aroused.

11

ST. PAUL, 1958

There is a color slide, probably taken by King, of his son at age seven: bundled in a snowsuit the color of blue sky. Geoffrey is sunk above his waist in mounds of snow, documenting the awesome northern winters in St. Paul, Minnesota. Behind him is their new home—a massive three-story colonial of fifteen rooms with a black marble entryway, a spiral staircase, a solarium, and French doors that opened onto a lovely garden in spring. Their street was on a high ridge overlooking the Mississippi, and at night in his bed, Geoffrey heard the ice groaning in the river far below. But this time there were neighbors on their long street of stately homes—Riverside Drive, where the elite lived. In St. Paul, Geoffrey learned how to add and subtract. Finally he could see for himself what other children were given or denied, and he toted these comparisons on a mental abacus. In St. Paul, his parents began paying attention.

A secret game: Geoffrey, naked, stood in his mother's third-floor dressing room inspecting himself in her full-length mirror, pressing his lips against tissue in a careful final blot. Using Ruth's makeup kit, he artfully applied her brushes, powder, paints, and pencils to recreate his image into someone entirely different. He glanced at the mirror and then at an open page of *Vogue,* showing a close-up of an exotic model with emerald eye shadow and moist, powdery pink lips. Satisfied that he'd copied well, he turned to the wardrobe he'd selected, laid out on Ruth's bed. His mother's silk panties were fastened to his waist with a safety pin; her bra dangled lifelessly at the bottom of his rib cage until he wrapped the back straps around his chest and filled the cups with wads of toilet paper. Next, he unrolled her silk stockings up the length of his legs, then lowered his head into her mauve satin evening gown, purchased for the country-club dance. He chose a single strand of pearls from her jewelry box before lifting the trailing hem and stepping into her strapless high heels. He wanted to be somebody else. Being Geoffrey was not much fun.

Staring at his dressed-up figure in his mother's full-length mirror, he judged that he had made himself into the pretty daughter of Robert L. King. This knowledge brought a smile of pleasure. So many times he overheard his dad state his disappointment at having a son. "Girls are so much easier to raise and more pleasant to have around," his father complained whenever the subject of Geoffrey was raised by family or friends. In his daydreaming fantasies, Geoffrey always saw himself as a pretty girl who had friends and fun and doting parents. These daydreams boosted his morale, but then made him feel worse when he became himself again.

One day he raced downstairs to show off to his parents. They were astonished and delighted. "Why, he's beautiful," Mother exclaimed. But too late he discovered the game's limited appeal. Repetition was discouraged, and finally Geoffrey was commanded not to repeat his game again. And when he disobeyed, his father escorted him into an upstairs bathroom and ordered him to drop his pants. His father gripped a silver-plated hairbrush.

"Now, bend over," he said sternly.

"It's the only fun I have," his son shouted angrily. He saw his father's strange look of distress. Geoffrey unbuckled his pants and leaned over the toilet seat. "And anyway, you wouldn't do a thing if I were a girl dressing up in a boy's clothes," he said heatedly.

He received two halfhearted smacks across his bare buns.

"Maybe this will convince you that I mean what I say," King said. "Now, keep out of your mother's things."

It was Geoffrey's first spanking, and he cried out of humiliation and wounded pride. King turned his back and left him with his pants still around his shoes. It was a first for King, too: the first formal spanking he was forced to administer, and, much more unsettling, the first time his son ever dared to talk back.

"Something is very wrong around here," his father shouted. "Now that there are children for him to play with, I don't want him hanging around the house. Hire someone to help you cook dinner. I want him outside playing." King accused Ruth of being a dismal disciplinarian without any gumption whatsoever. Which was true. The next day she halfheartedly pushed her son out the front door, zipping his snowsuit as he clung to her in tears. "Just introduce yourself," she said. "Tell them your name and ask politely whether you can play, too." Out he went, with an encouraging shove, as if to face a firing squad, even though the neighborhood kids were too engrossed in building a snow fort to pay much attention. He stood, shivering and miserable, watching them from behind the safety of his own snowbank. Years later, it occurred to him that Ruth should have invited over a few neighborhood mothers with their kids to help break the ice. But she was busy making her own new acquaintances; in St. Paul, his parents' socializing was at a peak; but even if she had time, the idea would probably not have occurred to her. He knew because he was a snooper and he overheard plenty.

From listening posts in the laundry chute, next to air ducts, beneath stair landings, he was always straining to eavesdrop on his parents' conversations, convinced that they began talking about him whenever he wasn't around. Sometimes he was right. And as young as he was, he was amazed at his mother's ignorance of children, as if she were raising some exotic pet whose habits mystified her. He overheard her asking women friends questions displaying her befuddlement: "Does Richard sleep through the night?" "Does he still wet his bed?" "What do you do when he's sulky?" "How do you handle temper tantrums?" The women were always eager to give advice, although their kids, he knew, were worse than he was. But occasionally he admired her. Mother could be pushed just so far by his father before responding to him in kind. "Listen, Bob," he'd hear her say, "what he needs is your concern and attention. That would go a long way around here. Why don't you face up to a problem instead of laying it off on me?" King had little to say after that.

When he was enrolled in St. Andrew's Boys' School, he encountered the complexity of organized athletics. He was certain that his was the only father for miles around who never played catch with his son, never showed him how to swing a bat, never hung a hoop over the garage and swished baskets, and never went to a sporting event, either with him or alone. Kids teased Geoffrey for walking and talking like a girl; he was hurt and amazed; he hadn't realized. Now, gym. One of the boys asked him a sports question and he just stared back blankly. Everyone snickered watching him throw a ball or trying to catch a fly with a pathetic slap of his hands as the ball thudded into his chest. Every Friday afternoon the school hockey rink was jammed with cheering fathers rooting for their sons on the third- and fourth-form teams. But never Bob King. And these fathers were just as busy and successful as he.

"I'm quitting gym," he announced at the dinner table. "I hate it. I'm so terrible that everyone laughs at me."

King frowned. "I didn't raise a quitter. Work at it. Look at it as a challenge to be mastered."

"It's no use. The other kids are so much better. And do you know why? Because their fathers showed them what to do long ago."

"Get your teacher to show you how. That's what he's being paid for. Athletics are important. That's how a boy makes friends. Believe me. I was shoved onto a piano bench when everyone else in town was playing ball. So I know what I'm talking about."

"But I hate it."

"With that attitude, you'll never accomplish anything. End of discussion, Geoffrey."

Usually, but not this time. This time he was fiercely defiant, surprising himself as much as his parents.

"You don't care about me. You only care about yourself and your stupid dinner guests. We only do what you want around here, and I'm sick of it. I hate this house."

King's face darkened ominously. "Listen here. No seven-year-old is gonna sit as my judge and jury."

"Well, somebody better," his son interrupted.

"Go to your room," his father shouted. "Immediately."

He did. And he practically slammed his door off its hinges. This was a historic moment, and although he was trembling violently, he felt elated, as if he had kicked a football for a home run. Or was that baseball?

1959

"Whoever heard of an eight-year-old insomniac?" his father complained, discovering Geoffrey padding around the house at three in the morning. He didn't need much sleep, and night was his peaceful time, when he crept down to the study and watched Late-Late Show movies with the sound off. In bed, it was more fun dreaming with your eyes open, inventing fantasy adventures. Daylight was synonymous with persistent aches and pains which were only partly attributable to growing bones. He lived with a despair that he barely understood, and a certainty that his unhappiness was permanent. He hurt with wants and lonely dissatisfactions, many as undefined as occasional seizures of fear that would engulf him for no apparent reason so that he burrowed beneath his covers with a racing heart. He figured he might be crazy.

He was willing to take risks, pushing himself beyond constraints to the narrowest ledge of safety. His impulsive curiosity was fearlessly daring: cutting an electric cord with scissors to see what would happen—nothing but a dead clock and an angry mother. In Parkville, racing his bike to the edge of bluffs and skidding sideways at the very last moment. He was only three when he had his first swimming lesson at the country-club pool and was seen next standing atop the high diving board. His mother saw him, screamed, and hid her face as he stepped out onto air with a crazy grin and plunged. He was obsessed with vehicles and their ability to carry him away. Impatiently he awaited spring, when he hoped his father would teach him how to ride the two-wheeler given him that Christmas. Cars—he couldn't keep his hands off them, playing behind the wheel of any car parked in their driveway. Cars were freedom, power, and escape—a metaphor for his needs.

But even he could not explain why he did what he did to the Nielsons' car. Maybe it was because it was such a beauty—a fire-engine-red Thunderbird which Mr. Nielson bought for Mrs. Nielson's birthday. Mrs. Nielson couldn't wait to show it off, and Bob and Ruth came out of the house to admire it. Geoffrey was very polite, asking if he could just sit behind the wheel for a while. For some reason, Mrs. Nielson had parked out on the street at the top of a steep hill where, far below, a bridge spanned the Mississippi. Maybe it was the posh interior, the wonderful scent of new leather, that excited him. He released the emergency brake. The startled adults looked up as the Thunderbird began to silently sneak away. Mr. Nielson and King began to chase after him, looking ridiculous in the rear-view mirror, running downhill and waving their arms frantically. Of course, he knew there would be hell to pay, but the thrill of steering this beautiful car, of working the foot brake and feeling the mechanisms obey, of hearing the wind rush against the glass, and then of bringing it to a graceful stop two-thirds of the way across Sullivan Bridge, was worth every moment of grief. It was Mother rather than King who was especially furious (Mrs. Nielson was her friend, after all). "You're grounded for a month," she snapped. "And that's that." They were livid, but he couldn't help noticing that they were more shaken than angry, as if scolding one of the Great Danes—"you bad doggie"—after he had attacked a house guest.

Unexpectedly that winter, his father took him along on an ice-fishing weekend with some cronies from the country club.

67

The lake ice was so thick that they drove halfway across in a pickup truck to a wooden cabin with a kerosene stove and bunk beds. The men just chopped a hole in the floor and fished. Geoffrey was curious about how King would fare in such intimate surroundings with other men: aside from Nick Hopps, whom King spoke with practically every night on endless long-distance calls, he had no close friends. In St. Paul, they were living more lavishly than ever before, in a house three times as grand as the one in Missouri, and entertaining a better class of strangers. The women shook snow off their minks before handing their coats to the maid, while overhead the chandelier tinkled and swayed each time the door was opened. Table talk reflected that his parents were putting down roots (he was older now and was a regular at dinner), and he was delighted to see both of his parents become embroiled in discussions and display a passionate intensity. He loved it! Passion was the missing ingredient in their lifeless living together. He ached for intensities from them—even if angry ones. Anything was better than their usual dull indifference. One night King, bouncing up and down in his chair, was under attack from practically everyone around him for having fired a fellow who cheated on his wife. "Of course it's my business," he argued. "If he cheated on her, he'll cheat on me, too." Everyone shouted at him simultaneously, but King, the stubborn German, was unyielding, and Geoffrey and Ruth exchanged glances and spontaneously laughed.

Geoffrey was the only kid along on the ice-fishing trip, so he fished for everybody. At last he had a chance to observe his father around those who were more than his equals. The men sat around the stove, passing a bottle of whiskey and smoking cigars. At first they glanced his way and lowered their voices while telling dirty jokes; but after a while they no longer bothered. He was one of them and pretended to be laughing too. He noticed that the men seemed to genuinely like and respect his dad.

The talk gravitated to women, and everyone wore serious, set expressions. Old Judge Galvin, whose cabin they were in, openly declared his contempt, while others nodded. "I tell you, boys, I wouldn't have a thing to do with women if it wasn't for that tunnel of love they got stashed down there," the judge emphatically stated with a grin and a wink. Everyone chuckled, but Geoffrey was shocked. Why did they dislike women so intensely? Then suddenly King spoke.

"Men and women may seem to belong to the same species, but that's just a deception. Of course they're a mystery to us. Of course we can never understand them. And I'll tell you why: they're as different as a crocodile is from an alligator. People who go to zoos think these reptiles are almost identical, but they're entirely different in every way. My point is, I don't think any man can really understand a woman's way of thinking or dealing with the world. We just can't cross over. I know I can't."

"Are we missing much, Bob?" One of the men laughed teasingly.

"I don't think so. Do you? I'm not saying women aren't smart; being married to Ruthie, I could never say that. No, I just don't find them *useful*. They have no real understanding of power, for example, which is at the center of a man's world. So, no, except for companionship and stuff like that, I wouldn't seek them out either."

"Oh, but, Dad, being a beautiful woman—what can be better or more fun?" Geoffrey blurted.

"You like the girls, do you, ol' Geoff?" The judge laughed, and so did all the others.

"He sure does," King agreed. "Never been a time yet when my son didn't make a beeline for the best-looking woman to walk in our door. Grabs 'em, takes 'em into a dark corner, and talks their ears off."

"Is that so, Geoff?" Mr. Malcomb asked. "What do you talk about?"

"Where they buy their clothes," Geoffrey replied. The men howled, and he grinned in embarrassment because he had only told the truth.

There were times in St. Paul when he thought he might be beginning to connect with his family. His father was home more often because of the terrible weather. Ruth looked fine, twenty pounds slimmer than in Missouri, a reminder of one of her brother's cleverest observations: "My sister's tears are fattening." King seemed thinner and tired lately, and noticeable gray was flecking around his temples. Geoffrey was never entirely sure what he actually did to earn a living and usually even forgot the name of the firm, although in this case he was proud of the fact that Dad's company had one of the most popular commercials on TV: "From the land of sky blue wa-a-ters," sung by adorable woodland cartoon animals. Hamm's beer. King was a vice-president. "I've been hired to carry this company into the twentieth century," he said, "but it ain't easy."

Dad was either gentler or disappointed with his job—Geoffrey could not tell which. But seated quietly with his parents, he never failed to feel a real affection, and on one such evening he impulsively cleared his throat and waited for the two of them to look up

"Can I say something? I'm real sorry about Mrs. Nielson's car. I don't know why I did it. Honest, I really don't. It was a bad mistake. I know that. I'm sorry I made you mad. I don't want that. I want you to like me, not be mad all the time."

His father sat up on the couch and put aside his report. There was a strange look on his face that Geoffrey failed to recognize. "Don't think—" King began, but the phone rang and he left the room, holding up one finger. "I won't be a minute," he said. "I know who it is."

When he left, Ruth leaned forward confidentially. "I don't like the way your father is being treated. Some of those people at Hamm's are not being fair. He's very hurt and upset right now." Geoffrey wondered if she was being critical of him, his outburst, but King returned with a benign smile. Before he could say another word, the phone rang again, but this time for Ruth. "Let's wait for Mother to come back, because I want her to hear what I have to say, too. I'm glad you said what you did. All of us make mistakes sometimes. Mothers and fathers, too. But there's something more I want to say about that."

He never did. Instead, he lurched up straight in the easy chair next to his dog, grabbed at his chest with a wild, terrified expression, gasped Ruth's name, and keeled over.

His dad's face was dark as leather and he was not breathing. Geoffrey ran from the room screaming for his mother, and although he was ordered to stay in the kitchen when the fire rescue squad came from the station house a few blocks away, he heard them say that King was dead. They worked on his father for an hour before they took him away. Geoffrey peeked from

behind the door and saw only King's limp, lifeless hand bob-
bing on the passing stretcher.

It was Good Friday. And although his parents were both
atheists, everyone in the family would remember that.

12

1960–1962

If Bob King had died, he had also carried them *all* to
heaven—courtesy of the Rexall Drug Company. On Christmas
Day, which Ruth might have expected to spend quietly around
a fire in widow's weeds, the family sat by the pool under a warm
sun at the exclusive Bel Air Hotel where they were staying until
King found them a house. They were staying in a three-hun-
dred-dollar-a-day hideaway cottage that Clark Gable had built
for Carole Lombard, but King told Ruth not to worry, Rexall
would pick up the tab. "We're traveling first cabin, Ruth," he
told her. "We finally hit the jackpot."

Only the precise dictionary definition of the word "miracle"
could explain how a man presumed dead could only six months
later bring them in glory to Los Angeles. But here he was,
flatteringly tan, looking trim and eager and confident after
being successfully courted for one of the most prestigious and
highly paid jobs in his field—and claiming never to have felt
better in his life. Ruth and Geoffrey did not doubt him, but
they could not quite believe it, either. King's heart had stopped
when the firemen rescued him—but for how long was uncertain, and there was real concern about brain damage after heroic efforts restored his breathing. His coronary was massive,
the kind one doesn't survive. He was in the hospital for six
weeks, and when he returned home fifty pounds thinner and
white-haired, his son had to hide his confusion at the sight of
the ghost claiming to be his father. King kept mostly to himself
for four weeks in an upstairs bedroom, suffering depression,

but gradually he recovered his strength and his senses, and almost three months to the day after his attack, he appeared at the breakfast table dressed for work, ate heartily and without particular comment, and left for the office with a bulging briefcase.

"Well," Ruth sighed, "that's that."

And now they were in Los Angeles. It was hard for his family not to believe what King himself believed and articulated: that the fates had resurrected him for greatness.

King drove his son to Marina del Rey, where hundreds of yachts and sailboats were moored. "Pick one," King said. Grinning at Geoffrey's dazed expression, he said, "I'm dead serious. Tell me what boat catches your fancy and I'll see what I can do." They strolled together down a long quay as if it were an aisle in a supermarket.

"I'll take that one." Geoffrey laughed, pointing to a trim, sleek thirty-foot sailboat with teak decks and polished brass fixtures called the *Stalwart Angel*.

His father smiled. "Fine," he said, marching up the gangway to peer into the cabin. "Anyone home?" he called. The young bearded skipper popped his head out. "Hello." King smiled. "I'm Bob King of Rexall Drugs and this is my son. We're looking for a boat to sail on the weekends. How much would you charge to make the *Stalwart Angel* available to us whenever we want it?" The skipper laughed in amazement. It so happened he was on board battening down all the hatches in preparation for selling a boat he could no longer afford. "No," King said, "I don't want to buy it, I want to lease—I'll pay a good retainer so you won't have to sell." They disappeared together into the cabin, and when they next emerged, Geoffrey saw them smiling and shaking hands on a deal. Who would not believe that King was master of all that he surveyed?

Sailing had been King's passion since his college days on Lake Erie, and the pitching deck of the *Stalwart Angel* created a camaraderie between father and son somehow not possible on land. The tensions between them vanished in the cathartic slap of a stiff breeze against stiff sails. King, braced at the tiller in a blue velour turtleneck, captained them with dreamy contentment. For Geoffrey, an enthusiastic neophyte, sailing provided clear parameters about how to please his father. They worked together in tandem, anticipating winds, tides, and currents with speed and dexterity; and unlike most Sunday sailors, they worked from nautical charts to reach specific destinations, establishing time frames, then working like hell to race the clock.

During their first months in L.A., King's fortunes had taken such a quantum leap that the exotic landscape merely added to the willful suspension of reality experienced by his family. They shopped for clothes in Beverly Hills—whatever they wanted—in preparation for a weekend at the Eldorado Country Club in Palm Desert, where they stayed in an opulent cottage suite directly next door to vacationing Dwight D. Eisenhower. The cottage belonged to King's new boss, Justin Dart, a close friend of Ike's. The first morning, Geoffrey hitched a ride on the president's golf cart and was invited to play a round of golf. "Do you like living in the White House," Geoffrey asked Ike. "Do you like going to school?" the president replied.

By the time Eleanor Lowe arrived for a visit in early February (only a few weeks after the Kings finally left the Bel Air for their new home), Ruth and Geoffrey couldn't help laughing at her disbelief as she stood in their driveway cradling her irrelevant New York lamb's-wool coat in her arms, staring at the megalopolis of Los Angeles stretched to the horizon—fifteen hundred feet below. Beyond the city, the beaches: the edge of the American continent and the bursting surf of the Pacific shimmering under a bright sun. "Why, this place reminds me of the French Riviera!" Eleanor Lowe exclaimed.

Ruth laughed. "Well, Mother, it's only the Hollywood Hills, but leave it to Bob to be King of the Mountain."

Ruth had initially resisted the move. "What all of us want most of all, Bob, is you. Give us your interest and attention and we'll be happy. I just don't understand you. Why can't you ever be satisfied? We have a good life in St. Paul. This move is wrong for you and wrong for us, and as far as I'm concerned, that's the end of it." To Ruth's argument that California was no place to properly raise their son, King responded by promising a family-togetherness they had never known before. He seemed intent about keeping this promise. At least at first.

"Is this the life?" King sighed from the stern of the boat. He had stripped to the buff and lay spread-eagled on the teakwood afterdeck like a vast blubbery sea lion soaking in the warm sun. Geoffrey was at the tiller. From the moment he arrived in L.A., he knew this was where he belonged. The bright air rang with radiant energy, and the opulent streets and flamboyant people seemed phantoms from his own excessive daydreams. He was at home in the Hollywood Hills in a way he never was in the drab, inhibited Middle West.

"I'm glad we moved here," his son said.

"Yes," King agreed, "we can't do much better than this. Business is a beautiful thing, Geoffrey, exciting as a horse race, except you're betting on yourself to beat the pack. I'm gonna stand this town on its ear before I'm finished—mark my words. I'll tell you a secret: it isn't so hard getting ahead. You've got to play the role you want to get. Most of the people Mother and I entertained over the years were earning a helluva lot more than I was. They never knew that. See, I was building up my contacts. But now I really am their equal—hell, I'm their superior, and they can watch my smoke. Rexall is expanding into plastics, buying up companies, and relying on me to find the right executives to run them. Once I do that, we're hitched to the gravy train forever."

"Great, Dad."

"You bet." King grinned. "One of these days I'm gonna take over a company and show those turkeys what a real executive can do. I'm not just saying that, either. It's gonna happen. And sooner rather than later, too."

King had become nouveau-riche-baronial. Having—not being—governed his passions. His house was run like a cruise ship. Everyone left early in the day, leaving a maid and a houseboy in charge. All day long provisioners arrived. The florist brought three dozen sprays of fresh flowers, which the houseboy arranged in several vases. Then the maid phoned in Ruth's list to the Beverly Hills food merchant whose van climbed the steep, curving Sunset Plaza Drive with so much food that the Kings owned two of Whirlpool's largest refrigerators. At various times during a typical day, the driveway was visited by the liquor store's truck, the dry cleaner's van, the carpet man's truck, the bottled-water truck, the Japanese gardener's pickup, the milkman's van, and the various department-store delivery trucks. King's household expenses were averaging about a thousand dollars a week.

There were days when Geoffrey never saw his parents at all. They left the house while he was still upstairs getting dressed for school, returned home briefly to change and freshen up while he was outside wandering, and arrived home too late for him to go downstairs to greet them. Although he enjoyed ample privacy these days, it was because nobody seemed to care what he did. He could spend hours in his mother's rooms, rummaging in her things, trying on her new clothes, experimenting with her new face glosses and eye shadows. His bedroom faced the city view and looked down on the patio from the second floor. His parents' bedroom, a floor below, opened onto the patio, and he often watched them in their evening clothes, standing together sipping a nightcap and watching the city lights, or, dancing in each other's arms, humming their own music. They talked quietly, intimately, their voices drifting into his open window mixed with night sounds. On balmy nights they sometimes slept with the sliding glass door open, and he thought he heard them making love.

He wanted some of the things the other kids at school had—ten dollars a day spending money, for instance—but when he asked for it, his father exploded: "Why, that's as much as some families are forced to live on!" Other kids may have less, he thought, but in the school he was sent to, nearly everyone else had so much more. They were delivered and picked up by the family chauffeurs in Mercedeses and Rolls-Royces, while he slumped down in the front seat of Teddy the houseboy's VW Beetle. He felt too poor to get chummy with kids who had their own charge accounts in Beverly Hills and took lessons on their own private tennis courts. One of his classmates had a real Renoir in her bedroom. Compared to the parents of these children, King was just a janitor. But try telling him that! These days his father seemed seven feet tall.

King had begun acting as if he owned Rexall. He was impatient and bristling with self-importance, waving aside menus in expensive restaurants and telling everyone to order what they wanted. Geoffrey knew to keep out of the way. But somewhere during the months of adjustment to L.A., Geoffrey also lost his mother. Ruth was seduced—there was no other word for it—and seemed hypnotized by endless rides on King's merry-go-round. Acting as if she had finally shed herself of a lifetime of worry and responsibility, she was in no mood to confront Geoffrey's moodiness, and annoyed that a boy given so much should seem so dissatisfied. "What's the matter now?" she would exclaim in exasperation. "I can't understand you when you're whining, and I'm late already. Now, be a good boy and zip me up in back." Hurt, he became withdrawn, but then his resentments would overflow in a flash of temper. "I'm not your entertainment director," she replied curtly. "If you're bored, you're just going to have to find friends and things to do."

King no longer bothered to take Geoffrey anywhere. He took Ruth on business trips back east, to brunch at the country club; and sailing on the beloved decks of the *Stalwart Angel*, he invited only businessmen. The latter stung most. "Maybe he'd take you, too, if you were more pleasant to be around these days," his mother said. Even being left out was his own fault. He couldn't believe how easily his father broke most of the promises made to him in St. Paul. But only he seemed to care. One day, in pique, he confronted King:

"What about our weekends together and family trips? We never do anything together. Boy, you never keep your word."

"How dare you complain," King declared. "By God, you're the luckiest kid in America."

Because he was hurt and angry, he easily saw through his parents' pretensions. They were living a farce. King was obsessed with trying to impress the world, and his family were bit players in his grandiose productions. But King wasn't rich. He wasn't powerful. On the night he was elected to Rexall's board of directors, he decided to fly his family in the company plane to San Francisco to dine in Chinatown, but they had no sooner taken off than a message was radioed that forced them to turn around and land. Mr. Dart wanted to fly up to Pebble Beach. Mr. Dart owned Rexall. Mr. Dart owned the plane. Mr. Dart was rich and powerful, and whatever King was given was on loan from Justin Dart and at his pleasure. King looked damned sheepish stepping off the plane.

Only Toby, their West Indian maid with a face as grim, as unknowable as an Easter Island totem, seemed to understand

Geoffrey's unhappiness. She was a secret tippler, and one night she came into his bedroom and slumped on the floor at the foot of his bed and began to weep drunken tears. "Oh, Geoffrey, I so lonely here. I so homesick for my people. I got no friends, no nothing. I just stuck here, like you."

Ruth finally took the initiative to find Geoffrey a playmate and drove him halfway down their hill to the home of Gail Westhorn, whose son, Jay, was in Geoffrey's class. Gail was a costume designer for the movie studios, separated from her director-husband, and very beautiful. Geoffrey adored her on the spot, but disliked her son. But it was arranged by their parents that they would play together, out of mutual concern and convenience. They were inescapably brothers in neglect. Jay was not even preferable to total boredom, but his mother was marvelous—chic, elegant, sophisticated, talented. He was mesmerized by her wardrobe and her mini-studio downstairs where she sometimes fitted movie stars. "Oh, Gail, I wish you were my mother," he told her. Gail laughed. "I'm a terrible mother. Ask Jay. But I'm perfect for you as your friend's mother." To Geoffrey she seemed to know more about glamour, business, and life than both of his boring parents combined. She took the boys to the studios and let them watch shows being filmed; but like King, she was wildly inconsistent. Sometimes, for no apparent reason, she slapped ten dollars in both their hands and told them to go get lost for the afternoon. "I need my privacy, kids," she said. Gail's cynical, twinkling eyes read Geoffrey perfectly, and she seemed to know all his secrets, including ones he had not yet revealed to himself. "Hey, Geoffrey, keep your paws out of my closet," she'd call from another room, as if she had left behind her eyes. She taught him fabrics, design, professional stitching. She amazed him with gossip from the studios. She was his real friend, not Jay. He wanted to be with adults, learn from them as much as he could, and one day own his own big house on the hill. Meanwhile, he and Jay faced endless days of unstructured boredom, wandering around neighborhoods as empty and lonesome as a prairie, filling their time with impromptu pranks, such as egging cars from a fence behind the street—until, bored again, they drifted downhill onto the Sunset Strip to seek higher adventure. They got adults to buy their tickets into R- or X-rated movies. Sometimes they hit dime stores or record stores to see what they could swipe. They were never in a rush to return home.

"Where the devil have you been?" his father shouted. "We were ready to call the police. My God, the moon is out."

Jay later recalled watching Geoffrey dress up in his mother's clothes.

"Is Bob upset having a son who's obviously going to be gay?" Gail Westhorn asked Ruth King one day. Ruth was so hurt and shocked by the question that she was absolutely speechless. She turned her back on Gail and walked away.

13

Behind the locked gates of his Bel Air estate, Skip Harte impatiently switched channels on the local six-o'clock news for word about the fate of Geoffrey King. But in less than forty-eight hours, the double matricide had been shunted aside for fresh outbreaks of violence, as if TV were the medium of record to document man's inhumanity to man and the vagaries of existence in a violent age. Fiery freeway crashes, gangland slayings, domestic arguments culminating in a shotgun blast, abandoned day-old infants killed and tossed in a trash barrel, an eighty-seven-year-old woman raped and found impaled on a picket fence—these photogenic horrors provided the backbone of news entertainment, more suggestive and shocking than prime-time police fiction, and infinitely bloodier. Geoffrey had had his moment of stardom, but *sic transit gloria,* so that Skip Harte searched in frustration through the back pages of the Los Angeles *Times* for a possible follow-up that would indicate whether Geoffrey was dead or alive. He was still too upset to make phone calls that might inform him.

Harte was a third-generation Californian, the scion of very old money of a prominent, ultraconservative La Jolla family actively engaged in shipping, banking, and cattle. In Europe, his family would have been titled, while he would have achieved wider renown as an expert connoisseur-collector of eighteenth-century Continental furniture. His twelve-room estate, bristling with sophisticated alarm systems, housed one of the great private collections of museum-quality art and antiques; and among dealers he was thought of as a latter-day Bernard Berenson, whose knowledge and purchasing contacts were peerless. His file of European sellers was guarded in a wall safe, and rumors persisted that Harte was silent partner in several of the best Beverly Hills antique establishments, although he insisted that his annual European buying sprees were a mere indulgence to his favorite avocation.

Only after the death of his elderly parents did Skip come out of the closet to live cautiously and privately as a homosexual. He was then in his forties, and moved from La Jolla to L.A., one hundred and twenty miles north, to be beyond prying eyes. Amid the Bel Air–Beverly Hills axis, he discovered a discreet, almost subterranean gay enclave of wealthy aristocrats like himself—a mix of new and old money, successful professionals and landed gentry joining together in common interests and paranoias. Among these rich, middle-aged gays, discretion was the common valor and they assiduously avoided the flamboyant Hollywood crowd or the gay bars and private dance clubs raided regularly by the police vice squad. Los Angeles Police Chief Ed Davis was on record as believing homosexuals to be "immoral, abnormal, perverted, disgraceful, degrading, and criminal," and the American Civil Liberties Union was busy filing harassment complaints against the police in behalf of gay establishments. Clearly Los Angeles was not the free and open mecca of a New York or San Francisco, but to cautious Skip Harte it was a paradisiacal playground for a gay of discretion and refinement. Through contacts in antiques, Harte had no trouble meeting men of similar interests. They all wanted the same thing: the most beautiful young boys they could find—the boy on the Grecian urn, bronzed golden by the Southern California sun. One saw faltering old men arrive at opulent dinner parties with stunning young men on their arms who might have been their grandsons. Every Sunday a caravan of Rolls-Royces and Bentleys arrived at the front door of Delsy Raymer's Beverly Hills mansion, depositing the town's richest dowager queens, many of whom arrived wearing diamond tiaras and other exquisite family heirlooms for an afternoon tea and dance. Everyone drank Dom Perignon and ogled the stunning male models and call boys rented for the afternoon's entertainment of dowager queens being naughty. Skip Harte was a Raymer regular, but only because he was vastly amused by the antics of these jewel-encrusted libertines. Harte was not promiscuous; he ached for romance and searched continually for a perfect boy to become his perfect lover.

Several months before the murders in Palos Verdes, Harte had discovered Geoffrey King and was instantly smitten. Geoffrey was Skip's fascinating opposite as an unpredictable manchild, but shared his tastes and enthusiasm with a sophistication dismaying in one so young. He was a gorgeous boy, dark and slender, with eyes like ripe olives—a sultry faun, but also a boy of style and breeding, who avoided the gay hangouts in West Hollywood and knew the difference between a Louis XIV and Louis XV chair. They met in the office of a brilliant but eccentric interior designer named Frank Estes, whose quarters above his office were transformed into a replica of a Pompeiian brothel. Frank was a young hawk-nosed redhead who lived near Hollywood, and every night throughout the raucous 1960s, his place was crowded with male revelers thirsting for his punch-bowl concoction of gimlets laced with LSD, the best orgy-inducing lemonade ever devised. Frank was a wild man. Once he crashed an ax into a sideboard when a customer complained it lacked a "distressed look." God knew what he was about, but seemingly he used the chaos of the Vietnam protest movement and the sixties' drug-oriented youth for his own hedonistic, destructive impulses.

Geoffrey was a regular at Frank's parties, wild, petulant, and a little too mad—inventing his madness from moment to moment—not quite in control. A kid who might set somebody's hair on fire to gain attention, Geoffrey fascinated Estes as a living exemplar of the current madness of youth and, unexpectedly, as a leading light in the adolescent process of information-gathering.

The printed word was not Geoffrey's forte; suckled on TV, he learned not by reading but by listening, asking questions, and using his eyes. The kid was also talented and clever. Brilliant. A brilliant boy who had accumulated sophisticated knowledge of art, furniture, antiques, fabrics, and interior design by watching and listening. Estes was impressed. Convinced that Geoffrey could achieve success in either antiques or interior design, he became his mentor, teaching him the intricacies of a complex and subtle industry. Frank hired him as his office assistant—where Skip Harte found him when he dropped by one afternoon to pick up an end table Estes had purchased for him at an auction. He chatted for nearly half an hour with the young helper before whispering to Frank, "My God, who is that boy?" Estes grinned sardonically. "I know," he said. "Now that you two agree on the glories of Versailles, you must go off together in a dazzling sunset."

Harte nicknamed his new lover "Amphion" who built Thebes by charming the stones into place. The perfect lover artfully inflames all of one's vanities, and Geoffrey's swooning enthusiasms upon confronting Harte's priceless possessions, his touching appreciation of the older man's gentle tenderness, his sensitive longing for romance and candlelight, his dreamy contentment and rhapsodical ecstasies, wrung from Harte the fullest measure of devotion and delight.

"I'm happy—at last," he confessed to the seventeen-year-old in his arms. If he had permitted it, Geoffrey would have moved in with him immediately. Skip was tempted; surveying himself in his bathroom mirror, he was now pink and glowing, a handsome, solid fifty-year-old man who looked at least ten years younger. But Geoffrey was a mere boy, a teenager, and at times Skip had to speak to him rather sharply. He was moody and impulsive and a restless night person, oblivious of Skip's habitual routines which began at six in the morning with wide-ranging calls to New York and Europe on business. They compromised: Geoffrey could spend weekends at the estate, and he left changes of clothes in Harte's bedroom closet. Both of them lived for the weekends.

"Where did you find such a treasure?" everyone wanted to know. He took Geoffrey everywhere: to private art galleries where viewing was by appointment only, to the best restaurants, to plays and concerts and the most important dinner parties. The boy's manners were impeccable, and all of Harte's friends envied him a lover who could hold his own among the most effete of the dowager circle, men who declared, "Sometimes when I'm in a silly mood and somebody asks whether my Bollaert is a Vuillard, I say yes. Why not? I only do it for a little harmless amusement."

Picasso, Geoffrey noted, thought that Bollaert was far more convincing than Vuillard. How, Skip wondered, did his young lover know these things? One answer was that he had been reading *Vogue* since he was six and *Architectural Digest* since age eight, and his eye unfailingly appreciated the best. One night, at the home of a wealthy art dealer, the actor Edward G. Robinson sat in a corner with Geoffrey, conversing on art and other matters with noticeable admiration. "Shall I tell you something?" Geoffrey could be overheard saying. "A genius like Picasso uses the gift of his childhood abilities to see and feel. That's mostly what genius is all about, somehow retaining those special powers we are all born with—to *really* see, to *really* feel—which our parents and society drain out of us." Robinson grunted with agreement and told his wife, "You see, dear, I'm not too old to learn from the young."

Harte, of course, glowed pridefully, and found himself eager at times to shed his inbred caution and follow Geoffrey's brash, bold lead. The boy's impulsiveness charmed him at first as he pushed Skip into uncharacteristic adventures. He actually talked him into attending the local Beaux Arts ball, a homosexual costume extravaganza for flamboyant young gays. Harte had only to wear a tuxedo; but Geoffrey threw himself into the event, extracting an agreement that Skip would pay for the costume bills, no complaints, no questions asked. So Geoffrey charged a two-thousand-dollar ball gown at I. Magnin in Harte's name, hired a leading Hollywood beautician to make him up, purchased a two-hundred-dollar wig, rented diamonds at Cartier, and descended Harte's spiral staircase after four hours of preparation looking no less stunning than Elizabeth Taylor in her prime. Geoffrey was the belle of the ball and won first prize for his costume, and to celebrate, Harte and a group of friends arrived at Ciro's for a late-evening supper. Waiting at the bar, they encountered a young and handsome attorney who began to flirt outrageously with Skip's beautiful date, trying to win her name and phone number. Suddenly Geoffrey pulled off his wig and stuck out his hand:

"Hi, Bill, Geoffrey King's the name. Still want a date?"

The usually introverted Skip Harte collapsed on a bar stool in helpless hysterics. And for several weeks his obsession with his man-child paralyzed his usually sharp critical instincts. He had noticed, for example, that Geoffrey was a shockingly heavy drinker for one so young, and several times had caught him searching in the medicine cabinet, presumably for drugs. He was also displeased by Geoffrey's overbearing manner with the servants at home, and his unbridled use of Harte's phone to make endless long-distance calls. He was spoiled, without limits, and would not be intimidated by scoldings or complaints. Most disturbing of all, he seemed to want much more than Harte was prepared to deliver.

"I don't want to know all of his problems and hear all of his complaints," Skip confided to Frank Estes. "He wants me to be his father. What should I do about him?"

Estes chuckled and told him to read *Lolita*. "That's who you are dealing with," he added. As a rich and worldly man, Harte did not shrink from the realization that perhaps both he and Geoffrey were mutually guilty of using one another—at times, callously. When Geoffrey wanted something, he pushed until resistance crumbled, and for weeks he had been badgering Harte to help launch him in the antique or decorating business. "Your contacts are even better than Frank's," he argued, while Harte resisted, not wanting to be drawn into that side of Geoffrey's life. Finally, though, he surrendered and called an acquaintance whom he knew on the shared level of antique expertise—the actor Laurence Harvey, himself a Geoffrey, a mad Hungarian child with Caesar-like taste in antiques, his statues too large, his bronzes too bronze, but always fascinatingly ahead of current fashions: an Eastern European excess transplanted in the excess of Beverly Hills. Harvey was looking for a young but knowledgeable helper to catalog a downtown warehouse crammed with his treasures and to work in his antique shop on La Cienega, a tax write-off protected against browsing customers by a fierce mastiff in the doorway.

Harvey hired Geoffrey, but Skip suffered instant regrets: L. H. could be impossibly demanding and was usually surrounded by a fast Hollywood crowd that was definitely not what

Geoffrey needed at the moment. Even while Skip was being showered with thanks and kisses by his grateful lover, he wondered guiltily whether or not he had unconsciously shoved Geoffrey out of the door and out of his life.

Harvey called Harte a few weeks later to report glowingly about his new assistant. "A bright and marvelous young man who's not afraid to get what he wants out of my upholsterers or framers. By God, if their work isn't right, he makes them do it over. He has a great eye." Harte barely suppressed a laugh, having heard from others how Geoffrey was driving around Beverly Hills, running Larry's errands in one of the actor's fleet of Bentleys. He also knew that Geoffrey was invited to L.H.'s estate in the evenings to help serve guests—mostly other Hollywood celebrities—at nightly screenings of new movies. Heady stuff for Geoffrey. Skip and Geoffrey were seeing less of each other. By midsummer 1969 they had a nasty quarrel when Skip disclosed he would soon be leaving on a five-week buying trip to Europe and refused to take Geoffrey along.

"What about your new job?" Skip remarked defensively.

"Oh, L.H. can spare me. Anyway, I'll learn more about the business watching you operate in Europe than I would a year on the job here."

Harte refused. His negotiations with furniture dealers involved only the intensely private side of himself, and when he explained his feelings, Geoffrey left in anger and hurt. Harte took off for Europe in late July and returned to Los Angeles on Sunday, September 7.

When his butler informed him of the tragedy that had occurred in Palos Verdes barely twenty-four hours earlier, Harte was so stricken with shock and remorse that he took to his bed, wondering if he would ever find the courage to get up again. He tried to recall Geoffrey's numerous complaints about his mother, voiced so dismally to Skip over the past months; but with added anguish, Harte realized that few of Geoffrey's complaints had registered in his memory—mostly because he had not been listening. He dimly recalled Geoffrey's desperate yearning to move out, but his mother somehow thwarted him with a desperation of her own.

My God, Harte thought, if only I had taken that kid to Europe, this might never have happened.

Frustrated by the lack of information on television and obsessed with knowing whether or not Geoffrey had survived his terrible wounds, Harte finally capitulated and called Frank Estes. He really didn't want to call Frank, not knowing how the interior decorator might have reacted to news of the murders. Indeed, Estes' voice seemed dry, almost detached.

"Geoffrey is touch and go," he reported. "He's very critical, but his doctors think he might make it."

"Thank God for that," Skip remarked. "What lies in store?"

"What do you think? He'll be tried for two murders. Listen, there's something I think you should know. Geoffrey was on drugs when he killed them, on LSD. Last Friday L. H. went off to Africa to make a film, and his shop manager didn't wait ten seconds to fire the kid. Pure jealousy, of course, and I told Geoffrey that. He came here in an absolute fury . . . well, you know how he gets, and he talked someone into giving him some very suspicious acid. I warned him against the stuff, but it was like whistling at a wall. I'm just sick about this," Estes said, sounding close to tears.

Skip Harte sent his private secretary, a bearded young Swiss, to the hospital in Torrance with a dozen roses and a note for the patient. The secretary was told that Geoffrey King had been transferred the day before to a downtown facility. When he arrived at that other place, the secretary handed over the note but was told that flowers were not permitted to patients in the prison ward of the USC Medical Center.

14

Geoffrey was carted like wreckage down a long, polished hallway lined with prison cells. He heard men wolf-whistling, calling out taunts, and laughing as he passed—a cacophony of noise echoing off the steep, solid stone walls.

"Hey, baby, you been gang-banged?"

He heard that remark clearly and was terrified. What were they going to do with him? No one had talked to him or told him anything since the murders, and he had no idea how long ago they had occurred. Was he even charged with anything? They wheeled him to the end of the hall, unlocked a cell door, and rolled him inside a small bare room dominated by a hospital bed. Gently he was lifted onto the bed, and a white-coated attendant took his temperature and then left, locking the door behind him. He was alone, surrounded by hardened criminals. He heard them calling out to one another, joking and teasing, sometimes brutal and threatening in their insults. A few claimed to have mutilated themselves to get in this place, calling the prison hospital "the country club," where they could put in soft time. For the first time, he sensed the very real possibility that he would be living with these animals in prison for the rest of his life, and he felt so sick with fear and despair that he attempted to will himself dead. Focusing all remaining energy on his eagerness to die, he held his breath until he passed out. Sometime later, in the night, he became aware of a loud argument outside his cell. He opened his eyes and saw a young white-coated doctor in his doorway, waving a paper in the faces of two impassive policemen. The doctor angrily waved his arms while the two officers studied the document with a maddening bureaucratic lethargy. They shrugged and moved on somewhere else, deaf to the doctor's heated arguments. But soon they returned to fetch Geoffrey.

"We made a mistake," one of the policemen told the patient. "You belong downstairs—not up here." He was wheeled back down the long corridor, and this time when he heard the prisoners' shouts and wolf whistles, he was tempted to raise his middle finger in triumphant disdain, but lacked the will or energy.

The elevator carried him from the thirteenth to the tenth floor, the intensive-care unit of the cardiac wing. They wheeled him into a crowded ward steeped in the silence of illness, and lifted him onto a new bed. Then they shackled his leg to the bed railing—a reminder that he was a prisoner among civilians—and left, telling him that a guard from upstairs would check on him every few hours and warning him to behave. He was too weak even to lift an arm, but so relieved to be out of the prison ward that even the sight of a dead man in the next bed failed to distress him. He was an old black man, yellow-tinged skin stretched tautly across his shrunken face. He still wore an oxygen mask over his nose, but the rubber bladders remained deflated and the man's unblinking eyes stared unseeing. When a nurse finally arrived at Geoffrey's bedside, he mentioned that he thought the man in the next bed was dead. "We'll get around to him," she said, and stuffed a thermometer in his mouth.

Drifting in and out of restless dozes during the long night, he was dimly aware of other people around him, of a sudden burst of activity down the long aisles, followed much later by laconic orderlies who removed the corpse and stripped the bed. As sick as he was, he knew he was in some sort of charity ward for seriously ill poor people who neither expected nor received any amenities, either in life or at death's door. The overworked staff was gruff and exhausted. The dead black man was replaced by a semiconscious Mexican woman, an old crone chanting piteously a prayer in Spanish to the Virgin. Geoffrey wanted to jump out of bed and run away, but he couldn't move. Suddenly he was feverish, thirsty, gasping for breath. Someone had filled his chest with hot sand. He passed out, but was painfully shaken awake and yanked upright into a sitting position.

"Ruff!"

A fierce dog barked into his face. Lucifer's dog, the size of a wolf with saw-blade fangs, had come to fetch him. He put up a weak hand to defend himself as the beast shook his shoulders. Brightness hurt his eyes, and he struggled to see.

"Cough!" the head night nurse repeated. "Do what you're told. Come on, I don't take any guff." She was enormous, and she shook him again like a rag doll. He was in incredible pain.

He coughed—anything to be able to lie back down.

"Again, and more," she bristled. "You've got to clear those lungs."

He began to cry. He couldn't. She left him and then returned with a doctor holding a syringe with a long needle. "Pneumonia," the doctor said, and explained what the needle was for.

The fluid was drawn from his lungs while the patient stared vacantly and never flinched from the usually excruciating procedure. "Didn't that hurt?" the doctor asked.

"Who cares?" His patient shrugged.

He was even less interested in pain than in living. He resented his body and its maddening, independent, stubborn will to survive. He was so disgusted by his stamina that he would have sat quietly while a spike was hammered into his skull, if that would end matters. Pneumonia was fine with him, although he lost count of his days of suffering. One day he awoke knowing that his body had again defeated his will. Nobody had to tell him he would recover, that the crisis was over, because he no longer struggled to breathe and he was hungry. But why? There was not a smidgen of hope remaining in him.

"You certainly are a remarkable survivor," a doctor told him after listening to his chest. Geoffrey turned away bitterly. That night he went berserk, shouting insults at the nurses while begging them to bring a psychiatrist to his beside.

"At least get me Valium," he pleaded.

"You'll get a swat if you don't shut up," the head duty nurse told him. One of the sheriff's deputies came down from the prison ward to warn him to behave, but finally a rumpled doctor arrived, claiming to be a staff psychiatrist.

"You're just going to have to be patient," Geoffrey was told. "I can't help you right now. The law prohibits that."

"Fuck the law! I'm going out of my mind, doctor. Do something—I beg you."

"I can't. Not until the court psychiatrists talk to you. You have to wait."

"I can't wait," he sobbed. "I killed two people. Don't you understand? I can't handle my feelings. Help me."

The doctor slipped him two Valiums.

A black lady whose son was recovering from open heart surgery in the next bed sat with him awhile each day. She brought him oranges and held his hand while he told her about his crime.

"They forgave you," the lady said, smiling with certainty.

"How do you know?" he challenged her. "How can you say that?"

She was very stout and religious and chuckled at his question while fanning herself with a magazine.

"Oh, I know because I'm a mama, too. I know exactly how your mama feel. If you done that to me, I'd of forgived you. Mother love is the strongest love there is. Yes, she forgive you, and so do your granny. I'm certain of that as the stars do shine.

Your mama up there in heaven this very minute shining a blessing on her darlin' boy."

"But I killed her. I took away her life."

"It don't matter what you done. A mama don't hold no grudges. You more precious to her than life. Don't fret about that. I'm telling you what truly is."

He was shackled to his bed with a twelve-foot chain and twice a day was forced to walk up and down the aisle in front of his bed to exercise, sweating in humiliation, dragging his clanking convict chain behind him, although the other patients were too sick or indifferent to notice. A nurse brought him a note in a sealed envelope that had been delivered to the hospital a week earlier. He saw Skip Harte's neat handwriting, but tore the note in half. That part of his life was over.

Early one morning, shortly after the night shift changed, a doctor removed his stitches. For the first time, Geoffrey saw what he had done to himself, and felt sick.

"I had to be crazy to do this, didn't I?" he asked the doctor.

"A safe assumption," the doctor said, shaking his head. The scars began at his collarbone and ended above his navel. He had raked himself with that knife. Less than an hour after they removed his stitches, he was removed, too. This time he did not ask where they were taking him and was prepared for the shouts and wolf whistles greeting his appearance in a wheel-chair rolled down the long corridors of the prison ward. A visitor awaited him in his cell: a homicide detective.

He looked like a detective: a big man with hard, unfeeling eyes. "I tried to see you in Torrance," he said, "but the doctors said you were in no shape. Looks like you're on the mend."

"Go away," Geoffrey said.

"I won't take long," the detective replied. "Just want to fill in a few details."

"I admitted I did it. I have nothing more to say. Leave me alone."

"Look, son, you're in the worst trouble imaginable. You'd better face up to it and cooperate."

"You don't scare me. I want to die for my crime. Right now. That's all I want, and that's all I have to say. So please leave."

The detective stood up and shrugged. "Can't force you, I guess, but you're only making matters worse for yourself."

"That's impossible," Geoffrey said. "Now please go away."

Geoffrey approached the thick glass window in the visitors' room cautiously, uncertain whom he would find waiting on the other side; and when he saw who was there, he shrank back, ashamed to be seen this way, in this place. Beyond the thick glass, two men smiled uncertainly, then sat down and picked up the telephone receivers to communicate with him. Each of them felt melodramatic, as if they were appearing in a Late Show prison movie.

Skip Harte smiled. "God, it's good to see you. You look okay, too. I didn't know what to expect."

It was a lie. Geoffrey looked dreadful. Pale and drawn, with dark circles under his eyes. He had lost twenty pounds off his slight frame and seemed almost moronically torpid. His chin quivered continually on the verge of tears, and his lifeless eyes avoided theirs.

"Geoffrey, you are one helluva survivor, I must say," Frank Estes remarked. "I never thought I'd see you again. Damn this glass: I wish I could give you a hug."

"A cosmic joke," Geoffrey remarked. "The kind you like, Frank. God is playing games with me. Keep Geoffrey alive . . . punishment for the crime. You can't know how humiliating it really is still being here. I did my best, you know. Thirteen stab wounds."

"Jesus, that many?" Skip exclaimed. "Well, how are they treating you?"

The prisoner shrugged. "I'm locked up in a cell all day. They feed me my meals in my cell, too. Thank God I'm a minor so they've got to keep me separated from the adults, because they're all animals, real criminals. I don't know how long I've been here. I've lost track. I have a lawyer now, a public defender from the juvenile authority. He came to see me a few days ago to explain everything. It sounds very complicated, and I can't remember. They want to test my sanity. I know that, but that's all I know."

He unbuttoned his denim prison shirt and displayed his scarred chest. His visitors stared solemnly through the glass as if observing a grotesque, exotic marine creature in an aquarium.

"I had to be crazy, didn't I, to do that, much less what I did to them? Frank, you warned me not to take that LSD and I didn't listen. I didn't listen, and now two people are dead. Anyway, it wasn't just the bad acid. My whole rotten life just caught up with me. I had a breakdown, just like my father did a few years ago. I cracked. Did you know I quit my job with Harvey two weeks before the murders? I was in such terrible shape I couldn't handle it; but then they called every day, begging me to come back, and I did, and then that fucker of a manager canned me! That broke my back, I'll tell you. That last week, I dropped acid about a dozen times, Frank. I found this boy on the beach, my age, and he had all this acid. We tripped together. He was as hurt and unhappy as I was. We were going to run off to Mexico, because he saw what I faced at home. But then he just disappeared. I don't know what happened to him. He was very beautiful and we had beautiful times. I wonder if I invented him? Maybe he really didn't exist. I don't know. I was really crashing."

Skip Harte flushed and looked away, wondering if Geoffrey was trying purposely to hurt him.

"I only wish I had taken you with me," Skip said sadly.

"Europe, you mean? Too late! I was too crazy to handle it. I was heading for disaster and couldn't be stopped. I even told my mother I was going crazy, but there was nothing she could do. But, dammit, they should never have allowed her to bring me home from jail. How could they do that? I was deranged."

He began to cry. "I'm scared," he whispered to them into the phone. "I want to die, not be in prison for the rest of my life. I can't face it. The fear, I mean. The fear."

Skip Harte leaned forward in his chair and saw Geoffrey hiding his face in his hands.

"Baby, we're with you. We love you. We'll stick by you, no matter what."

"Poison," Geoffrey whispered. "I mean it, Skip. If you love me, get some to me."

91

15

Under California statutes, murder is defined as the unlawful killing of a human being with malice aforethought, while voluntary manslaughter is killing without malice—an act of passion or impulse. In juvenile crimes involving murder, the district attorney's office is often invited by the juvenile authorities into the pretrial deliberations to determine whether or not the accused should be tried as an adult. At the time of Geoffrey's incarceration, the death penalty was still on the books. Deputy District Attorney John Provenzano read the reports on the King case and notified the juvenile authorities of his intention to proceed with a conviction for first-degree murder. The King boy was only months short of eighteen, the legal age of adulthood, and this case, a drug-related double murder, was disgustingly similar to the recent massacre in Benedict Canyon by the then still-at-large Charles Manson "family." The only mitigating circumstance in the King case was the questionable judgment of the Pasadena police releasing him to his mother. But the D.A. blamed the lenient California juvenile laws for that. The police report indicated that Geoffrey King was a chronically unstable psychopath with a long history of mental illness, but the brutality of the murders of his mother and grandmother—so similar to the Tate-LaBianca slayings—made it mandatory for the prosecution to push for maximum punishment.

"They can't cop an insanity plea if he voluntarily took drugs," Provenzano reminded his staff. "If the court psychiatrists find him insane, that's one thing; but if he's fit to stand trial, we can convict him."

The majority of serious crimes in the state were drug-related and caused by persons between sixteen and nineteen; and Provenzano, like a lot of other people, was fed up.

The decision was made to keep Geoffrey King on ice until his eighteenth birthday on October 10, and then try him as an adult for first-degree murder. On the case folder, somebody scribbled with a red marker, "No plea-bargaining."

* * *

Raymond Lowe had retreated into depression. With his actress-wife back east doing television commercials, he saw few people and spent his days in his small apartment drinking too much. In later years he would admit feeling tainted by his nephew's crime, which seemed to him to cast shame on all surviving family members. Social and business acquaintances were avoiding him, as if he, too, were responsible for the crimes. It occurred to him that those who were convinced that his nephew was mentally ill probably suspected a congenital form of insanity that rotted the entire family tree. He felt much like his old Aunt Jessica, who pledged her immediate family members to secrecy over the tragedy in California. He was bitter and ashamed. When the homicide detectives questioned him about his nephew, he carefully pruned Geoffrey from the Lowe side of the family and placed him exactly where he belonged: on the King side. He told the detectives that mental illness was inherited on the King side (the family rumor was that King's mother was "very peculiar") and that both father and son were certified schizophrenics. Both had spent time in mental institutions, and both had tried to commit suicide. He told them that at least one psychiatrist had warned Geoffrey's mother that a child who was suicidal often harbored the kind of hostile feelings that could cause harm to others. But of course she ignored the warning. Raymond's views were documented in a twelve-page homicide report filed by the detectives, and those involved in both the prosecution and defense of the case briskly underlined that Geoffrey had been in and out of mental hospitals since age thirteen.

Ray Lowe was the official family spokesman and the only family member whose views were represented in the report. Although he provided the name of Dr. Maurice Whitten, a psychiatrist who had treated his nephew for several years, no one in authority bothered to contact him or check on Lowe's statements, which became increasingly definitive as the trial date approached. Of course, he was unaware of his impact in a case presumably considered too open-and-shut to demand much investigatory legwork. The detectives liked Lowe and sympathized with him. He was obviously shattered by the tragedy, and they kept him informed. From them he learned his nephew would soon be undergoing psychiatric evaluation. "Those shrinks better be on their toes," he muttered. "That boy is the most artful deceiver they'll ever encounter. There's nobody he can't fool for an hour or two. That's part of his syndrome, his sickness. His father was the same way." Then he added that he wasn't being vindictive, but only wanted assurance that Geoffrey would be put away where he couldn't do any more harm. The detectives hinted that the D.A.'s office would be calling Lowe soon with good news on that score.

To far-flung family friends and relations who called him seeking information on what had happened, Lowe invariably failed to mention that Geoffrey was under the influence of drugs when the murders occurred, leaving the impression that his nephew had lashed out cold-bloodedly without reason. For years Ray had been extremely critical of the way that both of Geoffrey's parents had raised Geoffrey; but now he portrayed his dead sister as a saintly martyr, a Madonna of naiveté who mistakenly thought she could help Geoffrey. Of Ruth he declared, "The meek shall inherit the earth—provided the naive haven't already given it away."

Nevertheless, those who ultimately took charge of Geoffrey's defense believed that Lowe's statements in the police report represented the one shred of hope for keeping his nephew from a life sentence behind bars.

Geoffrey complained of severe chest pains and periodic seizures of breathlessness, and the doctors found several ventricular defects on the right side of his heart, either damage missed during repair surgery or a loosening of implanted sutures. He would need corrective surgery at some future time, but the situation was not life-threatening. He was judged fit for transfer from the prison hospital.

The idea of being moved—even from such a terrifying place as the prison ward, where guards escorted him to the shower room only after lights out—filled him with unaccountable dread. For nearly three weeks he slept curled in a protective shell, his face turned to the wall, pretending he was invisible, but the other inmates never forgot he was there, his youth exciting them as if he were a beautiful woman; and they called out to him from their cells and told him in the most graphic way all the things they were going to do to him when they finally got their hands on his soft flesh. Even so, fear of the unknown outweighed the fear he experienced daily.

A six-and-a-half-foot detective came to take him to Juvenile Hall.

"What's that?" he asked.

"A place for bad-ass kids like you."

How poignant, he would remember thinking, to be out in the world again, even though he was handcuffed in the backseat of a police sedan moving much too quickly through a sunny morning that failed to brighten the drab back streets of a Mexican barrio, its walls spray-painted in Spanish graffiti. They drove through neighborhoods where any sensible white man would lock the car doors and keep the windows rolled up, yet Geoffrey envied everyone on the streets. Even a drunk propped asleep in a doorway had more going for him than Robert King's son. He would gladly trade places with the meanest, worst person he saw. And he would give an arm to be able to spend an hour alone sitting under a tree or strolling in the park. Freedom! Privacy! My God, how precious . . . what losses! Without them, life was not worth living, and yet he had always taken them for granted.

He was already thinking like a convict.

16

1963–1964

Wherever the Kings lived, there was always a room reserved for Ruth's mother, Eleanor. If Ruth was asked, for example, where to find the sewing basket, she'd reply, "Look in Gram's room, on the top shelf of her closet." Her clothes and hatboxes were stored even though she had not been there in months. As a child, when Geoffrey heard of her impending visit, he drove Ruth to distraction, pestering her almost hourly on how much

longer until Gram arrived. He never understood why his eagerness for her arrival and sadness over her departure were the
direct opposite of his parents' emotions. Gram and Mother
bickered a lot, especially over Mother's smoking, drinking, and
weight. Dad seemed uncomfortable around her. But as a child,
Geoffrey adored her. His favorite moment was to sit with
Eleanor in her room and watch her write letters with his late
grandfather's thick black pen that looked like a cigar. She wrote
with lavender ink, and if he sat quietly, she let him lick and seal
the envelopes. Her handwriting was as precise and elegant as
she was. All of her belongings were treated as precious heirlooms, meticulously wrapped in tissue and stored in their original boxes. She showed him a silver vase that stood on her
nightstand throughout fifty years of marriage and always contained a single fresh rose, a daily gift of love and appreciation
from his grandfather, who had died only a few years before
Geoffrey was born. "The most tragic loss I will ever carry in my
heart," she sighed. "Love like ours is eternal. I'm sure of it, even
though Larry would chide me for being a sentimental fool. He
didn't believe in an afterlife, but, oh, he believed in a happy life
in the here and now. Our home was filled with love and laughter, Geoffrey. Everyone adored that man. Your own dad told
me at Larry's funeral that he loved him more than his own
father." His grandfather was a poet and self-taught scholar who
spoke six languages fluently and could translate books aloud
from French or Spanish into perfect English. As a young man
he rode down to Mexico on horseback and helped build a railroad. "They don't make men of his breed anymore," Gram
said. "I'm not just saying that out of pride, either, because I
wish it wasn't so. But that kind of man belongs to another age,
unfortunately."

He peppered her with questions about his parents, and her
responses stuffed him with pride and wonder. Ruth was described as a precocious student and gifted poetess who might
have been the next Edna St. Vincent Millay if she had only kept
at it. Oh, yes, she had had a wonderful childhood—both children had. She was taken to the Grand Canyon, to Canada and
Montana. She went hiking with her dad in the Rockies; and
later on, in college, fended off dozens of young men eager to
date a pretty, lively and sometimes naughty flapper. Mother

loved to dance. She loved fun. The joy of life shone in her eyes. "Your parents met at college. Bob was the one who pursued her. In those days, he was so thin that he reminded everyone of a gaunt Abe Lincoln. These were difficult times. Millions were out of work and your dad was very poor. He played the piano in cabarets and the organ in churches to help support himself through school. Believe it or not, in those days he was quite shy and blushed a lot. Your grandfather was a wholesale poultry-and-egg merchant, and he gave Bob fresh eggs and chickens to keep him from starving. That's a true story."

Sometime during his childhood, however, Geoffrey began to realize that while she stayed with them, Gram didn't really live with them, but remained aloof, like a regal houseguest demanding special treatment. Yet she remained an ally; she took his part with his parents, even stood up to his father, who accused her of using her mouth like a blunt instrument. But during her first trips to L.A., King seemed to cast her in his spell, too.

For her 1963 visit, Eleanor arrived shortly before the double birthdays of King and son and discovered Geoffrey living inside a fiberboard doll's house perched next to the garage. Geoffrey was living in there because his father ordered him to clean up his messy room or move out, which seemed to Eleanor a rather severe either/or, except that Geoffrey had been ignoring nicer requests for several days. Her grandson responded to the ultimatum by carrying down a pillow, lamp, and favorite scatter rug, hung curtains in the large window, and crawled through the doorway. He slept in there but ate his meals in the house. Eleanor peered through the curtained window and ordered Geoffrey to come out immediately. She was told to go away. When she insisted, her grandson spoke sharply and told her to get lost. Her visit did not begin auspiciously.

Eleanor Lowe wrote to her son and daughter-in-law:

Dear Ones:

Bob and I have had quite a row. For several days we haven't been speaking and avoid being in the same room. The donnybrook started after dinner several nights ago— after Geoffrey had left the table and gone upstairs to his room. Bob started in on Ruth about some minor matter, but in his typical arrogant way. I saw red and let him have it. As usual, he has dumped all of the family responsibilities in her lap, including the Geoffrey Problem, and then, of course, blames her when things go wrong, as they inevitably do. Here, too, he is afraid of failure and has made her his scapegoat. It is so unfair to Ruth, who is definitely not a disciplinarian. Nor is Bob much better. He is uninvolved and neglectful, expecting Geoffrey to be a perfect young adult, and when he isn't, he blames Ruth for being permissive. Geoffrey resents discipline but also yearns for it as proof that his parents still care. A few days ago he was screaming so loudly I thought I'd lose my mind, while Ruth tried to ignore him, until I finally told her that if he was my son I'd wash his mouth out with soap. Well, the look of loathing I received from that child! But the very next evening he came to my room and sobbed in my arms, telling me how miserable he was and how confused, with millions of problems. It broke my heart. Ruth showed me his latest report card with three F's and four D's and a note from the teacher saying he puts forth so little effort there is no way to evaluate his capabilities.

I asked Ruth what she planned to do about this and she said there was nothing she could do because it was Geoffrey's way of getting his father's attention. She said they were too alike not to be antagonists. Well, that's true. They are either sweet or nasty—no in-betweens. Thoughtful or rotten, without any restraints. One day Bob might take him sailing, and then not talk to him again for a week. Geoffrey can be loving and kind one minute and look as if he wants to hit you the next. Ruth has her hands full, I don't deny it. But she does so little to try to improve a situation that gets worse and worse.

Bob accused Ruth of never doing anything right, and I just saw red. I called him a weak man and a fool, a failure as a father and a husband, who absolutely was doomed to fail at everything unless he faced reality and became aware of his own destructiveness. I said he was a very limited small-town person in way over his head, and the sooner he realized his limitations, the better off he and everyone else would be. Well, his face turned that peculiar livid color and he went berserk. I thought he was going to punch me, but Ruth moved quickly, I must say, to protect me. He threw down his napkin and left the house, but not before screaming curses at me. It was very ugly, very tense, and believe me, he knew I had his number and always did. I'll be very interested to hear whether he dares to accurately repeat to you what I said to him.

I don't regret what I said. I hope it will do some good around here and help bring them to their senses. I hope I'm wrong, but I think Ruth has reached a point where she really doesn't care what happens to any of them, herself included. This family is a mystery to me and to themselves.

It is all very depressing, I know.

As ever,
Mother

17

1964

Gail Westhorn was incredulous at Ruth's news. "Why, you can't do that! That's like moving from Paris to Poland!" But Ruth was adamant: the Kings were moving from the Hollywood Hills to the San Fernando Valley. The hills were charming, but too corrupting—an enclave of affluence that was wearing down her family's values. Too many show people driving too many fancy cars. Too many wrong influences, especially on her impressionable son. Geoffrey was hanging around with some bearded, unemployed musician who was teaching him how to play the guitar and who made a living by selling drugs and renting out his Mercedes to young actors trying to make an impression at parties. Really! Gail laughed at her. "Ruth, you can run, but you can't hide from the world."

Ruth wasn't so sure. L.A., she discovered, was a community of enclaves within enclaves stretching across two mountain ranges equal in size to the state of Rhode Island, and although linked by a ubiquitous freeway system, people pretty much stayed within a ten-mile-square area where they lived and worked—their "neighborhood." The affluent West Side was moderate only in its sea-breeze climate. But the Valley, smog-shrouded and admittedly hot, was a flat bowl isolated by mountain ranges that represented a vast enclave of middle-class living. There, at least, people washed their own cars and mowed their own lawns. Families went to church and kids joined the scouts. She had found a lovely home in the community of Westlake Village, which a realtor told her was every bit as affluent as Beverly Hills, but without the phony ostentation that was so offensive.

Gail laughed again. "Oh, Ruth, all she meant was that West-lake Village doesn't have many Jews."

Ruth flushed with anger. They were moving. That was that. Even Bob agreed that they needed a change. Everything was just too much on their mountaintop. The new house had a backyard swimming pool, and Jay was invited to spend week-ends swimming with Geoffrey.

"Gail, I had to do something. We couldn't go on this way." Gail didn't understand, but Ruth's tight face did not invite fur ther questions.

A few months earlier, Ruth had been invited to lunch by Tildy Ridauer, the lively wife of one of King's staunchest foes at Rexall. But Ruth liked Tildy, and when they first moved to L.A., the two couples became friends. Then Barry and Bob had a serious falling-out at the office and the Ridauers headed King's black list. Ruth was delighted to see her again, and they spent an entire afternoon in the garden court of the Beverly Hills Hotel, talking even after the tables were set for dinner and the bar became crowded for cocktail hour. Ruth would later say that it was one of the most important afternoons she had ever spent, and in many ways, one of the most unpleasant. They talked mostly about Rexall, and Ruth was amazed at her igno-rance of the business world. Of course, she knew only what Bob told her, which was never very much, but Tildy opened her eyes. She had been an executive's secretary for years. That was how she met Barry. And she possessed a shrewd, analytical mind.

She told Ruth that Bob was right: there was a cabal out to get him. Usually a cabal is worn as a badge of honor by an executive who is out in front in the contest for power. A cabal signifies jealousy, which was certainly true in King's case because he got off to a very strong start and made a terrific impression on Dart. But jealousy was no longer the motive. Now most of those closing ranks against Ruth's husband claimed he was corrupted by power, and rumors were circulating that he was involved in some highly unethical stock manipulations. Barry had told his wife that twice this past year Dart had extended personal loans to King to bail him out of financial binds. Bob was always short of money. And frankly, his expense accounts were a scandal. The comptroller claimed that finding the bottom was like un-peeling the world's largest onion. She added that Bob called attention to himself from the first day by putting up his family at the Bel Air Hotel for a month.

"Ruth, Bob is not a kid," she said. "He should know better. That's amateur stuff, running up such bills. Dart wasn't pleased, I can tell you that. It wasn't the money. It was Bob's poor judgment. And it looked so déclassé for a new vice-president to do something like that. Oh, Ruth, I'm not trying to hurt you, please believe me."

Ruth felt ill. Physically ill. "I knew it was wrong," she said. "But you know Bob. He said we were in the big leagues now and not to worry." But suddenly she felt a surge of loyalty for her husband and surprised herself by lashing out against Rexall. "What do they expect?" she said. "They pump up these men, give them these enormous salaries, pompous titles, all these memberships and expense accounts and private planes . . . how can they expect them not to have their heads turned, not to feel above reproach or restraint? I mean, it really is laughable how Rexall continually claims to be a family and wants only good family men in the executive suite, and here Bob has traveled to New York and Chicago sixteen times already this year. Blatant hypocrisy, if you ask me. I don't know how many times Dart has called our house on weekends, so that Bob was afraid to leave and we all had to sit around on our hands. I'm not saying Bob's an angel. I'm saying they aren't playing fair."

Tildy's small smile of agreement was in part condescending.

"They're little boys playing games," she said. "That's life in the good ol' executive suite in nearly every company there is. Games on games. A lot of time is spent gratifying egos. Games and toys like the plane and Eldorado Country Club. But do you know what all of the baloney really boils down to? In the end, it really is the schoolhouse. Your immediate boss is your teacher, and Dart is the principal. Everyone gets report cards every year, just like your kids do. If you pass, you get a raise and a pat on the back. And they're graded just like seventh-graders: co-operates with others, gets to work on time, is honest in his dealings, cheerful with his colleagues, neat and orderly in his work, does his homework, and uses initiative and imagination. There's really very little difference in what the teacher expects from your kid and what Rexall and all the rest of them expect from their employees. Bob's been around. He knows all about that, but Barry thinks—and I happen to agree—that he is like our middle boy who rebelled like hell against authority and was always in hot water. Either that or Bob has become so arrogant that he thinks he's above rules. If so, he is sadly mistaken, because Dart plays strictly by these rules. You've seen his estate, haven't you? I mean, you'd better wear comfortable shoes just to walk the hallway; but he's the first in his office and the last to go home."

"Well, that was never Bob's way," Ruth said, staring at her barely touched fruit-salad plate. "He doesn't like paperwork or being tied down in an office."

"I know. That's a complaint against Bob. He's too eccentric. Three-hour lunches. Reports late. And he doesn't delegate very well. He should at least be where people can find him."

"Oh, Tildy, what should I do? What can I do?"

"Well, pressure causes different reactions in different men, but they all suffer from it, believe me. Rexall is a tough, competitive place, very demanding. Poor Barry is in charge of a regional sales division. I mean, you can't bluff your way if the figures aren't there. But Bob has it so much easier, Ruth. What is it? Industrial relations and public relations. Well, it's true he's had some tough assignments, but there are no black-and-white figures staring him in the face. He can talk his way around any problem because what he does is basically subjective. That's why it's so criminal for him to blow it. With Barry, if sales are down, so is he, and excuse my French, I've got to work like hell to get it up. Every New Year, he resolves not to take it so seriously. But he still worries too much, takes pills to sleep, gets nervous rashes. The pressure is there, and so is the insecurity. Let's face it: there's a lot at stake. He's making a very handsome living but he has got to keep performing. It's not easy. Especially for men in their fifties who see younger men edging toward recognition from the boss.

"Ruth," she concluded, "if I were you, I'd get the hell out of the Hollywood Hills and find a nice, quiet place in the Valley. Inject as much reality into your husband's life as you can, take over the bankbooks if possible, and give him a lot of sympathy and tenderness. Bob is not a youngster. He could be in deep trouble if things don't change dramatically, and soon. Excuse me for being so blunt, but you've got to get cracking and be strong, because if he should lose out at Rexall, well, it could be much tougher for you down the road."

The two women embraced emotionally saying good-bye, but Ruth had a final question before she departed: "Tildy, did somebody from Rexall ask you to take me to lunch?" Her companion laughed. "Now, that's a good question. It shows that you're finally thinking like a veteran wife of the executive suite." But Tildy Ridauer never answered her directly. Or, being herself a veteran executive wife, perhaps she did.

It was early in May when the two women met for lunch. The Kings moved to Westlake Village in mid-July.

"The Valley!" Jay exclaimed at Geoffrey's news. "That's where Mom took us to Warner Brothers. The Valley sucks!"

Yet it seemed a glorious place during the final weeks of summer, when King took a vacation, Nick and Marion Hopps and their four kids came to visit, two friends arrived from a study trip to Mexico, and Jay, whose mother was touring Europe with a boyfriend, slept on the floor in a bedroll. Everyone stayed in bathing suits and the backyard grill smoked constantly with the delicious aroma of charring steaks and hamburgers. They lived in the pool, playing tag and water polo until the bottoms of Geoffrey's feet were so sore that he could barely walk; his throat ached from squeals and laughter. Ruth shoved Nick into the pool in his slacks and shirt, and he surfaced holding his martini glass above his head. Someone accidentally dumped chicken soup into King's lap and the Hoppses' six-year-old boy laughed. "Oh, look, Uncle Bob boiled his weiner." Nick and Bob mysteriously disappeared for a couple of hours one day, and when they returned, they brought with them a beautiful gray weimaraner, twenty-seven inches at the withers, the most incredible dog any of them had ever seen. Everyone seemed to ache with joy and love. King strung Chinese lanterns around the pool, set up the stereo outside, invited over the new neighbors, and everyone danced—kids and adults—under a full moon, their faces cast in an eerie greenish glow from the pool lit under the water. Late one night Geoffrey sat next to his father in the den while he hoisted a few drinks with Nick. He was barely awake, cradled in his Dad's lap, and heard his father repeat what Ruth had said earlier, wishing the vacation would never end and that the Hoppses would forget Kansas City and move in next door. But then King turned solemn and told Nick that he had several hundred thousand dollars in stock and insurance.

"Nick, if anything happens to me, I want you to manage my estate. Ruth doesn't know beans. I'm making you my executor with full power for decision."

Nick was moved. "Well, Bob, I could abscond with everything." He smiled.

"You could, but you won't," his father replied.

Nick went to bed, but King sat up alone and Geoffrey never stirred from his father's lap, where he dozed contentedly until he felt a splash of water on his bare shoulder. He opened one eye, thinking his Dad's glass of liquor had dripped on him, but was shocked to discover tears rolling down King's cheeks.

Everyone thought it strange and sad when the day after the Hoppses departed, the weimaraner leaped over the backyard wall and disappeared. The family searched for him for hours, but finally gave up. The dog never returned.

18

KANSAS CITY, 1964

The humid Midwestern summer began to ebb, and by Labor Day early evenings carried an invigorating westerly breeze that swept away the thick, humid heat and scattered litter among the concrete arches of Kansas City's new shopping plaza and mall. The breeze sailed spray from the playing fountains in the courtyard, causing a well-dressed young girl to turn away and readjust the fur wrap on her slender shoulders. She walked quickly, as if late for an appointment, her high heels clicking across the stones. She was pretty, but stared straight ahead, avoiding the admiring glances of passersby attracted to the striking blond hair cascading across her shoulders. Too blond to be real, maybe, but the fur was real mink, and her clothes looked expensive. Her makeup was tasteful, not garish. She certainly wasn't a hooker, because if some lout blocked her path and attempted a pickup, she froze and then quickly zipped around him and ran toward the safety of other strollers. She usually appeared around ten in the evening, when most of the stores were closed, but found her way to the back rows of an auction gallery specializing in antiques and Oriental rugs. She never bid and never spoke to anyone. She left before midnight, driving away in a blue Oldsmobile with California plates. Anyone who had bothered to follow her home might have suspected that she was someone's mistress. She lived alone in a tiny studio apartment in a transient apartment-hotel.

"Geoffrey, I'm missing twenty-five dollars from my purse and I wonder if you know anything about it," his mother asked him not long after they had fled to Kansas City to escape an unhinged Bob King. He seemed indignant, but she found a sales slip for a twenty-five-dollar blond wig on his dressing table; and when she opened the closet in his studio apartment, she discovered her mink stole and three good dresses. The next day when he was at school, Nick came over and helped Ruth move all of Geoffrey's belongings back down the hall into the tiny studio apartment in which she lived.

It was Nick who found a Beretta pistol hidden in twelve-year-old Geoffrey's shoebox. Ruth found two empty bourbon bottles under the couch.

"Damn, damn," she muttered. "Another good intention bites the dust." There was no room in her small, crowded apartment, which was why she had allowed him to move down the hall by himself in the first place. Ruth and her son were living like political exiles who had run for their lives.

When Nick and Ruth questioned Geoffrey about the pistol, he told them the truth: Jay Westhorn had lent it to him in California in exchange for one of Geoffrey's jock straps. The Beretta was a war souvenir brought home by Jay's dad and forgotten in a desk drawer. Ruth solemnly produced the two empty liquor bottles—Exhibit B. He flushed. He didn't dare tell her that on some nights he was so tense he could drink nearly a pint without feeling any effect. He was petrified, not only by the real possibility that his father might actually come here and kill them, but also because he was now forced to tie his ankle to the bedrail. He was sleepwalking. One night he woke up across the street from the hotel and stared in bewilderment at his third-floor window. He was wearing only Jockey shorts and knew he was not dreaming. It was real. He had to wake up the building manager to get a passkey, explaining he had been locked out while going down the hall to visit his mother. Another time he woke up standing in the empty elevator.

"Well?" Ruth said, holding the two empty bottles.

"What do you want me to say? Really, Mother, I'm amazed that you'd even notice, the way you're emptying your own these days."

He saw her hurt and immediately went to her. He hugged her and began to cry.

"We've been shattered, Geoffrey," she moaned. "Look what he's done to us."

Through Nick, Bob King was consulted in California and reluctantly agreed to increase the weekly checks to pay for a psychiatrist for his son. Even more reluctantly, Geoffrey agreed to go, only because his mother begged him. It was the third psychiatrist he had seen that year; at least this one, unlike the two pompous frauds in Beverly Hills, seemed kind and caring.

"Your mother tells me you began dressing up in her clothes and stealing her car back in California. I'd be interested in hearing about this."

"I'm sure you would," the patient grimly replied. But he was ashamed to tell, not only for himself, but for his family. Who could believe his fear of his father, who had suffered a mental breakdown, who systematically drove them from his life, and even now, while living apart and legally separated from Ruth, called her almost nightly, shouting curses and threatening to fly there and kill her and Geoffrey? How could he recount the nightmare of the past year? Who would believe him?

It was the Year of Worsts. The worst wasn't when King had gone off somewhere and no one knew where he was—on the run in some distant city—and Rexall called the house wondering if they had heard from him. He would burst in on them, slamming the back door so violently that the glass panes shattered (that happened twice) to announce his return, only to closet himself inside the wet bar until he passed out on the couch. No, that wasn't the worst.

The worst was when he came home from work and without a word or warning slapped Ruth across the mouth so violently that contents of the pan she was holding splattered across a far wall. Often he chased her down the hall, ignoring her shrieks, dragged her into the bedroom, and kicked the door shut while Geoffrey listened to lamps overturning between the sounds of the slaps and punches. But even more disturbing was the fact that they were getting used to it. Ruth begged Geoffrey not to hate his father. He couldn't help it. He was cracking up under the worst strain imaginable.

One relatively calm night, watching *Gone with the Wind* on TV, they suddenly heard the ungodly racket of a car going berserk directly outside the front windows. Geoffrey saw Mr. Bourne, who lived across the street, racing his black Cadillac back and forth across the Kings' newly sodded lawn, smashing down flowerbeds and rosebushes and raising a defiant fist at Geoffrey's father. Ruth was forced to tell Geoffrey that King was having an affair with Kim Bourne, the flashy mother of one of his friends. His reaction was close to the very worst, although not as upsetting as finding his mother alone in the living room, drunk, her eyes vacant and glassy, knowing that she was at the end of her rope. The idea of losing her caused a rash to break out across his chest and stomach. "I won't let him win, Geoffrey," she gasped. "He can kill me, but I won't let him push me out the door. Too much invested." Because King insisted, she still slept beside him in the same bed, and they even went out together to certain parties and functions for appearance' sake, but only after he threatened to kill her if she told a soul what was happening inside the privacy of their home.

In the midst of all of this, Geoffrey began stealing the car at night. He dressed up in his mother's clothes, figuring the police might mistake him for a young woman rather that a twelve-year-old boy. Sometimes he stole the car keys right out of his drunken father's pockets, rolling him over on the couch and plucking away his keys. He had a duplicate set made so he never had to touch that bastard again. Then he would sneak out to the garage and push the Olds out onto the street, and off he drove in his mother's clothes and makeup, crowned by a garish redheaded wig his father bought for his mother as a joke when wigs were all the rage. Putting mileage between himself and that house, he was free! Only his mother's helplessness and lack of money kept him from driving across time zones, never to be seen or heard from again.

Sometimes he drove back to the old neighborhood and picked up Jay Westhorn, who copied him by dressing in *his* mother's clothes. They barreled around the hills till dawn. But the most fun occurred on the night he was caught. He had a crush on a guy who worked at a taco stand on Van Nuys and decided to go see him. He arrived at midnight and the guy fell on the floor, seeing a young kid in drag. The guy told him to hang around till closing and he'd take him to a party. Geoffrey followed him into Sherman Oaks, waited for him to go inside, then made his grand entrance. He threw open the door and threw out his arms, singing, "Well, here I am!" The teenagers were smoking dope and looked at him as if he had landed from Mars. Then they began to howl until the neighbors threatened to call the riot squad. They got him drunk and sent him home. He was in the process of pushing the Olds back up the driveway when he looked up and saw his parents. He took off his wig and grinned. "May I help you?" he asked. He couldn't think of anything else to say. "Oh, my God," his father moaned. "Well,

Bob, congratulations," his mother said, and went back into the house.

They sent *him* to a shrink. One night he found his mother so battered that he broke his solemn vow to her about not telling anybody and called Gail Westhorn. Maybe that was the worst of all—how nobody on the outside knew what was happening to them. Gail came over and immediately drove Ruth to the hospital. But then, when his father unexpectedly came home, Geoffrey panicked. What would he say if King asked for Ruth? But he didn't. He looked sick and awful. He changed into a pair of Bermudas and left, saying he was going out to buy them Kentucky Fried for dinner. He never returned. He wasn't even wearing a shirt, and when he was still gone at noon the following day, Geoffrey impulsively called Justin Dart's office. One of Dart's assistants came out to the house and stayed with him. They were about to call the police when King finally arrived home. He was glassy-eyed. "I don't know what happened," he said. "I think I've been driving the freeways all night." They called a doctor and put him to bed. Geoffrey waited a long time before peeking in the room, and was instantly sorry. His father's eyes grabbed him in a brutal stare.

"Your grandmother hates me," he said. "With all of her aristocratic airs, she doesn't have a dime. Neither does her precious son. He's a deadbeat, dead broke. I'll tell you the family secret. It's funny as hell. Eleanor, the aristocrat of aristocrats, got knocked up when she was eighteen. Yep, she and Larry were naughty-naughty. Had to get married. Ruth is their love baby. Absolutely true. Your Uncle Raymond told me. I don't even know if Ruth knows, but you can go ahead and tell her if you want. I don't mind. Geoffrey, you weren't a love baby. No way. You were legal. A thousand years of marriage behind you, and a thousand years ahead. But now the real question is—are you my son, or what? How could you betray me to Rexall? Don't you know what this does to me, having them see me like this? You've ruined me."

But there was no end to it all until one day King punched too hard and broke three of his wife's ribs. Geoffrey thought he had killed her. Ruth was carried unconscious to an ambulance, and Geoffrey went over to the Bourne house to fetch King. He was drunk, so Geoffrey shoved him over and drove them to the hospital. He left King sleeping in the front seat and went upstairs to his mother. He stayed with the Westhorns while Ruth recovered; when they returned home, they found the house in shambles and heard that King was in the hospital. Mr. Bourne had sneaked up on him on the patio and beat the hell out of him. Then he drove his Cadillac through two plate-glass sliding doors to ram and smash as much as he could. "I don't know whether to laugh or cry," Ruth said. "Either way, my ribs will ache."

They flew to Kansas City the next day.

Much of this Geoffrey told the psychiatrist, but not all of it, because he was just too ashamed of some stories.

"Oh, I know why I dress up. I really do want to hide in shame. I'm desperate to be somebody else. I've had it being me. Really, all that I can take. Especially now, because I think I've lost my mother's confidence totally. She's been relying on me for everything, and I've tried so hard to make her believe we can start a new life and maybe be happy. But now? I don't know."

Geoffrey saw the wounds King inflicted on his mother more clearly than his own, and was determined somehow to rise above the limitations of a confused, anxiety-ridden twelve-year-old boy to become her protector and the new family leader. His mother, exhausted, depressed, was drinking heavily and talking on the phone with her friends in a small, tired voice, her head ringing with advice that she never followed.

Ruth confided her guilts and frustrations to Geoffrey, and during their first weeks in exile he became her confidant and principal adviser. It was a role he relished. In the days prior to being forced to move in with her, he sat alone in his tiny apartment down the hall, polishing his bulletless Beretta, chain-smoking her Marlboros, and gulping her bourbon, his eyes shining with adventure, feeling like a gangster holed up and on the lam. His father called two or three times a day to threaten his mother. King was making her hysterical. "Oh, Geoffrey," she wailed, "he's coming here. He's coming to kill us." From then on Geoffrey tried to intercept King's calls and hang up on him. He stayed alert, listening for King's heavy tread in the hallway. He would point his bulletless pistol at his father's heart and hope that fear would stop him in his tracks. If not, hand-to-hand combat. He was resolved to protect Ruth at all costs, not only out of love but also out of fear of losing her. His weak, vulnerable mother was his only bulwark against ever returning to his father. If anything happened to her, he would commit suicide or run away.

His mother felt adrift after a lifetime of dependency. "I have no skills. Being your father's wife is all I know. How will we survive? That man has no conscience. He's hoping I'll have a complete breakdown and become institutionalized so he won't have to pay alimony. He told me so on the phone. Can you believe it? So here we are in a dingy hotel, eating off paper plates, while he's back there with everything: our china, our furniture—everything. Oh, but I had to put space between him and us. He's too wild and dangerous. But mark my words: between him and that terrible Bourne woman, we'll be cheated out of everything."

Geoffrey tried to raise her to his own idealism, to see beyond her insecurities. "Mother, we can live without fresh flowers every day or swimming pools. Who cares? I know it won't be easy for us, but we can do it. We can be happy—a real family. Believe me, you won't ever be alone. I'll be at your side. I promise. Mother, you were a brilliant student and there's so much you can do with your life if you'll only give yourself a chance. You're free! Doesn't that excite you? You can finally live your own life. We can be happy!"

At times she nodded agreement, although she was too absorbed in unhappiness to really listen. He began to feel claustrophobic in those two stifling rooms he shared with her and started wandering alone, a grim-faced boy, his hands thrust deeply into his jacket pockets, resentful of the changing seasons which mocked his perpetual winter. His only consolation was finally being free of a father he now hated. King had made him an emotional and physical wreck. Already, at age twelve he was a developing alcoholic, an insomniac and occasional sleepwalker, impulsive, hostile, melancholy, and brooding about death. It shattered him to admit that at least as King's son he possessed a future, instead of being stuck in a hotel for losers with a drunken mother who could not even go grocery shopping.

How could he—a mere boy—keep them afloat? He could

envision himself as a bag boy in the supermarket, charming tips out of housewives to put bread on his own table; and he sagged into gloom, knowing he was inadequate as the new man of the house. He just wasn't ready; yet somebody had to do it. His only hope was to push Ruth onto her feet and keep her standing.

One day his mother confronted him with an extraordinary request—a favor that seemed to him so irrational that he just stared at her openmouthed. King wanted to spend October 10, 1964, in the company of his son to celebrate their joint birthdate together. "Do this one thing for me, not for him," Ruth begged her son. "Go along. Otherwise he'll think I put you up to saying no. He'll make my life more miserable than it already is, and, Geoffrey, I can't take very much more."

He agreed, but he would never forgive her for doing this to him. Nor would he ever forget zipping across Missouri farmlands in the Sprite sports coupé King rented, heading for a jolly weekend at the Lake of the Ozarks, his smugly content father driving as if without a care in the world, humming and whistling and grinning as if nothing had happened between them at all, until he finally pulled over to the side of the road, stopped the car, and invited his son to drive. "Go ahead, let's see what you can do." Geoffrey climbed behind the wheel and gunned the Sprite to the floor until the speedometer quivered past ninety. For a moment he flirted with an impulse to aim them off the road and blow them to pieces, but the idea of dying with that man was too repulsive. Whether or not King read his son's thoughts, he sat silent and grim, staring straight ahead at the accelerating road blurring past, his lips pursed with tension, until Geoffrey finally slowed down and pulled over. "*That's* what I can do," he declared.

They drove the remainder of the way in silence, arriving in late afternoon at their rented cottage on the lake. King had also rented a motorboat that was tied to their dock, and while he hurried down to inspect it, his son entered their cottage, raced for the bathroom, and threw up.

19

After six bleak months in Kansas City with nothing much happening, Geoffrey wondered when his parents would actually begin divorce proceedings. Word filtered back that King's behavior was more unstable than ever—drunk at work, running around town with floozies.

Ruth learned that King had attempted to take his life with an overdose of sleeping pills, but was rushed to the hospital in time and had his stomach pumped. Then came word that Robert Luther King, vice-president of Rexall Drugs, was in the slammer for drunk driving and resisting arrest—raving on the concrete floor of the drunk tank at the Los Angeles County Jail while under the restraint of a straitjacket.

As a result, the Rexall comptroller's office had declared all-out war against King's flagrant abuse of expense accounts and launched a thorough investigation of his financial affairs. The word was that he was actively maintaining at least twelve women around town, including Kim Bourne, whom he insisted that he planned to marry the moment he divorced Ruth, although Mr. Bourne was reportedly determined to deal a mob contract on his rival's life. Several of these women were seen waiting for King in the Rexall parking lot, and Tildy's husband recognized one of them: "My God, he's screwing my manicurist!" she reported Barry as saying. On days when King showed up at the office, he was either drunk or woefully hung-over. There was also a rumor that a woman from Chicago had blackmailed him for a considerable sum by threatening to reveal to his Rexall bosses their employee's penchant for extremely kinky sex. Even worse, company investigators uncovered unethical, if not criminal, stock-manipulation deals; so that shortly before Christmas 1964 Justin Dart sent for him and demanded a full explanation. King swore that the situation looked worse that it actually was, but asked for a few days' respite, by which time everything would be clear. He then took off and disappeared.

"Your father is at the end of his rope," Ruth informed Geoffrey. "He's ruined."

* * *

King was fired. But in a phone conversation with Justin Dart, Ruth was assured that the company was seeking a humane ending to the tragedy—a generous settlement, the promise to help him find future employment provided he agreed to immediate hospitalization; he was obviously a very sick man and Ruth was urged to fly back to L.A. immediately and help settle her husband's affairs. Her family and friends urged her to stay away. "I'm still his wife," she insisted. "My duty is to be at his side." She asked Eleanor to fly to Kansas City to stay with Geoffrey. "I'll be back in two weeks," she promised. She was gone two months.

Everyone had enough of him running loose and out of control. They had finally cornered him, cut off his escape routes, and dumped him like a wild animal into a psycho ward. He lay in his bed curled in a fetal position, his face turned to the wall, refusing to eat or talk to anyone. He saw clearly how the world hated and despised him. He knew they had put him here not so much to punish him (that would at least denote caring), as to be rid of him and of their responsibility. They told him it was done for his own good, that they were rooting for him to work hard and make progress. The bastards! Acting as if they were entirely innocent of all that happened to him. Their hypocrisy ate at him; and he hated them for ignoring how hard he had tried to please them, for their rejection of him. They had never accepted him. From the moment they saw him, they contemptuously shunted him aside as an outsider. He had a keen nose for rejection; he couldn't be fooled. But why? How could he be a threat to them? There was only one ruler in that place, who held all the power.

They told him this hospital was one of the best, costing a bloody fortune, and urged him to make good use of it. But for the first couple of days, the staff just let him cry in bed. They checked on him often because they felt he was suicidal, and gave him Mellaril, an anti-depressant. The nurses felt sorry for him, he could tell, but not nearly as sorry as he felt. The world had destroyed him. Nobody ever walks out of a mental ward without that stigma following him forever. He knew his capabilities. He knew what he could've been if only they had given him a fair chance. He had barely begun, and now they had purposely hobbled him for the remainder of his life. He was once a golden boy, but now he was tarnished forever; they had pulled the plug on his future, making

him a pariah, an outcast, a certain loser. Give Bob King ten sticks of
dynamite and he knew exactly where to plant them for sweet revenge.

Maurice Whitten, the psychiatrist assigned to King's case, finally visited. He was a pudgy, cherubic little man and King showered him with his pent-up rage. "I won't be treated this way," he shrieked. "I'm not a goddamn psycho and I demand—"

"Shut up," the doctor told him. "You're not running this ward. I am. And if you ever want to get out of here, I suggest you do what you're told. Because you'll only leave when I say so, not when you want to. You got that straight?"

He began his psychotherapy sessions the next day.

"Why are you here?" Whitten asked him.

King just laughed. "Why ask me? Ask those lovelies who sent me here."

"I'm asking you," Whitten persisted.

"I'm here because those I trusted turned against me. I've been betrayed. Everywhere I turn, there are just knives out. My family, if you can call them that, dragged me down. They're all glad I'm in this place, happy to be rid of me. They killed me. This is murder, can't you see that? A legal murder with all the right papers signed."

"But why are you here?" the doctor repeated.

Dr. Whitten diagnosed him as a textbook psychopath—egocentric, unstable, perverse, conceited, and lacking common sense, social feeling, self-control, truthfulness, and persistence. Because he exhibited so little curiosity about his problems and was so resistant to introspection, the doctor decided to attempt pragmatic counseling and try to stabilize his relationships at home and reduce the stress and tensions. Ruth King, whom the doctor liked, was reluctant. She preferred psychotherapy for as long as necessary to induce permanent change. "We simply cannot go on this way," she told her husband. "Your behavior has ruined us. We won't put up with it, ever again."

What could he say? She and the doctors held all the cards. He agreed that he caused his family terrible grief and he was determined to change his ways if they gave him another chance. He sat down with her and Whitten and began to express some of his deeper feelings. At the final session, he truthfully claimed to be feeling much better and was convinced he'd made real progress.

On the day that Dr. Whitten signed his release, Robert Luther King felt reborn.

His wife, who had remained at his side for the month-long hospitalization, agreed to set up housekeeping in a small efficiency apartment while he continued another month of treatment as an outpatient. After only two months of treatment, King was pronounced fit. Then Ruth, not Bob, flew to Kansas City to get Geoffrey.

The whole way back to Los Angeles Ruth drove hunched over the steering column, lost to her own thoughts, her arm on the open window frame growing crimson under the hot sun. Geoffrey lay prone across the backseat like a loaded shotgun. Not five words were exchanged by the two passengers the entire trip. The car was stifling: no air conditioning. Well, of course not: his father had bought it for her. But you'd better believe that his own had air conditioning.

Geoffrey saw his mother's eyes reflected in the rearview mirror. She was driving without hope; neither of them wanted to be in this car; yet, here they were. He couldn't believe this was really happening. Dr. Fraser, Geoffrey's psychiatrist, had flushed with anger when he was informed by his patient. When Ruth told him they were going back to live with his father, Geoffrey had grabbed his mother by the front of her blouse, yanked her out of her chair, then slammed her back so harshly that her eyes rolled up in her head. Nick Hopps, only a few feet away at the time, did not try to intervene.

Now they were crossing the plains of Kansas, heading west.

Geoffrey, watching billboards periodically sweep past, felt more dead than alive. He wished Ruth would suddenly doze off and slam into the back of a tractor-trailer so they could end quickly and mercifully. They were like shackled galley slaves in a sinking ship. Nick Hopps had said, while saying good-bye, "Geoffrey, I'm sincere about there always being a place for you with us if things get too rough back there."

"Nick," he had replied, "tell me why she's doing this."

Hopps shrugged and told him that it was easier to predict what Ruth would do than to try to explain her actions. "I knew from the day you arrived that you'd be going back," he said. Marion Hopps refused to even say good-bye.

Their future was evident on Ruth's tense, unsmiling face as she stubbornly steered them westward.

"Ruth, for God's sake," his grandmother warned, "think of your son. How can you do this to him? You're going to lose Geoffrey forever."

"Your father is a changed man," his mother had insisted. "The psychiatrists have worked wonders. I'd never go back to him if this wasn't so. He's like someone who's awakened from a terrible dream. He's so sorry. He begs our forgiveness and wants another chance. I've decided to give him that chance."

In the end, Geoffrey screamed at her: "You've betrayed me. I'll never believe another word you ever say. All this talk about 'Oh, Geoffrey, what are we going to do? Tell me. I'm so lost'—you just set me up, and you know it." He had told Dr. Fraser at their last session that he would battle to his last breath for his rights. "I'm growing up," he said. "I'm not just a sack of potatoes. Believe me, Doctor, if they do anything to me, I'll take them down to hell with me."

20

Los Angeles, 1965

"My graduation day," King joked self-consciously to his psychiatrist's receptionist. She smiled to hide her surprise, remembering Mr. King as a gaunt outpatient with a stricken look who often left Dr. Whitten's office blowing his nose. In only three months, he looked years younger, probably because he had put back twenty lost pounds. He had done beautifully, just beautifully. The doctor was delighted with the progress reports received from both Bob and Ruth over the past weeks.

At first Geoffrey did not want to go to the sessions, and his father said he understood and nobody would try to force him, but that the point of the meeting with Whitten was to cement their accomplishments thus far and establish criteria for the next phase of their family relationship. But that was precisely Geoffrey's unspoken objection. He was fearful of rocking the boat and disturbing a delicate balance of affability. He also knew they had all avoided the central issues surrounding their return—as well they should have during those first touchy weeks—but maybe it was time to explain themselves. His parents avoided definitions, seemed to fear them, while he yearned to know what they expected from one another, what their roles were in a family unit, what their goals and responsibilities were not only to the outside world but also to each other. Why were they living together under the same roof—merely because the law said they must? What did it mean to be a family? If that question could be thoroughly aired and agreed upon, then perhaps he would understand their mysterious hold on him and the urgency he had felt from birth to be central in their lives. So he sat in Dr. Whitten's waiting room mulling over the way he would raise some of these issues and clearly articulate their importance. But he was amazed that things had evolved even this far. The mystery was his mother. After arriving in Santa Monica, she deposited him with King, then, pleading total exhaustion, took to her bed and was seldom seen again. It was as if she were living in her own upstairs apartment and avoiding new neighbors. Never was there a more loveless, passionless reunion between husband and wife; and Geoffrey was convinced that if King ever felt an urge to mount his wife, he would probably be better advised to try a marble slab. No, things were not exactly the same as before. King had definitely changed. Whether it was an act or whether it was truly lasting— who could tell? Perhaps his defeats and ordeals had hammered him down to more manageable size, making him more approachable as a human being. His son began to think that King's doctors had had his brain sent out for dry cleaning. He was that different.

King located for his family an unpretentious but comfortable apartment in a very middle-class section of Santa Monica, where neighbors pampered their six-year-old Fords with STP and eagerly searched the bargain bins at the supermarket. He was neither defeatist nor hyperbolic about the future; and on that first night back, he told them he knew the road back from where he had been was long and tough, in both his career and his family life, so much so that if they had decided not to come back, he would probably have given up even trying. But now that they were all together again, he was determined to try like hell. He quietly confessed his sins, but without gratuitous breast-beatings. "I was like someone running in flames. That's what those last months were like for me. I must've had a complete emotional and physical breakdown. Toward the end, I was drinking a quart of gin daily." In response to his son's pointed question, he said he had not been in touch with Mrs. Bourne since the day he was thrown in jail and called her, pleading for help. "She hung up on me," he said. He did not really apologize for the pain and anguish he had inflicted on his family, nor did he explain why he thought he had gone off on such a tangent. "The pressures at work were fierce," he said, "and there were a lot of people out to get me. But my doctor thinks I was heading for this for a long time. I just don't know." That night when he went to bed, Geoffrey found himself choking on tears into his pillow, crying not for himself but for all of them, his father, too.

They sat together as a family only at the dinner table. Ruth, who spent her days in a tattered J. C. Penney's housecoat, no longer fussed over meals, and returned to the bedroom after doing the dishes. Geoffrey, too, retired to his room after dinner because he did not want to be left alone with his father. King was now as effectively shut out of his family's life as his son believed himself to be throughout his childhood. It was sweet, unexpected revenge against his nemesis; but perhaps because it cut so close to the sorest of his own wounds, he found himself disturbed by his father's isolation. King's face registered his losses, a face grown soft with velvety folds of flesh like a partially deflated beach ball, but his back was straight and his thick jaw was firm. In spite of his reverses and self-inflicted humiliations, he was more manly than when he had been king of the mountaintop. Diminished, he became gentle and blazed with a dignity that commanded admiration. "I'm here if you need me" was his clear message in the face of his family's rejection. Pity drew Geoffrey toward his father; over the next several weeks, they began to be friends.

With a burst of apologies for being delayed at the hospital, Dr. Maurice Whitten ushered King and his family into a Danish-modern inner sanctum.

"So," he said, digging in behind his large desk. "How's it going, Bob? How's the job?"

King shrugged. "As you know, Rexall worked out this agreement with a local talent-search firm. I'm under a one-year contract. Frankly, I haven't been swamped with work. I think there's a little distrust on both sides. But it pays the rent."

"Well, these things take time," Whitten remarked, then asked Ruth how things were going at home.

"Much smoother and more pleasant than any of us had a right to expect. Bob has been thoughtful and involved, and that has made a big difference."

"You had some tough encounters right here in this office, but you now can see some results. It isn't easy to admit mistakes or use alternative methods dealing with one another. But I imagine you feel real satisfaction now—isn't that so?"

Both adult Kings nodded. Geoffrey spoke up. "I must say my father has made a tremendous effort that I never expected from him, and he deserves enormous credit. Believe me, I never thought I'd ever say *that*, because as you probably know, Doctor, I fought like hell against coming back here. To say I didn't want to live with Dad again is the understatement of the century, but he really has been trying, and I must say, I've been trying, too."

"Absolutely," King interjected.

"I hated him as much as I could hate," Geoffrey continued. "I still hate what he has done to us, but I feel we've made a start at understanding each other. I feel real hope that we can have a good relationship."

"How do you account for that?"

"Because, for once, he really seems to care."

"May I interrupt?" King asked. "I want to say something about that. Doctor, I recently discovered that my son became interested in art during the separation in Kansas City. A few nights ago he invited me into his room and showed me some of his work. Doctor, until that moment I never realized the extent of the pain I've caused my family. Geoffrey showed me sketches of faces . . . well, I'm sorry, I feel emotional right now . . . of faces so haunted by loneliness, so tortured! It was as if he showed me his own heart. I never felt closer to my son and, you know, he's wonderfully gifted. I bought him all the supplies he needs and we're gonna get him the best teachers money can buy."

"Wonderful," Whitten remarked.

"I'd like to say something," Geoffrey said. "That was the closest I felt to Dad, too. But the point is, we are going to have to start talking soon and discuss our problems. I'm glad we haven't so far, because we all needed time. But we've got to get down to business here."

"About what?" King asked.

"About everything," his son replied. "How this family is going to be run, for example. I think all of us expect to have a voice in decisions that affect all of us."

"I agree completely," King declared. "I know we have a long road to hoe, but I think I'm proving that I can be a good father and husband."

"Absolutely," Whitten agreed. "Your father dropped off somewhere into a deep, dark hell. He never wants to go back— am I right, Bob? That means being a caring, sharing human being. Am I correct, Bob? Tell me, please, because I don't want to put words in your mouth."

King responded, "If I learned anything under your care, it is the importance of expressing and sharing my feelings . . . unbottling them before they blow, and not presuming to know how others feel without bothering to ask. All of us have got to express ourselves. And as head of this house, I will never decide on a matter without hearing everyone out."

"Excuse me?" his son interrupted. "Did I hear right, or what? Are you saying we can discuss an issue till we're blue in the face, but only *you* decide it?"

"No," King insisted, "that's not what I said. I'm saying my decision on an issue will reflect the views and feelings of every one of us."

"But you're the only one deciding—isn't that so?" his son said pointedly.

"That's my right as head of this house, isn't *that* so?" King countered.

"Well, you can count me out, Dad. No more dictatorship for me. And this is most definitely not what Mother said would be happening if we came back. You said we'd live under a democracy, didn't you, Mother? We'd decide things mutually."

"Yes, I did," Ruth said. "That's what your dad agreed to with Dr. Whitten and myself."

Everyone looked to the psychiatrist, who merely extended an open hand in King's direction.

"There's no conflict here," King insisted. "I'm not proclaiming any dictatorship. But every family needs leadership, and I'm merely saying that as head of this house, I will weigh and consider everyone's views before—"

"Bullshit, Dad!" his son exclaimed, and jumped from his chair. "Listen, you're not the Rexall bigshot anymore, pushing people around. We've all had a bellyful of that. I can't speak for Mother, but I won't allow you to dictate my life to me ever again. And if you're smart, you won't even try, because, believe me, you won't win. Dr. Whitten, you'd better take back your patient and work on him some more, because this is what got him into your hospital in the first place."

And he walked out. His mother rushed outside to retrieve him. He angrily brushed off her grip, but returned inside to hear the psychiatrist urge him to calm down and give his father a chance. Geoffrey wagged a finger under Whitten's nose and declared: "Who are you talking about, anyway? What about the fortune he squandered on women? We're supposed to forget about that and pretend it didn't happen? Why should you ask us to blindly trust this man to lead us in the right direction? What right does he have to tell any of us what to do?"

Outside, by the car, Ruth confronted her husband. "Bob, what's come over you? You're acting just the way you did before when you brought hell down on us." But King's eyes were fixed in a hostile stare with his son.

King's graduation day was indefinitely postponed.

Sprouting pubic hair was evidence that puberty had not forgotten him. In the mirror, Geoffrey could see traces of how he would look in maturity: a swarthy, elongated face dominated by flashing dark eyes and white, even teeth—the face of a sensitive artist who dreamed of staging the first teenage one-man show at the Wildenstein gallery in New York. He wore his dark hair sloped across his right temple; and in subdued light with one eye closed, he thought his mirrored reflection resembled a photo he had seen of the youthful Picasso seated in a Paris café around the turn of the century. He knew he was very handsome. But somehow, puberty ignored his boyish voice and beardless face in its transformations. He was girlish, nellie, a cause for grief at Lincoln Junior High, where tough Chicano kids parodied his mincing walk and soprano register. "Hey, sister," they ragged at him. He tried to ignore them, but was no more successful than in trying to deny he was different at a time of life when being different was a particular curse. His penis sprang up stiffly a dozen times a day for no apparent reason other than to test its prowess; and his first wet dream was stunning but incomplete: Geoffrey, in the locker-room shower, reached for a bar of soap and accidentally grabbed Mr. Burns's cock. Mr. Burns was his gorgeous English teacher. With awareness of what he was gripping, he awoke to a mess.

These were confusing but hopeful signs that he was growing up; no ninth-grader was more impatient to reach manhood. "Let's get on with it," he muttered to himself. Even so, he felt much older than his classmates and secretly superior, having seen, suffered, and experienced so much more than they probably would for the next dozen years, at least.

His teachers found him conservatively well-groomed (King saw to that), but not dissimilar to other moody, mercurial, intense teenagers who blurred together in the schoolyard. He was clever and quick, very independent-minded, and would not be bullied by anyone. He was also lazy, a daydreamer, who got by on a minimum of effort. His quick temper annoyed some of his teachers, especially when he intruded his opinions in matters that did not concern him. When a teacher complained that one of the boys in class needed a haircut and violated the dress code, Geoffrey shouted: "That's unfair. You can't just send Carlos up on charges! Maybe his family can't afford a haircut every week! Why don't you talk to him privately first, before you send him up to Dr. Fleason's office?"

He was sent to the vice-principal, a disciplinarian who looked as if he once had roped steers.

"King, when are you going to learn to keep your mouth shut?"

"When are you people going to learn to be fair?"

"King, one of these days I'm gonna slap you silly."

"Try it and I'll tear your office apart."

Mr. Burns was his favorite teacher. He was tall, rawboned, and raised horses. He lived alone, recently divorced, and

Geoffrey volunteered to help clear brush in the high-risk fire area where the horses were corralled. There was a moment, during a pause for an iced-tea break, when Geoffrey admitted his infatuation. They were seated next to each other and Burns was plopping melting ice cubes from his emptied glass into his mouth, when Geoffrey blurted his feelings: "Stan," he said, "I'm dying to kiss you." The young student saw surprise register on the young teacher's face, and then something else—consternation perhaps. But then Burns began to chuckle. "You would, would you?" he replied. "Come on, back to work." From then on, Burns made certain they were never alone together.

This infatuation became a quickly forgotten prologue to Geoffrey's love life. At the home of a classmate, he was instantly smitten by a seventeen-year old two heads taller, lanky, and slim-hipped, with a lopsided grin smeared across a freckled, boyish face. Geoffrey grinned back, feeling dazed and light-headed as he introduced himself. They shook hands as if sealing a secret agreement, a firm, manly grip.

Her name was Annette.

She was slightly bowlegged and as feminine as a rancher. She loved horses, body-surfing, bowling, tight faded jeans, and dirty worn-out shoes without socks, McDonald's cheeseburgers, paddle tennis, and overnight back-packing. She drove her own jalopy that was minus floorboards: an ancient Chevy convertible without a top or windshield wipers.

They fell madly in love and began to go steady.

21

Following the fiasco in Dr. Whitten's office, Geoffrey decided to go his own way. But it did not work. Irresistible forces intervened: the Geoffrey who released the hand brake on Mrs. Nielson's car or who jumped off the high dive as a toddler was always in the forefront in his dealings with his father. Somehow, King stood between the child Geoffrey and the man he hoped to be. There could be no peace until King surrendered either in love or in bitter defeat to a greater will. It was not a conscious decision but a restless itch inside himself that became more insistent with each passing year. What was it? A primordial father-son battle for the leadership of the herd? King sensed it coming, had probably anticipated it years before, when he bounced baby Geoffrey on his lap and told Nick Hopps that he had never wanted a son. Ruth saw it coming, too: those two were so alike in their inability to forgive or forget, storing their anger like sharp-pointed stones. King would later admit as much and tell his son: "You stood up to me the way I would've." By then he was a beaten man.

"Dad, we can't stay mad forever."

"Geoffrey, some other time. I've had a rotten day. Here, pour yourself a drink and turn on Channel Two; there's a good movie on."

He took the bottle of gin but did not turn on the TV.

"There's just too damn much selfishness in this house," King muttered darkly. "Everyone stuck away in a separate corner. Might as well have stayed away."

"Dad, I don't want to hurt you—honest."

"Then don't," his father replied, and raised his glass. "Here's mud in your eye. Now, turn on the tube, or I will."

"No, please. Why can't we talk this out? You've got to understand—"

"Oh, I understand," his father interrupted. "You're just one of dozens who think my corpse is beginning to stink, so why not bury it? Well, I have news for all of you: I've been down before, and I'll be on top again."

"Of course you will."

"'Of course you will,'" King mimicked. "Listen, I'm not quite ready to turn over the reins to you yet. I'm still your father. This is still my house. When I really am dead, you can do what you damned well want; but while I'm still breathing, there are certain rules and standards I expect you to obey. Now, I want to watch my movie."

He flipped on the set and sat back down rather heavily.

"Dad, I was always proud of you. That's the truth. You're a great man and you'll be great again."

His father's eyes blazed agreement and his chin trembled. "Well, then, act like my son, not my enemy. I've got enough of those."

My father, my friend. My father, my enemy. Geoffrey soon had the full measure of both—simultaneously—and later admitted that it was always the son, not the father, who triggered their fights, although it was always King who instigated them. Perhaps because the world turned so rancid, King withdrew into the family circle and reached out for his son, seeking his companionship to an extent that would have transformed forever the sad, lonely, younger version of King. There was too much solitude in King's life, and he eagerly declared his intention of becoming the kind of caring father his son always wanted. They biked and sailed together, visited art galleries and swam at the downtown Y. The attention was unexpected and overwhelming. His dad wanted something from him that he didn't know how to give. He was too young to deal with all of King's poignancies, and the need for King's companionship at times froze Geoffrey in guilt, since he would rather be doing other things. He could act as cheerleader because he really did believe in his father's abilities, but there were times, when King bared his anguish, that Geoffrey hung his head and turned away, not knowing what to do or say. One day, on impulse, they drove to Georgie Fallow's house up in Bel Air, to drop in on one of King's few friends from the old days who still called once in a while. He lived in a massive Tudor house overlooking the country-club golf course. King rang the bell, but nobody was home, and Geoffrey followed his father around to the back, remembering several pool parties he had attended with his parents. The backyard was designed to approximate a Roman spa; they sat down on a marble bench next to a statue of Venus.

"Do you miss this?" King asked his son.

"Not really," Geoffrey lied.

"Well, I do," King said quietly.

Suddenly his father put an arm around him and pulled him to him. Tears ran down King's cheeks, and with his free hand he covered his eyes.

"What have I done to us? I can't believe what's happening to me, Geoffrey, I just can't. What have I done to my life? Oh, my God!"

The world was merciless. A few days before his father's year-long contract came up for renewal, he overheard his mother phone for an appointment with the man who headed the firm.

She returned home looking too grim and forbidding to question. King expressed real joy to be on his own at last, and "ROBERT L. KING ASSOCIATES" was freshly painted on the door of the third-floor suite of offices in downtown Santa Monica.

King hired a full-time secretary and left for the office with his family's good wishes ringing in his ears. At first he complained that men who owed him significant favors now did not even bother to return his calls, but rather soon he lapsed into silence and changed the subject if Geoffrey asked how things were going. One day King had a special phone line installed next to the wet bar so that when the phone rang at the office he could pick it up at home. He was around more than ever.

"Where are you going?" he asked, an edge of disappointment in his voice, seeing his son about to depart.

"Oh, Bob, leave him alone," Ruth exclaimed. "He needs time to be with his own friends. He's growing up. You can't turn back the biological clock."

But then one day King pushed himself out of his chair, walked to the door, and slammed home the bolt lock. He turned around and confronted his son with a pinched, hurt look on his face.

"Not tonight, my friend. You're too young to go steady. I will not permit it."

He was jealous of Annette. Jealous of his son's puppy love. He disapproved of her and thought her common. Anyway, Geoffrey had been out three nights already that week, and tonight he would stay home. Period. End of statement.

His son's hands formed determined fists and he marched toward the front door as his father barred the way.

And so it began.

22

The only concession to youth in the maximum-security wing of Juvenile Hall was that the corridors were free of uniformed guards and there were no cells. Geoffrey was kept locked all day in a small room with an observation window, allowed to mingle with the other inmates only at meals. Like himself, they were awaiting trials and detention. They were tough kids, housed in "max sec" for serious, adultlike crimes—although some of the boys were as young as eight and ten years old. He sat across from a ten-year-old arrested for shooting up a liquor store, and someone pointed out a twelve-year-old arrested for attempting to rape a forty-three-year-old housewife. Two fifteen-year-olds were in for attempted arson. They were mostly poor kids, unloved, uneducated, alone, and abandoned. Nobody knew what to do with them; they spent their time during meals whispering bold plans to escape, and treated Geoffrey with grudging respect. "Hey, man, we hear you wasted two people. Is that true?"

He would spend nearly a month inside his small room with a stack of comic books, and began to think that the authorities had run out of criminal statutes. How do you punish someone who killed his mother and grandmother? Do you pluck out his eyeballs with a teaspoon? Do you impale him on the ground and then stampede cattle over him? What were they waiting for? He wondered how much longer he would be ignored; someday, someone would have to tell him about the charges filed against him. Every night in the cell was the same: it began with one of these tough boys whimpering behind his locked door; and soon, like a band of frightened young animals, others joined in and began pounding in anguish on the doors.

Nora Lowe raced the sunrise across the continent aboard the "red-eye" flight from New York, arriving back in her North Hollywood apartment in time for breakfast, only to discover there were no eggs in the refrigerator. The headache-powder commercial had gone well. The fee and residual payments would keep Nora and her husband eating for a while. She was forty-six, and producers thought of her when they needed a worldly wise mom to advise a teenage daughter on the blessings of Tampax. Nora was fair-skinned and full-figured, so she wore wide-brimmed hats to avoid the California sun that in one summer could age a woman ten years; and she counted each and every calorie.

Nora and Geoffrey shared a special rapport. From the moment she first saw her nephew (he was barely out of diapers), he touched her heart. He was such an eager, loving child, so physically beautiful. Like all children (to her mind), he was a precious possession which his parents unaccountably abused and mishandled, only to later complain about their damaged goods. She was heartbroken for the child long before the murders. During annual visits with the Kings, she alone of the relatives had spent time alone with Geoffrey, drawing him out, listening sympathetically to his problems. There was little she could say or do for him when he confessed his confusion except to hug him and tell him how much she loved him. Nora wished his parents would do the same, but the situation was hopeless. So Nora knew the rage in Geoffrey's heart—all too well—but now this terrible tragedy threatened to destroy her life as a wife and actress. In one moment of passionate revenge, Geoffrey had proved the futility of her hopes to resurrect her career, which had been promising before her marriage to Lowe. She and Ray had moved to Hollywood to get her parts in movies and television productions. But the murders shattered Ray, and Nora knew it would be a long time before their plan was back on track.

Nora knew Ray's feelings of guilt, that he had done too little to help his mother and sister avoid the tragedy. He said nothing, but she knew he blamed himself, and worse, secretly acknowledged his fear of standing up to his nephew. Like his mother and sister, he was no match for Geoffrey's rebellious contempt. He blustered and fumed about what should've been done to curb that boy, but it was Geoffrey who tore up Ruth's checks to Ray and threw them contemptuously in his uncle's face, calling him a sponger. It was the truth of the charge, as much as anything else, that rendered Ray impotent. Geoffrey always said things nobody else would dare to say; he saw through his uncle. But Nora also saw through Ray and knew that guilt and shame were destroying him. "I want this over," she told herself, and yet could not surrender to a callous disregard about her nephew's fate. She became determined to visit him without her husband's knowledge.

Only when she arrived at Juvenile Hall and entered a small conference room did Nora wonder what she had hoped to accomplish. She wanted to help and comfort Geoffrey, but steeled herself at the sight of him: he was so pale and slight, so thin and drawn, that he seemed several years younger than she remembered him. His eyes were rimmed with sadness as he hesitated in the doorway, unsmiling at his favorite aunt, caught off guard, not knowing what was expected of him. Nora wanted to embrace him, but the prison chaplain blocked her way and told her he would be in the next room if his services were needed. When the chaplain left, she and Geoffrey embraced briefly and Nora managed a small smile.

"How are you?" he asked her.

"How should any of us be?" she replied honestly. "Your uncle and I are trying to understand how and why such a thing could happen. I thought if I could hear from your own lips . . . maybe somehow I could help you. . . ."

He shook his head. "I don't know," he said so softly that she had to lean forward to hear him. "That's all I've been thinking about since it happened. I don't know. I just don't. I've asked them over and over to let me talk to a psychiatrist or somebody who can help me work this all out—but they refuse. I'm so confused."

He raised his hands helplessly, then let them drop on his lap.

"Did you know what you were doing when you killed them?" she asked. "Were you aware?"

"I guess so," he replied laconically. "The moment I came to in the hospital, I knew what I had done. So I must've known."

Nora thought of her sister-in-law, a woman who wanted only to live in mutual happiness and tranquillity. To be murdered by her own son was a gross obscenity.

"It was all mixed up with LSD," Geoffrey said. "I was having a bad trip. That's an understatement: the worst trip you can imagine, flashing back and forth between hallucinations and reality. It's all a mishmash—what I knew or didn't know. The worst part is that I may never know, and I can't live with it. It's killing me."

"Please tell me the truth," she said. "Did Gram see you kill your mother?"

He shook his head. Nora felt relief. From the moment they had learned from the police that Ruth was his first victim, Nora had been tortured by imagining the old woman witnessing her grandson's act of matricide.

"Gram was in the living room when I killed Mother at the kitchen door. My God, I didn't mean to hurt them, please believe me. I loved them. I could never do such a thing if I wasn't out of my mind . . . deranged, crazy. It wasn't that we had an argument and I just turned on them; it wasn't that way at all. Mother should never have let me come home. I needed a hospital. I was out of my mind the night before. Why didn't they get me to a doctor? I'll never understand."

"Everyone is trying to understand," Nora said kindly. "We're all so hurt, Geoffrey, we just don't know what to do. Uncle Ray, myself . . . we don't know how to deal with this."

He wiped at his eyes with his sleeves and seemed to stiffen.

"Well, what do you want from me?" he asked, shifting his weight in the chair. "I killed them. I took two lives that I loved. I don't know why, except that LSD must've opened up my unconscious, or whatever. I didn't plan it, if that's what you think. But it happened. God knows, it happened. You want me to go on my knees to you and beg your forgiveness? I don't mind; I'll do it."

He began to get up, but his aunt's hand reached out and restrained him. "That isn't what I meant," she said.

"Well, what do you mean?" he replied. "Why should you or anyone else care what happens to me now?"

"I meant that each of us—you included—will have to find a way to live with this," his aunt said. "And I do care what happens to you, Geoffrey. I care very much."

"I love you," he cried, and ran from the room in tears.

Nora brooded for several days; Lowe had told her Geoffrey would be tried in February for first-degree murder. She knew that was wrong: he was sick and needed hospital care, not a prison. Then late one afternoon while Lowe was out, she gathered her courage and called the one person she could think of who might be able to help Geoffrey.

"I'm glad you phoned," Judge Tom Hemmings told her. "I've thought so often about my meeting with Ray and your sister-in-law. We all should've done more to avoid this tragedy, and I can't help feeling that a human solution must be found to help this poor kid. Frankly, he wouldn't survive very long in a prison setting. The public has little awareness of what happens to a young boy in prison, particularly a young gay boy."

"What should be done?" Nora asked. The judge replied that the case would be tried in his Municipal Court. "There are four sitting judges here, so it will either come before me or one of my colleagues. If I were Geoffrey's lawyer, I'd avoid a jury trial at all costs."

23

OCTOBER 10, 1969

The most pathetic eighteenth-birthday celebration imaginable was observed in stony silence when a counselor entered Geoffrey's locked room holding a cupcake with a single lit candle.

"Happy birthday," he said. "Come on, give us a smile."

It was one of the darker ironies of the King clan that Geoffrey and his father were locked to the same birthday observance. If his father had lived, Robert Luther King would have been fifty-seven on this day.

Suddenly Geoffrey was being informed of his rights and expectations, of court appearances and hearing dates, of examinations and interviews, but he was unaware of the cause-effect relationship between this activity and achieving adult status under the law as an eighteen-year-old. He felt like a weary traveler who had been waiting interminably for his luggage. During the next several weeks he was in and out of hearing rooms and courtrooms with nothing required of him except that he attend. He usually did not comprehend the precise nature of the proceedings. Two or three different public defenders were assigned to each of these procedures; they all briefed him, but the criminal statutes were of interest only to its practitioners or to clients anxious to be defended. He wished only to plead guilty and to get it over with. But the law was a dental drill: he faced a Juvenile Court hearing to determine whether he should be turned over to the adult authority so that he could be eligible for life imprisonment or the gas chamber—options not available to underage killers. Then he would be examined by two court-appointed psychiatrists who would determine whether he was sufficiently sane to understand the charges against him and participate in his own defense. There would be a hearing on this in psychiatric court. If found legally sane, he faced a preliminary hearing—a mini-trial, actually—to explore whether there was sufficient evidence to charge and try him for his crime. Only after this could he go on trial for killing his mother and his grandmother.

The lawyers who visited him at Juvenile Hall seemed sympathetic and tried to help him, but he was too disoriented and depressed to really concentrate on their explanations, especially knowing how useless all of these maneuvers were when he and everyone already knew what the end result would be: he was going to prison for a long time. Nevertheless, he was startled and incensed by some of the things they told him. He couldn't believe, for example, that he could commit murder as a seventeen-year-old and be held until his eighteenth birthday so he could be charged as an adult. That seemed stupendously unfair, but not nearly as unjust as the legalisms dealing with the insanity issue. The lawyer from psychiatric court told him that if the examining psychiatrists found him to be insane and thus unable to stand trial, he could be shipped off to an institution for as long as it took to regain his wits, then be recharged with his crime and forced to stand trial as someone now able to participate in his own defense.

"You mean they could send me away for, say, ten years to an institution, then hold my murder trial?"

"That's right," the lawyer replied. "The time served in one place has nothing to do with the time served as punishment for the offense, especially in a murder case."

He was incredulous. But he was also petrified by all of these possibilities and options. It was one thing to wish sincerely for the gas chamber, but quite another, he discovered, to allow his vivid imagination to seal him inside an airless steel vault, strap him to a chair, and watch a cyanide pellet drop into a container of acid. He could see himself holding his breath, gasping, smelling the acrid almond fumes. When they lived in the Hollywood hills, he and their Great Dane, Timber, were allowed to run wild, and a neighbor poisoned Timber by spreading cyanide on a piece of meat. Geoffrey had watched Timber die in a vacant lot, so he knew what it would be like. He welcomed death, but still . . .

A psychiatric social worker visited him. She became convinced that he suffered from a peculiar form of mental illness often experienced by those who commit a violent crime and endure incarceration. It was called the Ganzer Syndrome, named for the psychiatrist who first identified it, and the symptoms of abject depression, disorientation, and confusion perfectly described Geoffrey King. She filed her opinion with the Juvenile Court judge who would soon be determining Geoffrey's legal status.

He discussed his case with a few of his cellmates during meals in the chow hall. "Hey, you're gonna probably pull ten years, no matter what, so why get your balls in an uproar," they said. One of the fifteen-year-old arsonists added, "Whatever happens, you'll be the last to know."

24

1966–1967

Why Annette? Maybe it was the way she walked, her hands thrust into the back pockets of her jeans, a kind of slow, rolling gait as if she were strolling through tall prairie grass. Maybe it was how she closed one eye squinting at the bright sun, or the way the wind tossed her soft hair. Maybe it was her freckles and the healthy scent of her body, or the silly way she lit his cigarettes in the center of her mouth. God knew, she was neither chic nor beautiful like some of the women he had been drawn to in his parents' living room over the years. She wasn't even pretty or bright, which made her attraction amazing, since he was usually disdainful of those lacking looks and brains. But he adored her; only in later years would he speculate that maybe Annette, in her boyishness, represented a tentative statement about himself that he wasn't ready to acknowledge. But that was probably wrong, because his sexual energy could have fueled a moderate-sized city. They nuzzled at red lights and necked on beach blankets, the warm sun and sand no less arousing than the rock music on the portable radio, so that not even the pounding ocean surf could cool their bodies. Her car was their shabby bedroom; but despite the writhings on the torn vinyl, her virginity was an inflamed boil that refused to burst. "No, no, we can't, we mustn't," she gasped. Did girls mean yes when they said no? At fifteen, he was too uncertain and inexperienced to do anything but stop when she said so, and spend a lot of time pleading through clenched teeth. But her older sister had recently given birth to an illegitimate child. And her Catholic parents were devastated, telling her sister that she would roast in hell. He sulked. He fumed. He tried manipulative techniques to wear her down by evaporating her fear in a rush of passion. But he never succeeded in penetrating Annette's mysteries. She was eager to do "everything but" and was brought to dozens of orgasms; he, never. If he had, he might have gone on to other women; but instead, he returned home night after night seething and frustrated to encounter his father waiting up and demanding to know why he was two hours late.

"Do you know what time it is? Where have you been?"

He could have killed that man. Right then and there, he could have killed him.

"Nowhere."

"What kind of answer is that? You were supposed to be home at ten. It's ten past twelve."

"So what? Who cares? There's no school tomorrow. Go to bed."

"What? Don't you dare talk to me like that! You're grounded, young man. Weekend or not, you're staying home the next two nights."

"Yeah, you love that, don't you? God, why don't you just go away. Nobody wants to be here with you. Take a hint and leave. We're all sick of you."

"You little bastard! Go to your room."

"Oh, go to bed, you old drunk. You make me want to puke."

King shoved; Geoffrey shoved back. His father was slow and lumbering from booze, and Geoffrey easily blocked his attempt at a slap and pushed him backward so that he fell onto the sofa. Now they were both enraged, their fury unchecked, and they snorted and bellowed, hurling words like spears, scoring wounding insults.

One night, Geoffrey actually opened the front door so that the neighbors could more clearly hear him accuse his father of being a disgusting fornicator and crook who disgraced them all. King countered by calling Annette a whore, whereupon his son opened the window to shout to the world that his father had fucked his neighbor's wife. The walls shook, and at times lamps crashed as they took turns chasing one another around the room, until, spent and exhausted, they ran from the sight of one another and threw themselves into bed, dazed and bug-eyed. Occasionally—but only occasionally—Ruth intervened, coming downstairs wrapped in a robe to find them ludicrously circling one another with feints and jabs.

"Stop it, you two! The neighbors are going to call the police. Come to bed immediately before the landlord throws us out."

Sometimes she was a convenient face-saving device to quit, but if they weren't finished with one another, they ignored her until she finally went back upstairs. Geoffrey noticed that she never intruded while they were shouting insults at each other; he was much more damagingly articulate than his thick-tongued, boozy father; but when things turned physical, she seemed to fear for him and made her appearance at that point.

He was saying things that she was probably dying to say but would never dare. These battles erupted anytime that King attempted to exert parental authority. His son never backed off. But in their overwhelming ferocity, they assumed a life of their own as both combatants unleashed a lifetime of resentments. It was terrible and pathetic—damaging to both of them—but they could not stop. It was a battle of wills now out in the open, and neither would back down, despite mutual shame. Geoffrey especially. He felt torn between guilt and elation, taking on King. But it wasn't the awesome King of his childhood.

King, the timekeeper, stood firm, and fights developed over curfews, haircuts, cleaning his room before he went out, and even about telling where he was going and with whom. Geoffrey was grounded, docked allowance, deprived of TV. One consequence of these fights was that Ruth reappeared at the center of the family circle. She tried to arbitrate a truce.

To both of them she said that the fights must stop. It was a miracle that they hadn't killed each other by now or that King had not dropped dead from another heart attack. They didn't disagree; but each blamed the other for perpetuating the conflict. The tension in the house was unbearable. King spent most days behind the drawn louvers of the wet bar, morose and unreachable. Geoffrey gobbled his meals and then rushed for the door. But some days he was so depressed that he could not get out of bed to go to school—which triggered a new round of confrontation. Finally he turned to his mother in desperation. "Talk to him," she advised. "A little kindness would go a long way around here."

He agreed and opened the louvers to the wet bar.

"Dad, please don't fight me. I don't want this. We became so close. Please, Dad . . ."

"You're talking to *me*?" his father replied angrily. "I know what you want and I know what you need. You want to run circles around this family to prove what a big shot you are. What you need is a swift kick in the ass for the spoiled, rotten brat that you are. I reached out for you—father to son—and you kicked me in the balls. Yes, don't try to deny it. That's exactly what you did. I'll never forgive that. Never."

"How can you—"

"Get out of my sight!" his father shouted, and slammed the louvers closed. His son returned to his room and flopped on the bed. He had given up.

Into the maelstrom marched Eleanor Lowe, arriving for a long-delayed visit. Ruth's mother had not been to California in two years, mostly because of the "unsettled situation," as her daughter phrased it—meaning that King did not want his mother-in-law around to witness his plight in reduced circumstances. Indeed, it was only because Ruth knew that her mother's presence would inhibit father and son that she insisted on inviting her.

Eleanor did not have to be informed that the family was undergoing crisis—one look at Bob and Ruth told all—and she extended a particularly warm and affectionate greeting to her son-in-law. At the evening meal, she steered only toward pleasant topics and asked Geoffrey when she could meet his "friend Annette." She was told tonight, as a matter of fact, because Annette was picking him up in less than an hour. They were going to hear Joan Baez in concert.

King darkened. "Well, that's swell," he said to his son. "Gram just arrived and you can't even spend some time with her?"

"Oh, Bob, I'll be here for a month at least. Geoffrey and I will have plenty of time to be together."

"That's not the point," King insisted. "He knew you were arriving today. He hasn't seen you in a couple of years. Any grandson worth his salt would not have made a date tonight. That's the point. Annette may come in for a few minutes and meet your grandmother, but then she's going home, because you're staying home where you belong."

"But, Dad, we bought tickets."

"Exchange them. You should've known better. End of discussion, Geoffrey."

It was. Because Geoffrey stood up and splashed his glass of milk in his father's amazed face. Everyone gasped. Geoffrey dashed from the table as King overturned his chair and bounded after him. Geoffrey raced upstairs, but his father caught up with him at the top of the landing and delivered a resounding slap to his son's face. What happened next became frozen in the memory of the King family as an act of defiance which everyone knew—even at that moment—would change their lives forever. Geoffrey's fist slammed against his father's jaw and sent him crashing backward down the staircase. The women screamed. Eleanor grabbed at her chest, while Ruth dashed to her husband's side. Geoffrey stood above, glaring down at his father sprawled below. Blood trickled from King's lip. For a moment he lay stunned, but then slowly sat up and shook his head like a bad actor decked in a fight movie. Geoffrey and his mother exchanged a quick glance, and he was certain he saw her flash a small smile.

"Bob, are you all right?" she asked.

He pushed her away and slowly got to his feet. Then he glanced up at his son.

"You want to try slapping me again?" Geoffrey called down. "Come on up, you bastard."

King grabbed his wallet and keys and left.

Oh, God, he felt great! His hands were shaking from exhilaration as he unscrewed the cap on the bottle of bourbon he kept hidden in his closet. But before he could take a swig, his grim-faced mother stood in his doorway. "I'm not saying you weren't provoked," Ruth said, "but I just don't know where we go from here." He knew she was right. Look at how he had ruined their lives! Here he was, a fifteen-year-old boy, regularly drinking a pint of bourbon daily, nearly as much as his parents consumed.

It was very late when he heard his father unlocking the front door. He tensed. He heard King's heavy tread on the staircase and sat up. His father was standing on the other side of his door. He heard him breathing. Then the doorknob rattled, at first tentatively, but then with vigor. And by the time there was a cracking sound and the door flew open, Geoffrey was standing in the center of the room with upraised fists.

"Relax," his father said quietly. "Go back to bed." Even in the dark, he looked very drunk and weary. He sat down heavily on Geoffrey's bed and rubbed his eyes. "I'm sorry," he said. "I was wrong. As wrong as a man can be. Wrong about everything." And then he began to sob. It was crying different from any that Geoffrey had ever heard before—a painful gasping like a sick man trying to catch his breath. He cried for a long time with his hands limp at his sides. His son sat beside him, knowing what his father wanted, but he couldn't deliver. Not now. It was too late.

"Dad," he finally said, "it's real late."

King stood up unsteadily and looked down at his son in the dark. "From now on, you can do whatever you want," he said.

"Okay, I will. That's all I wanted."

"Well, you've got it. Have fun."

"You'll be surprised, Dad. I won't do anything to upset you."

"You bet you won't," King replied. "Because I couldn't care less from here on. You and I are finished."

"You just got through saying you were sorry," his son said hotly.

"Sorry that I ever cared in the first place," King replied, and departed, not bothering to close the door behind him.

King sat sullenly, avoiding Dr. Whitten's stare.

"Don't you see, Doctor," Ruth King said, "my husband doesn't give a damn about what happens to Geoffrey or any of us as long as he rules the roost. That's all he seems to care about. He's furious because he showed his son a little kindness and Geoffrey hasn't licked his hand in gratitude. So now he's gone to war. This has got to stop, and right now, before we are all carried to an asylum."

Dr. Whitten agreed. King agreed. But the psychiatrist later recalled this meeting with a particular sadness. "I tried to shame and shock that guy into changing, but it was all just talk. Right then and there, I knew there was nothing that I or anyone else could do to improve the situation. They were all locked in, acting out aggressions that they didn't quite understand and didn't want to. They were less afraid of killing each other than of coming to grips with their core feelings. I gave Bob less than a year before he was back in the hospital. The son? I wouldn't have hazarded a guess."

Unfettered at last, Geoffrey saw his future brightly outside the open door as he hit the streets on the run. Who he was and what he wanted to be were unclear, but by sampling life's wares, by picking and choosing in trial and error, he figured the process of elimination would ultimately reveal his destiny.

He was coming and going as he damn well pleased, staying out past midnight and offering no explanations, since none were requested. King brooded silently and left a room whenever his son appeared, often with a peroxide stripe dividing the front of his dark hair from the rest, wearing a lemon-yellow silk shirt purchased with birthday money. There were no fights and there was less tension in the house.

Geoffrey's anger at Annette's sexual ambivalence made her

cry. "You're the last virgin in Santa Monica High," he said. "You may be the only seventeen-year-old in all of L.A. who's never been laid! Aren't you ashamed? God, you're retarded!" They began to drift apart, and he didn't really miss her.

His newly dyed hair and modish clothes were rebellious growls, an intent to wade more than knee-deep into the lively sixties and flex his libido. He was naturally cautious, slightly reticent, until he unexpectedly won a citywide art contest for promising students that entitled him to admission into a special art class held on Saturdays. Burt Sardo's class in a second-floor loft above Westwood Plaza evaporated Geoffrey's tentativeness. The moment he entered the studio, waving aside a suspended cloud of marijuana smoke in the doorway—self-defense against his fear of drugs—he sensed he had found his spiritual homeland. The first morning, he volunteered to model in the nude, and although he stepped onto the platform with his hand demurely cupped over his groin, when he stepped down an hour later, he was a hero of sorts who had overcome shyness by displaying to his classmates privates that had unexpectedly become extroverted under public scrutiny.

"I was so afraid of getting a hard-on, that I did," he explained to grinning classmates, all of whom were either college or high-school art students. Bearded Sardo congratulated him on his excesses, urged the kids to draw quickly and capture a rare opportunity—"like a solar eclipse," he said. It was that kind of class, whose free-spiritedness unleashed Geoffrey's own, and no one had to tell him that most of these classmates were living his daydreams. There was Vi, a dark-eyed giantess in a flowing plaid cape and de Sade-style pointed high-heeled vinyl boots, who ironed her long black hair with a steam iron for the Cher look, then applied so much lacquer for shine that once when she lit a cigarette in class, the vapors ignited in a shocking whoosh of blue flame. Only quick thinking by several students who enveloped her inside her cape averted a possible tragedy. Vi was "tight" with Arnie, a UCLA space cadet, who accompanied her to class and sat in back in jeans and leather thongs, pushing his long hair out of his eyes and rolling joints from a leather pouch holding Mexican grass which he sold to the class for "inspiration" for half a buck each. Then there was Simone, a frail and tragic birdlike creature with a luminous third eye painted above the bridge of her hawklike nose, who went barefoot year-round and wore see-through blouses to bare her tiny breasts and hard, defiant nipples. Her roommate, Amanda, wore Indian saris and brass hoops on her wrists and ankles and didn't shave her legs. Sklar, an angular youth who wore thickly knitted turtlenecks in all weather, sketched with the skill of an accomplished draftsman, often while mumbling to himself in an incomprehensible language that he claimed was Aramaic. Other kids winked and whispered that he was "U.T.I."—under the influence. These exotics raised the consciousness and temperature of the classroom, so that even Sardo, a working artist struggling to support an Indian wife, became avid and provocative among his students and after class led the way like a middle-aged piper onto the crowded streets of Westwood Boulevard, wearing garish war paint like everyone else to stage "joy dances" or "mime confrontations" with curious onlookers.

Sardo would remember Geoffrey King as being the most talented in the class, but also the most raw and undisciplined of the students, who was often resentful of criticism and sulked defensively. On his second Saturday, Geoffrey brought to class a five-foot canvas and began work on his Opus One—a major oil painting which, without much question, he envisioned hanging one day in the Metropolitan Museum of Art. He painted a professional female model, using her torso and likeness as starting points for his own creative inspirations. He painted quickly, feverishly, attacking the canvas with a palette knife, as if sculpturing his intentions. Sardo had to laugh, but was damned impressed and offered to drive Geoffrey home with the large wet canvas. The student went in first and shooed his family away like a farm wife scattering chickens. Only after the canvas was hung on the living-room wall was his family invited back into the room. His big, burly father flushed. His mother gaped, then turned away. His visiting grandmother clapped one hand to her mouth and the other to her chest. The picture, *Marie Antoinette in Repose,* depicted a headless, flabby-breasted old crone seated in a straight-backed chair, her pencil-thin legs spread apart as far as she could get them. The young artist, mesmerized by his own creation, remained oblivious of his family's reaction. "Well, what do you think?" he asked, suddenly aware of their presence. "Interesting," his father replied, "but maybe it would look better in your room." Sardo burst out laughing. He couldn't help it.

Vi and Arnie, Simone and Amanda, and a few others became his close friends, forming a surrogate family, and King and Co. were no less shocked meeting them one Saturday after class while they were still in war paint than they had been meeting Marie Antoinette. King blinked at Simone's luminous third eye and then froze when she embraced him and declared, "Isn't life a groove? Aren't you glad you're you?" A put-down, of course, which he interpreted as something incomprehensibly else. Most of these new friends, meeting King, informed his son that they had one at home just like him. But at that point Geoffrey no longer cared. The group had helped him to shed his inhibitions. He felt loose and daring—ready to howl.

25

MARCH–JUNE 1967

For weeks Geoffrey had been carrying in his wallet an item clipped from the personal column of *The Advocate*, a local gay newspaper. The clipping represented a conscious decision to experiment, to take a chance. One word had leaped from the tiny type to seize his attention. The word was "art." The paid solicitation read: "Gay. W-M. 25. UCLA grad student, seeks gay roommate for small apt., Westwood district. Must like art, good music, share cooking, be compatible." A phone number was provided, and he had memorized it long before he finally found the courage to dial it.

"I'm calling about your ad in *The Advocate*. Have you found a roommate yet? Oh, good. I'm still living at home, but that might change quickly. I'd like very much to drop by and meet you."

The voice at the other end sounded dubious, slightly suspicious, and asked him his age.

"I'm nineteen," the fifteen-year-old lied. "But I'm very mature for my age." He also claimed to be an art student, more of a deception than a total lie. I'm into good music, and as far as cooking goes, I'm almost gourmet."

"What's your name?" he was asked, the voice distinctly friendlier. Geoffrey told him. "Hi, Geoffrey King, I'm Ted Larrick. Why don't you drop by on Saturday?"

For the next three days he imagined himself as the passionate plaything of Ted Larrick, who sounded "gorgeous," which, to Geoffrey, meant strong and masculine. A limp-wristed faggot would never interest him. He was nervous, of course, almost terrified. He kind of knew what homosexuals did together: they "Greeked" and had oral sex. Would he like it? The idea was both arousing and intimidating. Did it hurt? He hoped that Larrick would resemble Michelangelo's *David*, but he feared being physically mauled. He prayed the guy would be gentle and romantic. Above all, the latter. But what if he were an ugly brute who forced him into the bedroom? What if he expected Geoffrey to do things he, Geoffrey, had never heard of and refused to do? He fussed over himself for more than an hour on Saturday morning, dressed in slacks and a cotton shirt, then boarded a bus for Westwood, his mind spinning erotic fantasies.

Larrick, his muscular upper torso coated with a beach tan, greeted him in freshly pressed faded jeans and a warm smile. He was short and lithe, with the body of a trained gymnast, which he had been in high school—handsome, with a boyish face dominated by clear blue, lustrous eyes.

Larrick stepped aside and he entered a modest, sunny and immaculate apartment.

"Oh, Mary Tift!" Geoffrey exclaimed at an etching hung over the sofa.

"You know her work?" Larrick asked in surprise.

"God, she is one of my favorite artists."

Geoffrey stood in the kitchen doorway and watched his host toss a luncheon salad. They prattled about the best California Chardonnays and the few local bakeries where one could find crusty French bread. By the time they sat down to the meal, they were both glowing in camaraderie, and something more. "Well, cheers and welcome, Geoffrey King." His host grinned as they clinked wineglasses. Ted was working on a Ph.D. in biological research. From Enid, Oklahoma. Recently lost his roommate to a Stanford scholarship. "Sad," he admitted, "but, frankly, we both knew it was time for a change. Three years together ..." Ted loved Los Angeles, especially for the freedom it afforded gays. "You can't imagine what a prison a place like Oklahoma was." He shuddered.

"Do your parents know?" Geoffrey asked.

Ted laughed. "My father is an executive for an oil company. If he was an engineer or a mineralogist, I might have told him. Funny, though, the son of one of his colleagues was arrested in a motel room with an underage boy, and my father just couldn't believe it! I mean, he knew the family. He said to me, almost with tears in his eyes, 'You mean to tell me that John had another boy's penis in his mouth?' Is that hysterical! I felt like saying, 'Well, Mother does that for you all the time. At least I hope she does.'"

"You said *that*?" Geoffrey exclaimed.

"No, no, I thought it. If I had said it, he would've keeled over on the spot. Sexually uptight, you know."

"Oh, I know. I don't think my parents have had sex together in a couple of years. Isn't that sad? I wonder if they ever had one good screw together. I think about that a lot. There's no passion there."

"But you're not like that, are you?" Larrick teased. Geoffrey blushed. "I'm going to tell my parents. And soon. I won't live a lie."

"Well, good luck," Larrick remarked with casual irony.

They talked for a long time, each intent on avoiding silence that generated sexual tension between them, until Ted suggested a stroll on Westwood Boulevard. Geoffrey took him to a small gallery, where Ted found an inexpensive Tift etching to add to his collection, and they returned to the apartment to hang it. Ted opened another bottle of wine and they sat together on the sofa, pretending to be relaxed side by side, talking about art and travel.

"I dream of living in Paris or Rome," Geoffrey said. "I figure I can do it once I get a following for my pictures. It shouldn't take too much money to live, although I do love nice things. The point is, I just refuse to believe that the world has only one face—the scowling, unhappy one, which is practically all I've ever seen. I just won't give up hope. I've got to make good things happen for me."

His new friend smiled. "Oh, you will. I'm sure. You're audacious, the kind who gets his way—am I right? But tell me the truth, Geoffrey, how old are you *really*?"

"Oh, Ted, what difference does it make?" he replied. "I'm so hungry for somebody to love and who'll love me in return. I'm starved. You just can't imagine."

Larrick nodded, looking touched. "I know," he sighed. "I know all too well where you are coming from—believe me."

"I'm much older than my real age," Geoffrey added. "I've been through so much, you wouldn't believe it. I can't believe it myself. I've got a million problems right now, otherwise I'd move in with you tonight, if you'd let me. I want you so much."

Larrick kissed him—the first time Geoffrey ever kissed a man. What began as a tender, almost exploratory kiss quickly became something else. Even as it was happening, Annette's face flashed onto his mental screen and he realized that not even the sum total of all their feverish necking sessions condensed into one glowing atom of passion could compare with what he experienced in Ted Larrick's arms. They stood up, light-headed and laughing, and walked into the bedroom. Larrick's bed was covered by a quilted comforter, a family heirloom, which he and Geoffrey carefully folded back. Larrick lit scented candles, then drew the drapes as Geoffrey impatiently unbuttoned his shirt, then unbuckled his belt, stepping out of his jeans and kicking them aside before scrambling onto the bed a moment before Ted.

"It was the night I was born," he would say later.

With the stealth of a cat burglar, Geoffrey entered his bedroom window at dawn. He was a fearless, impetuous, and insatiable lover, but the miracle was not that his parents never caught him sneaking out late at night and returning just as the streetlights extinguished, but that they failed to read his secret blazing like headlines on his happy face. If they had merely cocked an inquisitive eyebrow, he probably would have blurted everything, but in their deadness and alcoholic stupor, he was all but invisible to them. He wanted to shout and sing and dance; and some nights after returning home, he flipped on the stereo, hungry for the Beatles or the Stones, uncaring whether he woke his parents.

He wanted out of their monosyllabic lives to crown his own at his lover's side. He ached to be eighteen and on his own, and never once did he return home from Ted's without seething with impatient resentment.

"Ted, you can't imagine what a turning point I'm at. I'm finally on track now. This is who I am—right now—in bed with you. It's like a magnet—that's who you are—a giant magnet who put all of the pieces of me into place. I fit now, don't you see? I've come together. Oh, stop it, you pig! You know what I mean. Oh, Ted, be brave: let me move in with you. They'll never find me. Not in a million years."

Larrick chuckled. "Oh, sure, wouldn't the vice squad love that! Corrupting the morals of a minor."

"It's so unfair," Geoffrey sighed. "They're so useless. Two drunks who ruined their lives completely. What right do they have to tell me what to do? I wish they were dead—I really do. That's the only way I'll ever be free of them. Oh, Ted, I could be so happy living with you. And I'd make you so happy, too. You're so gentle and loving. Do you love me?"

Larrick rubbed his hand across Geoffrey's firm, flat stomach. "You're my gorgeous boy. My gorgeous, gorgeous boy."

"You can have me at your side always. I'd cook for you. Do the shopping and keep the house clean."

"You're adorable." Larrick smiled and cut him off with a languorous kiss.

He was a boy in love: starved for affection, bursting with a desire to please—arriving with flowers; rearranging the living-room furniture in the small apartment for more dramatic effect; serving his lover meals in bed; appearing unannounced at Ted's study desk in the research library with a wicker basket of cheese, breadsticks, and wine. He was playful, endearing, and passionate . . . but he was a boy and Ted Larrick was an ambitious young man, working to become a research associate at the Rockefeller Institute in New York. As the months of their intense relationship flashed by, Larrick began to feel as if he had been relocated at the calamitous edge of the world where storms are born. Geoffrey was a funnel of desire and desperation, swirling Ted's lecture notes over the rooftops and crowding his life with an intensity that made it difficult to breathe. He was incessant and unpredictable and ignored limitations. "But I've got to study," Larrick complained, even as ardent kisses melted his resolves. "Oh, Geoffrey, you bitch, you know how to get your way." At times Larrick felt as if his young lover was feasting on the living marrow of Ted's own bones. Geoffrey asked not only for sex and affection but also to be saved from his family and himself. "Help me to become a man" was his plea, and that responsibility was too much. A B- at mid-term stiffened Larrick's resolves.

"You know, Geoffrey, my ad in *The Advocate* still remains unanswered," Ted said one evening. "I need a roommate to share my expenses."

"But why?" Geoffrey asked. "Your father is loaded."

"Geoffrey, we all have our problems at home, don't we? I don't feel like explaining mine at the moment."

"Okay, then I'll talk to my parents tonight. I'll make them support me, I'll just tell them I'm moving out. If you want, they can write a letter saying they approve."

Larrick shook his head. "No," he said sharply. "Absolutely not. Geoffrey, I can't risk going to jail over you. Forget that, please. Once and for all."

Well, Geoffrey could not claim he wasn't warned, and yet there was treachery in the way that Ted seemed to drop the subject, so that as weeks went by, Geoffrey began to think his lover had abandoned the notion of a roommate, or at least shelved it as a threat now that they saw each other only on Friday and Saturday nights. Finals at UCLA, a nervous, hectic time, and Ted seemed preoccupied and tense, barely smiling when Geoffrey arrived at the apartment with an expensive body oil and an instruction book for giving a sensual massage. Geoffrey was proud of his self-discipline, resisting dozens of impulses during the week to pick up the phone and hear Ted's voice, no matter how briefly. But then, one Saturday at noon, he arrived at Ted's place and was greeted at the door by a tall, thin stranger. "Oh, Ned," Ted said, "this is my friend Geoffrey. Geoffrey, meet Ned Bales, my new roommate."

He acted the fool, stamping his foot, blushing with humiliation and confusion, barely resisting an impulse to tear the apartment to pieces. "Oh, well . . . I see . . . lovely. Barely room for three, is there? Or did Ned bring his own bed? No? Oh, fine, I should've brought a housewarming present. Maybe a jar of Vaseline, or did Ned bring that, too?"

Then he departed with a thunderous, dramatic door-slam.

On the third day of the bleakest depression he had ever known, his mother came to his room and urged him to eat something. He refused. She was able to coax the family's doctor into a house call, and he diagnosed mild exhaustion and depression, and prescribed Valium. That night, Geoffrey lit some incense, turned on his stereo, and drank a couple of glasses of straight bourbon. Then he swallowed the entire contents of the plastic container holding the Valium. He closed his eyes. Mellow. Detached. Indifferent.

26

July–October 1967

KING, GEOFFREY. Mental Status Report: 15-year-old patient admitted via Psychiatric Emergency Room accompanied by his parents and wearing pajamas.

He appears moderately obtunded, but is easily aroused with tactile or auditory stimulation. He frequently closes his eyes and lies back to fall asleep. He can communicate only with difficulty and is confused attempting to carry out simple commands. He is oriented as to person but misses the date by three days. He is cooperative within the limits of somnolence. The patient's mood is generally one of depression, although a normal range of effect is demonstrated.

Diagnostic Impression:
        1) Intoxication from Valium, overdosage
        2) Psychoneurotic depressive reaction

Initial Management Plan:
   Careful observation, routine psychological testing; milieu therapy and individual
   therapy with Dr. Maurice Whitten.

Geoffrey smiled when the psychiatrist told him that he was
only three doors down from the room his father had occupied
as a patient in this same ward. And then he reminded himself
that King had also been brought here for, among other things,
attempting to take his life with an overdose of pills. But that
wasn't why he was smiling. "I was just wishing that my parents
were Rexall and they would fire me the way they fired him." Dr.
Whitten shook his head. "Not likely, I'm afraid. Now, what is
this all about? What happened, Geoffrey?" The patient
shrugged. "A million problems." He sighed. The psychiatrist
asked if he and his father were battling again. He shook his
head. "We hardly talk to each other anymore. Anyway, you're
his doctor, not mine. I want to talk to somebody else." Whitten
flushed with annoyance. "You let me worry about that," he said.
The patient turned away. "How can you help me if I don't trust
you one bit?" Whitten thrust his hands into the pockets of his
white coat and glared down at the bed.

"You're just like your father," he said. "He wanted to make
his own rules here too. So I'll tell you exactly what I told him:
I'm calling the shots around here and you're going to do what
you're told. Speaking of which, your parents are hanging
around to see if you're all right. They're very upset, as you can
imagine. Just say hello and let them see you're alive. Then we'll
let you sleep awhile. Come on, Geoffrey, get up. Or do you
want me to have the orderlies carry you down to the visitors'
room?"

He felt wobbly negotiating the long hallway and clung to the
wall for support. There was a moment, though, when he stood
in the doorway of the small visitors' lounge, unobserved by his
grim, silent, preoccupied father and mother, that he felt like
their small child again and ached to run to them and be embraced. King sat cross-legged, propping his felt hat on one
knee, staring glumly into space, probably barely in control
seeing his son in this very same place—his own mental ward.
Ruth looked like a traveler waiting in a distant place without

any means of getting back home. Geoffrey entered, and his mother looked up first, greeting him with a small smile as faded and functional as her old housecoat. Then King saw him and the blood rushed to his father's cheeks. He stood up and slammed his hat to the ground. "Well, by God, you've done it now, haven't you? You've done things your way, and you see where you ended up. You landed right in the pits, Mr. Big Shot. I watched it all happening and never said a word. But that's finished. You can forget all about that! From now on you're gonna do things my way. You got that straight? You're gonna shape up and fly right. By God, you will! You've run loose for the last time, friend. A goddamn wild animal, that's what you are. Well, we're gonna tame you. We'll cage you. You will shape up. Get that straight. You will shape up. You will!"

Geoffrey closed his eyes and told himself that King was shouting only to keep from sobbing, that for his father this must be the most terrible, guilt-ridden moment he would ever face, and he tried to block out that bellowing, bullying voice, to find compassion beneath the ugliness of it. He blanked it out by unleashing a shrill, deafening primal scream that caused his ears to ring and brought the orderlies running.

"Get that man out of here. Get him out. Out, out."

His father gasped, and with a fresh burst of fury rushed at him, but two hefty orderlies intercepted King and lifted him off the ground in restraint. His father was in an incoherent rage, flailing his arms as he was dragged off down the hall, shouting and struggling. "You will!" he kept repeating. "You will! Do you hear me, you little bastard, you will shape up." The orderlies didn't wait for the elevator, but hustled him down the stairwell.

Geoffrey found there is no respite from yourself in a ward for the mentally ill, no let up from pain and grief, no place to run or hide. The biggest surprise was the tenderness of some of his fellow patients, virtual strangers who reached out, either to comfort him or to be comforted themselves. The ward was a tiny enclave of intimacy in an indifferent world.

In group therapy one day, a middle-aged man remarked: "I wish I had cancer. Maybe then I would get some sympathy and understanding from my family. Right now, they just hate me.

They think I'm a monster. I know they're glad to be rid of me, even for a little while. My wife would've left me long ago if it weren't for the children. They're all stuck, you see, with this terrible monster. Me." Geoffrey knew that the group-therapy room had heard those words before.

Whitten stood aside in his case and turned it over to a young staff psychiatrist named Bernard Draper, whom Geoffrey suspected of being gay. He liked Draper and ultimately disclosed to him the real cause of his suicide attempt. The doctor told him, "If you're going to be crushed by every romantic breakup, you'll never survive your teenage years." The alternative, he said, was to grow with each experience and face the disappointment of a broken love affair as part of the overall growth experience. "Hopefully, there will be dozens of Ted Larricks in your life from now on. Anyway, look how much you received from this first experience." God, how true! He would never again be tortured by sexual ambivalence. He knew what he was and he was committed to his own nature. And he discovered a tremendous capacity to love as well as the selfless joy of giving.

"Why do I always react with such extremes?" he asked. The doctor turned the question back to him.

"I get desperate. I'm so greedy! I want it all. And more. I guess that's how I was raised. My father was never satisfied, either. But you've got to understand: Ted brought me the first happiness I've ever known. God, what if I've lost it? Happiness, I mean. What if that was my only chance and I blew it?"

"There will be other chances," the doctor assured him, "but first you've got to feel as if you deserve to be happy."

In the end, he agreed to participate in family counseling sessions with his father and Dr. Whitten, even if it was the psychiatrist's idea. Whitten told him that while he had done extremely well in his therapy with Dr. Draper and made real progress, it made no sense sending Geoffrey back to the stress of the King household. "In this hospital, we face reality," Whitten said, "and the reality of your situation is that you'd be much better off living apart from your father. But the sad fact is, you have nowhere else to go." So he gave in. His father was apologetic for his wild behavior on the day his son was admitted, and seemed sincere in trying to find reasonable grounds to get along. Whitten surprised Geoffrey by being extremely direct and at times brutally frank with his father.

"Bob, somehow I get the impression that your determination to master your son—make him toe the mark—is all tied up with your current struggles and disappointments. Am I right?"

King replied that he honestly didn't think that was the case—not consciously, anyway—that his only motivation was to try to keep his son in line by setting minimal standards of behavior.

"Well, Bob, then we've got to improve your tactics, because they are obviously counterproductive. Your relationship has become damned pathological. Those battles have distorted both of you emotionally. That's why Geoffrey is here. And, Bob, if you aren't careful, you could be back here sooner or later. Bob, you've got to learn how to accept Geoffrey's challenges for what they are: an inevitable part of growing up. And, Geoffrey, flexing your muscles and making growling noises is both acceptable and your right. But you've got to learn that you can defeat this guy without destroying him and losing his love."

They agreed to try.

One afternoon, while father and son were talking, the psychiatrist slipped out and phoned Ruth.

"I want you to think now, before there's another crisis, about how we can give that boy the chance he deserves to grow up. I know you're financially strapped, but isn't there any place you can send him to get away from his father? That's *the* question, isn't it?"

The day his parents came to take him home, Whitten sat with Geoffrey for a while. "There's still one item you and I haven't discussed."

"My homosexuality?" the patient asked.

Whitten nodded. "I'll tell you frankly, I suspect you're more interested in tantalizing your parents with being gay than anything else. In any event, you're still very young. Hell, you had a girl a while back. These are years for experimentation, so my advice is, just keep an open mind about it. Get ahold of *Playboy*. Look at the centerfold. Play with yourself. Don't grin, I'm serious. Try to turn on and masturbate. See what happens."

"Look, I'm gay," Geoffrey replied heatedly. "You and my parents are just going to have to accept that fact."

"Well, I'm not fighting you on this. I'm only urging you not to think you are totally committed at this point. Because you probably aren't. Who knows? A week from now, you might be in love with a beautiful blond."

"If so, his name will be Tom or Jerry." Geoffrey smirked.

"Maybe. But maybe not. Whatever, this is something you should sit down and discuss with your parents one of these days. This is exactly the kind of issue that can blow up in your faces, isn't it?

"You think Robert L. King can really accept this?"

"I don't think he has any choice, do you? Anyway, I don't think your father will give a damn, as long as you're discreet and don't rub his nose in it. I really think the old boy has lost his appetite for these battles. Do you know why?"

"Because he's losing," Geoffrey said.

"Exactly," Maurice Whitten agreed.

KING, GEOFFREY.	Discharge Summary
Length of Stay:	Five weeks, four days
Official Diagnosis:	Psychoneurotic Depressive Reaction
Manifestation:	Moderate; feeling of depression resulting in suicide gesture
Stress:	Moderate; difficulty within family setting and confusion over personal identity
Predisposition:	Mild; adolescent struggles with dependency, difficulties establishing close relationships
Condition on Discharge:	Improved
Prognosis:	Good

27

NOVEMBER 15, 1969

One of the peculiarities of prison life was that the most aggressive, flamboyant homosexuals were usually the least sexually harassed by other inmates, probably because of their outrageousness. Other gays called them "flamers": shrieking, screeching, overly effeminate drag queens who pranced through the corridors of the old county jail as if on an outing, oblivious of the hot, stinking cell floors as they greeted guards and prisoners with the boldest good humor—"Hi, you gorgeous hunks, how are you? Have a good day, now!" Not even the sourest guard could keep a straight face when these queens were stripped down and searched for drugs, often concealed in the damnedest places. "Oh, God, girls, don't you just love it!" they shouted when ordered to bend over and spread apart their buttocks. "Oh, hon, you just take your time and look up there as long as you want to." They descended on the clothing room like squalling bargain shoppers, stampeding the bins to find the tightest pair of denims and exclaiming in disappointment when the shirts weren't pressed. Many of them were transvestite hookers arrested while soliciting on Selma Avenue in Hollywood, arriving in jail in their dresses and wigs that Dolly Parton would one day make famous. These queens and any other prisoners that the guards could identify as being homosexual were kept in isolation on the top floor of the jail in a cellblock known as the Queen Tank.

Geoffrey was terrified of being sent up there, unaware that it was the only place in that hellhole where he could possibly survive without being gang-raped or murdered. Twice within his first day in jail, guards questioned him about his sexuality. He vigorously denied being gay, but caused such a commotion in the maximum-security wing that he was finally carted off to the queens. "Lisa will take good care of you," the guards told him.

Lisa stood six-feet-two from the floor on a pair of size-thirteen feet. He was a black trusty who ran the Queen Tank with guile and ruthlessness, calling all the shots and nicknaming all his minions with girls' names that stuck. Lisa, "herself" a transvestite hooker, could body-press two hundred and eighty pounds, and nobody in her block dared to cross her. "Really, Sally, what a turd you are. Clean up that pigsty of a cell immediately or I'll whup your ass." Sally, a hefty six-footer, reached for a broom.

Lisa looked over her new charge, who, terrified that morning, had thrown up the breakfast in the mess hall before two prison inspectors. His mere presence in the chow line had almost triggered a riot.

155

"Welcome, hon," she said. "Stop lookin' so scared. I got you a sweet little roommate."

His name was Dennis, a slender, pale boy with delicate features who had been arrested for committing oral copulation in the May Company's rest room. He seemed very ill, lying under blankets in the stifling cellblock.

"Poor thing," Lisa whispered. "She got pneumonia and the fucking pigs won't let us take her to the infirmary. So me and the girls been nursing her. Can you believe how much they hate us? The poor thing almost croaked. But I think she's over the worst, and anyhow, it ain't catching."

Lisa studied Geoffrey. "Well, hon, what you in for?"

"Murder," he replied.

"Your lover?"

Geoffrey told her, and Lisa whistled. "Well, hon, seems like you gonna be with us awhile," she said.

Lisa dispensed her charge's Queen Tank name. She told Geoffrey, "From now on, you be called Gerrie."

NOVEMBER 18, 1969

"Enters tearfully," Dr. Sanford Bode noted on his worksheet. Bode was a court-appointed psychiatrist who earned three hundred dollars for a sanity evaluation. On busy days, he could do five or six. "Do you know why you're here?" he asked the prisoner. Dr. Bode was brisk, efficient, and in half an hour he had fulfilled his obligation to Superior Court and made his evaluation. Actually, he could've done it more quickly than that, except that the prisoner became extremely upset providing a shortened version of events surrounding the murders and sobbed uncontrollably while trying to reconstruct the actual killings.

After lunch, the prisoner was returned to a small office in the basement infirmary and met with Dr. Albert Farber, a second psychiatrist and an expert on drug-related cases. Again, Geoffrey cried continually. The two doctors filed their reports with Superior Court. Both believed Geoffrey insane at the time of the murders, although Dr. Bode thought that an element of malice was present—an opinion that could convict Geoffrey for first-degree murder. Dr. Farber thought the prisoner was legally sane to stand trial, but too depressed to cooperate fully in his own defense. He recommended Geoffrey be transferred to a psychiatric hospital. Dr. Bode thought the prisoner legally sane and able to stand trial.

A few days later, Geoffrey sat with his public defender assigned to psychiatric court and heard the same two doctors testify about him. In less than ten minutes, a judge ruled that he was legally sane to stand trial. And although he had told both of these psychiatrists that he had twice been admitted to a psychiatric hospital not ten miles from the jail, neither they nor anyone else connected with his case bothered to request his hospital records or question the psychiatrist who had treated him.

NOVEMBER 20, 1969

Geoffrey wore his conservative blue suit to his preliminary hearing at the Torrance Municipal Court. He sat on the prison bus chained to two other prisoners, and was startled when one of them poked him in the ribs, winked, and whispered his name. He was a handsome man in his thirties named Larry, and he introduced his brother, Frank, next to him. The two were mob assassins, going on trial for the slaying of a Long Beach politician. The brothers knew all about his case. "Nothing happens in the can that we don't know." Larry said, winking. They knew what he had done and felt sorry for him. They smiled condescendingly at some of his questions and told him he was lucky to have a public defender because they're in court every day and know all the judges and prosecutors, which is invaluable when you're trying to swing a plea bargain—although in Geoffrey's case it would be open-and-shut second-degree murder. Diminished capacity because of the LSD. Out in seven years. "Next case!" Larry chuckled.

Before the bus reached Torrance, they told him everything he needed to know to survive prison. After conviction, he would be sent to Chino, a clearing house, and from there be assigned to a prison. Stay away from Soledad and San Quentin, they advised. You want to be either in Vacoville or California Men's Colony, the only decent prisons in the state. At Chino, the prison trusties do all the interviewing and screening. The brothers gave him a couple of names before he departed, trusties who'd take care of him.

Being so young and handsome, he would "marry" one of the top four inmates in prison. Marrying meant living in the cell with his "Daddy," or protector, who would make certain that he got whatever job, liquor, or drugs he wanted. But there would be fights to own him, and constant danger from the former "wife" who had been dumped to make room for him. They advised him to start weight-lifting and get as strong as possible as quickly as possible. If your Daddy gets killed, find another immediately. Don't be unmarried for a single day, if you can help it.

"You want a Daddy that not even the craziest nigger would mess with," Frank whispered. "You want a Daddy with connections."

Larry poked him. "Don't worry, kiddo; we'll end up in the same prison, and you'll do just fine."

Geoffrey barely remembered the preliminary hearing. He was buoyed by what the brothers had told him. It was now within the realm of possibility to believe he might actually survive a prison ordeal. In the courtroom, they called his Uncle Raymond to the stand and asked him if his mother and sister were alive the last time he saw them. Yes, he answered. And when they asked him if both were now dead, Lowe began to cry and needed several minutes to compose himself. Geoffrey's lawyer tried to question Lowe about his nephew's drug habits, but the judge overruled him.

"Your Honor, I understand that the People are trying to prove malice and premeditation in this case, and I want to show—"

"No, no," the judge interrupted. "All we have to determine here is, one, did the murders occur, and two, is there reasonable cause to believe that the defendant did it. All other matters are beyond the scope of the preliminary examination."

Finally Geoffrey was told to stand up, and heard himself being bound over without bail on two counts of murder. The arraignment in two weeks was a mere formality; and then, please God, he could finally go to trial and get it over with.

DECEMBER 9, 1969

Prisoners who were not yet convicted of a crime were not allowed to work, so up in the Queen Tank there was nothing to do except their hair and nails. The inmates snipped green from Salem cigarette packs for eye shadow and the red from Marlboros for lipstick, and manufactured their own mascara from cigarette ashes and toothpaste. They set each other's hair, using toilet-paper rolls. Meals were served in their cells, carted up to them in large metal containers. At eleven every morning an old vendor appeared to sell the Los Angeles *Times* and candy bars, the highlight of the day. The guards controlled a loudspeaker system plugged to local radio stations, and if inmates yelled for them to turn it up, they most often turned it off. Whenever Diana Ross and the Supremes—supreme in the gay community—were heard, the entire cellblock began to boogie. The cells remained open most of the day, and nearly everyone socialized, griping about the awful food, especially "jute balls," meatballs filled with noodles that tasted like plaster of paris. They bitched about the brutality of the guards and the cruelty of Lisa, the overpowering smell of "Magic Shave," a depilatory the black queens used to remove their facial hairs, scraping off chin whiskers with tongue depressors. Even in the Queen Tank, where there was common ground between the races, tension sometimes exploded into violence. "You goddamn nigger bitch!" someone would shriek and set it off. "I don't know how you feel about race," one of the queens said to Geoffrey, "but I guarantee, hon, before you leave jail, you'll be ready to join the Klan." Geoffrey had known few blacks before jail; he was frightened and intimidated by them.

Among the sixty inmates in the Tank, he was the most morose, and with good reason: his crime was vastly worse than theirs—matricide versus a lavatory blow-job—so they pampered him with candy bars and tried to cheer him up.

"Oh, Gerrie, just make believe you're on sorority row and all those handsome fraternity boys are just drooling to get inside your pants," they urged.

He laughed. But like them, he was a segregated freak, confined to a zoo on the thirteenth floor—a zoo within a zoo—an outcast in a terrible old building swarming with the worst dregs off the streets. At times be participated in their laughter, but he never felt one of them: he was gay; most of them weren't. They were drag queens, transvestites, creatures who thought of themselves in the feminine gender, who took silicone injections to grow breasts and yearned for the sex-change operation. He became friendly with a five-foot-two, chubby young kid named Billie, with dyed blond hair, whose idol had been Jayne Mansfield and who lived most of his life as a woman, so that even next-door neighbors never suspected the truth. "She" was married to a bank robber and was arrested driving the getaway car. Now Billie sat in the Queen Tank, heartbroken because she wasn't going to the same prison as her husband. They would be apart for at least ten years, and Geoffrey asked why, when they both had good jobs, they had tried to rob a bank.

"That's just the way he was." Billie sighed. "That's what he wanted to do."

There was sex in the tank, but it was not nearly as rampant or brutal as on the lower floors. Lisa, exacting tribute from her minions for favors rendered, tapped them to turn tricks for their keepers. One night she appeared at Geoffrey's cell.

"Oh, Gerrie, hon, I got a little favor I want you to do."

Directly behind her, an off-duty guard began unzipping his fly. To say no to Lisa invited a savage beating and continual cruelty. And even though he was depressed, staying alone in his cell and crying a lot, Lisa showed no mercy when angered.

"Hon, fuck yo mother and grandmother. Fuck 'em. You ain't got no sympathy from me. Yo watch yo ass or I'll break it." And this was said merely because he had used too much toilet paper.

On Sunday, most of the black queens went to chapel. They spent hours doing their hair, nails, and eyelashes to get ready, and went because they loved to sing gospel songs and flirt with the other prisoners. One Sunday they caused such a commotion in chapel that all of them were thrown into solitary for a week, and when they created a disturbance there, were given an additional week in the hole. Lisa was among them; so, unexpectedly, life in the Queen Tank became relaxed and relatively tranquil for the survivors. Even the guards seemed slightly less surly. And on the first day of this undisturbed calm, Geoffrey was sent to the client room to meet his trial lawyer.

His name was Leonard Stone, a short, intense, forty-year-old who seemed about to charge through a wall. They talked for a while, and Stone was appalled. "I never defended anyone before or since who cared less about what was going to happen to him," he later recalled. "Geoffrey had killed, knew it, and hanging, gassing, the guillotine, were all equally fine to him. I much prefer a hard-nosed bastard who insists on a course of action, so if I lose, I can then blame him."

Stone was a senior P.D., one of only four attorneys in the busy public defender's office qualified by experience to try homicide cases.

"Your crime turns my stomach, but I'll work my ass off to get you the best possible deal," he said.

"I want to plead guilty and get it over with," Geoffrey told him.

"No, you don't," the lawyer replied.

"I don't want a trial," his client insisted.

"You don't want a jury trial, but you sure as hell want a trial, fella. I'm gonna try to get an understanding judge who'll sentence you to a hospital rather than a prison."

Stone laid out the case. One of the psychiatrists who had examined Geoffrey—Farber—thought he should be hospitalized immediately; the other one—Bode—felt that Geoffrey had killed in malice. So Stone needed a third psychiatric opinion to bolster Farber's. Unfortunately, the court was obligated to provide only two, unless the defense declared its intention of pleading insanity, and then the court would provide a third. Otherwise, the defense pays for its extra psychiatric opinion. "I tried to tap your uncle," Stone added, "but he says he's broke. So the only alternative is for us to plead insanity."

"Well, I must be crazy to do what I did," his client said.

"An insanity plea is very risky for many reasons," his lawyer admitted. "I want you to know that up front. Right now, your psychiatric reports are privileged; but if we plead insanity, the prosecution gets access to them and could tear us to pieces. If you go to prison for second-degree, you'd probably be out in seven to ten. But if you get sent to Atascadero, you might be there much, much longer, on an indeterminate sentence."

He saw Geoffrey's puzzled expression. "Atascadero," Stone explained, "is the state's maximum-security mental institution.

Your keepers won't be anxious to release a murderer who might embarrass them by killing again. In fact, they could be held liable by your victim's family. So, in the battle between your rights and their job security, you can guess who wins."

"I know I need help," Geoffrey replied. "I want to get well, or I might as well die on the inside."

"Well, okay," Stone said. "We'll give it a whirl."

28

Having spent most of the summer of 1967 in the hospital, Geoffrey returned home aware of budding changes in himself that may have been planted by his doctors or that perhaps signified he was finally growing up. He had been gone five weeks, although he had been out of touch with his family much longer than that, considering his preoccupations with Annette and then with Ted. To his surprise, he noticed that his parents seemed to have achieved some sort of reconciliation during his absence, a rediscovery of intimacy, and they acted as if they were sharing a secret that had drawn them closer. They had both added heft in recent months—never a good sign—but there was something *different* between them that was revealed in the way his mother glanced at King at the breakfast table, or the way he lightly touched her arm on his way out to the office. His father had acquired contracts to hire salesmen for an Oldsmobile dealership and a large furniture store—no big deal, but enough to keep them going. On his first day home Geoffrey impulsively called his old girlfriend. They met on the beach and Annette surprised him by the warmth of her welcome: a tight hug and murmurs of delight. "You made it!" she declared with a laugh. "I've been delaying and delaying shopping for clothes until you could go with me. I almost gave up; I'm starting college on Friday." So he spent most of that first week with her and became caught up in her excitement, prowling with her around the bargain racks of department stores and dress shops.

They sat up all night during a rap session, a bottle of wine between them, sharing confidences and giggling and lapsing into sadness at each other's vulnerabilities. He told her about Ted Larrick and she told him about several of her own traumas that he had never imagined. He didn't know her at all, this surprisingly independent, feisty Annette. And it saddened him. But he was so proud of her: a scholarship winner.

She told him that his instincts were probably right about his parents. "I think what happened to you must've really shocked them. You can bet they've been doing a lot of talking about you and themselves."

"Annette," he asked, "what is my family all about? Have you ever figured it out? You know us by now almost as well as I do."

She pondered in somber silence. "I don't know why they married, so I don't think there's an answer. I would never just hitch my star to some guy and say, 'Okay, wherever thou goest, so go I.' Their generation was so *different*. You once told me your dad was very poor and she was very lonely, so if they talked about their future together, it was probably in terms of him being a success. I don't think a man like that was really meant for marriage. I don't think a domestic life meant very much to him at all. I'll bet your mother was disappointed in him early on, but women of her generation just went along. I'm guessing, Geoffrey. I really don't know. They're like my folks: they'll take their secrets to the grave. I just think that when two unhappy people marry, they produce an unhappy family. It's that simple. It's strange, you know, your fights with him, because he reminds me so much of my dad, who's really not a confronter at all. My dad hates that; he's just like yours—one of the world's great ostriches. Ask Mr. King how his business is going, he'll tell you, 'Oh fine.' He hates to face up to problems. So your folks are the last who would ever sit down together and say, 'Hey, why are we living together? What do we want and expect from each other? Why did we have a kid and what do we want from him? Why did we want a family in the first place?'"

"In the hospital," Geoffrey said, "we talked about basic values that people should be living by . . . you know, loving each other, sharing their lives, caring about one another, all that good stuff we never had. It made me physically ill when I thought about how deprived I was in this house."

"Well, Geoffrey," Annette replied, "your parents didn't have it for each other, so they couldn't give it to you either."

"Disgusting," Geoffrey muttered.

"Well, that's why I always wondered why you allowed them to *matter* so much. You saw what was coming down. I never could figure why you tried so hard to matter to them when it was so obvious what *did* matter to them."

Yes, that was the central question. But what could he tell her, except that they were his *family*, his life-support system, his protective circle, his makers and his breakers. He had poured all of his emotional energy into them, and yet he couldn't say why. They were his family. They were everything. He was glad he was gay, but if he ever did decide to marry and have children, he would sacrifice everything for their happiness, and said so to Annette.

"But what if your mate saw things different?" she replied. "What then? Your poor mother! Who knows what she might have become. I used to think the Kings were the sorriest excuse for a family there ever was, but, Geoffrey, there are so many kids as unhappy and screwed-over as you are."

"I know," he said. "There were times in the mental ward when I actually felt lucky, if you can believe that! God, how do we all get so fucked up?"

She shrugged. "Nobody means to, I guess."

One day Geoffrey impulsively picked up the phone and called his father at the office. The secretary answered and they chatted for a while before she put him through to King. "I'd like an appointment to see you this afternoon," he said.

King chuckled. "Well, I think that can be arranged, sir. Shall we say three-thirty?"

He dressed in his good suit and arrived licking his dry lips, remembering that Dr. Whitten had preached "creative encounters," by which was meant rational discussions to find a middle ground to differences, although in this instance there was no particular discussion involved, but merely an open and honest statement of fact. Man to man. In a business setting. Serious business.

He was precisely two minutes early for his appointment, but the moment he entered the outer office, he heard his father buzz Miss Walsh and tell her to show in his son the moment he arrived. In he went. King's big desk was cleared for action. His father smiled seeing him in his good suit and extended an open palm at the visitor's chair.

"Well," he said, "what can I do for you?"

"Just listen, I guess," his son replied. "Dad, if we really are serious about trying to get along, then there's something I want you to know. I'm a homosexual. I want to be honest and not sneak around trying to deceive you."

His father nodded and thanked him for his honesty. "You've chosen a very lonely life," he said.

"I know, but I didn't choose it. I have no choice. That's what I am."

"You had a girlfriend."

"But then I had a boyfriend and, Dad, there's just no comparison."

"I see. Well, I'll tell you my honest feelings. I'm not too surprised. You've been interested in fashions and decorating for as long as I can remember. I honestly don't think the less of you, but I am more concerned for your well-being. It's kind of like role reversal, Geoffrey, and right now you're a new, attractive young thing in town, and there is no shortage of older men ready to pounce and take advantage. You've got to watch your step. Be careful. It's a dangerous world out there."

"Dad, I know it. I'm just amazed that you know it."

"Well, I've been around, kept my eyes open. Just because I'm your father doesn't mean that I'm a dodo."

"Do you feel ashamed of me?"

"Not at all, Geoffrey, I swear it. We've never talked birds and bees, but the facts of life are damned simple: men want to screw. Young men, especially, and sooner or later they find their sexual outlet. The sap's really flowing, and right now, sex is the biggest thing in your life. You should be experimenting. God knows, it's much easier nowadays than when I was your age. Make the most of it. Have as many different kinds of experiences as you can. You are awfully young. Who knows? Maybe this is only a passing thing."

"Dr. Whitten said that, too."

"Did he? Well, I guess then I'm on the right wavelength."

"Dad, thanks for being so understanding about this."

"Thank you for coming here today. I can't tell you how much this means to me."

They stood up and embraced warmly. "Don't ever think I'd

be ashamed of you for something like this," King said. "A person can't help being what he is. I guess that's my only excuse with you: I couldn't help it most of the time, either, when things went sour between us. Take care. Promise me that you'll be very, very careful."

"I promise. I'm really a very cautious person, you know."

King threw back his head and laughed. "Oh, Lord, Geoffrey. I'd never have guessed *that.*"

The meeting was terrific and he felt real pride in himself and his father, but his mother surprised him when he told her the good news. Ruth turned on him, became accusatory. "Why do you find it necessary to rub your father's face in things you know he detests? What possible good will come from it? You could've gone your way and been discreet. Really, I thought you were much smarter than that. I just despair, I really do. Why can't there be a moment's peace around here?"

He was furious. "How can you say that?" he declared. "You act as if nothing has happened around here. Don't you realize how hard Dad and I tried these last few weeks to really sit down together and work things out?"

"Oh, spare me," she replied angrily. "Sometimes you're such a child."

29

His mother was right. The result of his discussion with King was that he was sent packing. The day after he had revealed his homosexuality to his father, they both came to him and backed him into a corner. They were so open, honest, and reasonable that for him to refuse was to invite blame as the unreasonable brat who exacerbated his family's miseries. He felt hurt because he really thought that he and his father finally had reached an accommodation on getting along, but he had to agree with their plan. They needed time alone to put his dad's career and their marriage back on track. They could move into smaller quarters and save considerably on the rent if he left, too. Primary was their overwhelming need to make one final effort to shape up. He could understand that. The plan: spend this school year with Nick and Marion Hopps, who had recently moved to Flagstaff, Arizona. Mountains, sunshine, and horseback riding. The Hoppses, being the world's greatest friends, were happy and willing. Think about it, they told him; no rush. And of course, he would spend holidays with his parents.

He spent the entire night packing and left the next day, surprising them with an eagerness prompted by hurt. He arrived in Arizona to find that Marion and the two kids had just arrived themselves. Nick had picked up stakes and moved them from Kansas City onto the moonscape of desolate northern Arizona.

The place was a ramshackle adobe ranch house with a nice view of the mountains and a steep arroyo that became a raging torrent during the winter rains. Nick bought two hunting dogs, a case of whiskey, two dirt bikes, a shotgun, and a hardwood rocking chair.

That first night, Geoffrey and Nick sat down together next to the blocked fireplace for a serious after-dinner talk.

"Nick, I know why I'm here. I want you to realize that up front, so there won't be any misunderstanding."

Nick reacted with a quizzical look. "Well, I think I know why you're here. It's because I have very deep feelings for that crazy father of yours. Hell, he's as close to me as my own brother—maybe closer, in fact—so when he asked me to take you for a year so he and your mother could try and straighten out their lives, what could I say? Hell, you can see yourself that it's not exactly the most convenient time . . . but you couldn't say no to them either, I guess, because here you are. Anyway, Geoff, it has got to be a goddamn good thing to get away from them for a while."

"I suppose, but that isn't what I'm talking about. I'm certain my father told you I am a homosexual, and I'm just as certain that's why he sent me here . . . in exile. As far away from my friends as he could get me."

"As a matter of fact, Geoffrey, this is news to me. He never mentioned a thing. That pisses me, not because I would have said no to him about you, but only because it's sneaky. Look, what you are is your business. I don't give a damn. I'm not about to impose my moral judgments on you, and I'm not at all interested in being a watchman. But I'll say this: you and I won't have a single rough moment as long as you play straight. You are still a minor and I'm responsible for you as long as you're under this roof. Now, if somebody gets it in his mind to come a-courtin', he is definitely gonna have a problem. Why? Because he's breakin' the law. You're under age, and that means the rock pile, which he's sure as hell gonna get if I catch him. Now, I've said it and that's all I'm ever gonna say about this particular subject. Fair enough?"

Nick kept a loaded shotgun in the hall closet, and you just didn't cross Nick, ever. Geoffrey was a virtual prisoner, cut off from self-discovery and his own kind, under house arrest in a desolate wilderness. He seethed at his parents' treachery, and on the fifth day there, when Nick was away on business and Marion and the kids were shopping in Flagstaff, he impulsively called a taxi to take him to the airport. His father had provided him with one hundred and fifty dollars in spending money, and he determined to fly back to L.A. and go underground in the gay community, in hiding from what he felt certain would be an army of King's private investigators.

But when the plane landed in L.A., a familiar figure stood at the gate glowering. "Good flight?" his father asked sarcastically. Geoffrey was too stunned to flee, and without resisting, was boarded back on the next flight to Flagstaff. This time his father sat beside him. Geoffrey's mistake had been leaving an apologetic note for Marion ("Sorry, I can't handle this situation") taped on the refrigerator. The cab ride was quickly discovered by police, who spotted him waiting for the flight to L.A. Meanwhile, King conferred by phone with Dr. Whitten to evolve a game plan.

The two flew back to Arizona in icy silence. King rented a car in Flagstaff and drove them back to the Hoppses'. Marion was thunderstruck, seeing them at her front door. "Bob," she protested, "I won't take Geoffrey back under duress. It makes no sense, Bob." They used her living room to talk things out.

"This is it," King told his son. "Nitty-gritty time. No, don't say a word. Just listen. We've had it, your mother and I, up to here with your impulsive behavior. Geoffrey, you're not making any sense. You're down to two final choices: you can stay here with Nick and Marion or come home. If you decide to return to L.A., it won't be very pleasant, I can tell you. Because you're going straight back to the psychiatric hospital, where you belong. The choice is yours. Which is it going to be?"

Geoffrey flushed with anger. "Think you can bully me? Well, think again. That's no choice, and you know it, but if you think I'm going to knuckle under . . . well, that mental ward better be ready, because they won't know what hits them if you take me back there."

Marion Hopps supported his decision. "Good for you." She smiled sadly. "They have no right doing this to you." And she said this to King's face, too. They drove back to the Flagstaff airport stiff with tension, only to discover they had missed the last L.A. flight for the day. They registered in a nearby motel, King ignoring Geoffrey's demand for a separate room. "You're not gonna be out of my sight one second," he muttered, bolting the door. They sat together at a small table poking at cold room-service steak sandwiches and watered-down vodka martinis.

"Goddammit, this is a ridiculous situation!" King sighed, looking miserable. "Why did you paint us into such a tight corner?"

"*Me?*" his son shouted. "*Me?*"

"*You,*" his father insisted. "What did you expect us to do: turn our backs? Jesus Christ, what's got into you? What do you want? I'll be damned if I can figure you out."

"Why can't you just leave me alone?"

"If you want to hate me, that's your privilege, but you're bringing all of this aggravation down on yourself. Be honest with yourself: you're out of control. For your own good, you've got to be reined in."

His son stood up so violently that he almost knocked over the table. "I'm going to bed. God, what a manipulator you are! *My own good* . . . What bullshit! You're putting me away for the same reason that Rexall put you away: I'm an embarrassment. I don't obey. Why that hospital ever released you is a mystery to me. And how that fucking psychiatrist can go along with you on this, I'll never know. Well, he'd better be ready for me . . . and you, too. I'll never give you a moment of peace again."

169

King rubbed his eyes dejectedly. "Oh, Geoffrey, stop this or we'll never make it through the night together. It's so useless and terrible. I've had enough."

"*You*'ve had enough?" Geoffrey ripped back the bedcovers. He turned out the light, leaving his father in the dark, in his chair, an empty glass in his hand.

At noon the next day King turned his son over to the keepers.

They had betrayed him. When he told his fellow patients in the third-floor mental ward what had been done to him, he sometimes received a strange look, as if he was full of schizoid delusions. But a young political activist down the hall had hung a "Free Huey Newton" poster in Geoffrey's room, scratching out the Black Panther leader's name and substituting Geoffrey King's name instead.

He would be allowed to attend his freshman year at Santa Monica High—traveling between school and hospital, because, as both Whitten and his bastard father informed him, the ward was where he was going to be living, like it or not. Think of it as a hotel, kind of. That's what they told him at first, until his rage forced them to lock him in his room and use other disciplinary devices.

But late one afternoon, all of his fury evaporated in a smile of joy. Geoffrey was driven to the Beverly Wilshire Hotel and taken to a large banquet room on the second floor, where, crowded inside, were nearly all the familiar faces of the Kings' past. His father had decided to celebrate his thirty-third wedding anniversary with a dinner dance in honor of his wife. Ruth arrived on a ruse of some sort. The doors opened and the orchestra King had hired struck up "The Girl of My Dreams," while the mob cheered. Geoffrey's smile was not quite full. It was the sight of his father—not merely seeing him again, but the shock of how he had changed in only (what was it?) three, five, six weeks since Geoffrey's second hospitalization. A detractor once described King as "two hundred pounds of bullshit piled into a two-hundred-dollar suit"—a description Goeffrey adored—but now you could make that three hundred pounds, maybe three-fifty. His father, beaming and moon-shaped, waddled into the room, his dark suit billowing even with his jacket unbuttoned. His son's jaw gaped. Later that evening, he would observe something that would wrench him—his father's shoes: King's ankles were so swollen he could lace them only halfway.

The guests raised their glasses to the couple and remained standing while King scooped his wife onto the dance floor. The band played Cole Porter's "Night and Day," her favorite song, and everyone applauded. At one point King seemed to stumble, which drew an audible gasp from those watching.

His father's appearance shocked him and he fought against a growing conviction that King's days were numbered. It would be a day of liberation and release, but also of numbing fear. King's death would signal the end of Geoffrey's childhood.

King arrived at the hospital late on the afternoon of October 10, 1967, and invited him out for a quiet dinner to celebrate their joint birthdays: he was fifty-five; Geoffrey sixteen. Ruth joined them and they ate in a small Italian restaurant.

His father picked at his food but drank a good deal. There was a silent understanding that this was to be a pleasant evening. King said he was negotiating with a publisher to write a book. "About your life?" his son asked in surprise. His father grinned. "No," he said, "about something I understand: personnel work. Talent-searching. They're very interested." Ruth looked down at her plate and said nothing; several times, King excused himself to go to the bathroom.

"His heart," she whispered. "He won't see a doctor even though it's so weak that none of his organs can function properly."

His father was drowning in his own liquid excesses; the final time that King got up from the table was not to seek a urinal but to summon a taxi for his wife. "I want to be alone with my son," he said rather mysteriously. The drive back to the hospital took only ten minutes, but King said nothing until he parked at the entrance.

"Oh, goddammit, Geoffrey," he suddenly erupted.

"What's the matter?" his startled son replied.

"*You.* You're what's the matter. You're fucking up, fella, and time is running out. You should've been out of this place by now. Listen, you little fart, it's almost midnight! Wise up before it's too late. Get out of this car and get your silly ass back upstairs and go to work. God, I raised a fool! Get out! Do you hear me? Get out and go to work! Out!"

He half-shoved his son out the door and drove off in a squeal of tires, leaving his dazed son on the hospital steps.

On the morning of November 5, he was told he had a visitor, a highly unusual event for nine o'clock on a Sunday morning. He entered the visitors' lounge and saw King looking surprisingly chipper and animated. His father grinned at his frown and raised both hands in mock surrender. "Don't lash out, please. I've already kicked myself in the ass a dozen times for the other night. I just wanted to be a cheerleader for you and, as usual, everything came out the wrong way. I want you to know I really do believe in you. I'm proud of you, too. Believe me, you'll make it and do fine in this world. I know it." He glanced at his watch. "I've got to run. Anyway, I said what I came to say. I'm really sorry if I upset you. You didn't deserve it. Come on, walk me to the elevator. Beautiful day outside. Take a pass and get yourself some sunshine."

The elevator doors opened and King stepped inside. "Goodbye, Geoffrey," he said. "Take care."

The next day a nurse told him he had another visitor. A staff member came to fetch him to the administrator's office, where, in amazement, he greeted his Uncle Raymond. Lowe had been in town several weeks, house-hunting, because he, Gram, and Aunt Nora were moving to the Coast now that Aunt Nora had the only productive career in her family. To pacify her frustrated acting ambitions, they agreed to stage a final twilight assault on the Hollywood Everest. Lowe's nephew greeted him with a smile. "Well, I'm suddenly very popular," Geoffrey said. "Dad was here yesterday." His uncle momentarily studied the tops of his glossy black loafers. "I'm not much good at beating around the bush," he said, "so I might as well tell you straight out. Your father died last night."

30

On the eve of Geoffrey's trial, Leonard Stone thought the chances of winning an insanity verdict were not better than thirty percent. Without a jury, success depended upon having the case tried by a humane judge, and he was pleased that the trial was scheduled in the courtroom of Judge Thomas Hemmings. A sound jurist. Fair. Willing to compromise. But when his client informed Stone that Judge Tom was a family friend, the lawyer marched on the judge's chambers and requested that he eliminate himself from the case

"You're within your rights, of course. Prepare a letter of request and I shall withdraw immediately," Hemmings said.

Stone was apologetic. "Your Honor," he said, "I've decided to go for an insanity plea in this case, and I just couldn't take a chance—because of your family connection, I didn't know how much you'd be willing to bend over backward."

The judge smiled. "Well, I think my friend Herman Kelso will receive this trial. He's been known to bend and twist to do the humane thing."

Stone told his colleagues in the public defender's office that the King kid was lucky to be going to trial in Torrance, an out-of-the-way locale for news-media coverage. He was also delighted about the media obsession with Charles Manson and his gang, recently captured. "A perfect climate," he remarked. "Because of Manson, the D.A. probably has lost all interest in little Geoffrey King. We're just a crumb on his plate."

Judge Hemmings spent an evening with Ray and Nora Lowe, discussing their nephew's trial. He told them that Geoffrey's chances to be found insane were now more favorable than he had imagined they could ever be. "I know his trial judge," he said. "He would not want to send an obviously sick boy to the penitentiary." Ray Lowe peppered the judge with questions, but in the end seemed wholly satisfied. He thought Judge

Tom's most significant remark was: "I've seen a lot of men sent to Atascadero, but very few leave. They don't release inmates unless they are healthy and sound."

FEBRUARY 13, 1970

Geoffrey felt minuscule entering Judge Herman Kelso's magnificent courtroom in a now-rumpled suit. The majesty of the place seized him by the lapels, forcing his submission to the law's supremacy in this vast wood-paneled amphitheater. "Most judges," his lawyer had told him, "operate on the principle that justice has to look good, even if it isn't." Judge Kelso's courtroom seemed like Mt. Sinai for somebody on trial for murder. He had been primed for this day by two visitors the day before. The first was his uncle, who stopped by to wish him well and tell him that Judge Tom, his mother's friend, knew the trial judge and thought him to be "compassionate and humanitarian." He was surprised that Judge Tom cared, figuring he was hated by all in his mother's circle. In parting, his uncle said to him: "This hasn't been easy for any of us, Geoffrey. We want to do the right thing, but there's also a duty here to make certain that you're well when you're released and no longer a threat to yourself or to others." Geoffrey told Lowe not to worry. He doubted he would be coming out, no matter where they sent him. His uncle didn't respond. The second visitor was Leonard Stone. If Geoffrey cared more, he would have requested a new lawyer, because he disliked this man intensely. Stone, however, was ebullient, telling him that Dr. Rose, the third psychiatrist, who had examined him a few days earlier, agreed completely with Farber. Geoffrey was insane at the time of the killings and needed hospitalization now. Stone didn't say that Dr. Rose offered a very pessimistic prognosis for an eventual cure.

Under California law, Geoffrey's trial was bifurcated: the murder charges were considered first, and if a guilty verdict resulted, the second trial immediately began on the issue of the defendant's sanity. His prison friends, the two mob brothers, warned him to expect a rough trial. "The D.A. will say some fucked things about you, but just stay cool and count to ten," they advised him. But his trial for double matricide wasn't that way at all. The first morning, there were only six spectators:

Skip Harte and Frank Estes sat on his side of the aisle, countering his family; also present was a reporter from the Palos Verdes community newspaper, scribbling occasional notes, who never returned after that first day. At one point, some teachers arrived with what seemed to be a junior-high civics class in tow. At first, the students seemed appropriately awed to be witnessing a murder trial, but soon grew fidgety, he noticed; and when next he looked back, they were gone. The fact was, his trial was low-keyed, and the defendant hunched in his chair doodling and disassociated from proceedings that seemed remote and strangely irrelevant.

Geoffrey's last psychiatric examination had been the best; Dr. Rose, unlike the others, had been warm, sympathetic, and intensely interested in him. They talked for two hours in the basement infirmary, and at one point the doctor surprised him by asking: "How would you sum up your life in a single sentence?"

Without hesitating (as if he had spent weeks preparing an answer), he blurted: "My desperation to be loved." Among other things, his murders were an act of desperate passion; but if he had been seated among those civics students, he would be restless and bored, too. Because this trial was not about him, but the legal ramifications of what he and LSD had done together. In both trials, the evidence under discussion was the three psychiatric reports submitted to the court, and the three authors were the only witnesses called to testify. Among them, the three doctors had spent a total of four hours questioning him, and now they took turns on the stand explaining Geoffrey King, particularly what he was capable of thinking and feeling while locked inside a delusional-hallucinogenic system. At times they were prescient, but often they spoke about a stranger. Theirs was supposedly expert testimony; and in citing credentials to the court, each claimed to have participated in approximately ten thousand sanity and drug-related cases. They were veteran experts at being trial witnesses: smooth, unruffled, self-assured, talking about Geoffrey with an intimacy belied by the shallowness of two of the three interviews. When Geoffrey listened closely, they were talking generally about the paranoias of a person under LSD and applying it specifically to Geoffrey's

175

frame of mind before and during the tragedy in Palos Verdes. It was a game, a charade, and he tuned out for long periods. Impulsively he scribbled a note to his lawyer at his side: "Let me testify and tell my side of what happened." Stone crumpled the note and put it in his pocket without even glancing at him.

His trial was a droner, with all participants going through the motions to satisfy their obligations to society against the most serious of antisocial behavior, and the defendant could not help thinking that the verdict was already known and decided upon and that in due course they would inform him as well. He felt very disappointed to be left out so entirely. The truth, even at its earnest best, could only be approximated in this case. He had killed in delusion and passion, and it was so difficult to try to convey his feelings months later. But he could come close, he was certain, if they allowed him on the stand. It mattered to him, but only somewhat. No one in the courtroom seemed gripped by his tragedy, and he doubted that his grief could move them, either.

But he enjoyed watching his uncle's face freeze when Leonard Stone twice mentioned Lowe's name that first morning. His uncle's statement in the police homicide report was eagerly quoted to the court as his lawyer asked each witness whether he had read that particular statement of Lowe's that Geoffrey King harbored no malice to his mother and grandmother. The defendant was amazed that his uncle would say such a thing in his favor. Raymond knew how bitter his nephew was, being forced to move to the Palos Verdes duplex after losing the battle to move out. But each of the psychiatrists was asked whether he agreed with Lowe's opinion on the basis of independent interviews with the defendant, and they responded affirmatively. Uncle Raymond winced.

The prosecutor, a stout, middle-aged, unexciting little man named Peter Bates, tried to make the doctors say that if Geoffrey knew what he was doing while trying to steal a helicopter from the Jet Propulsion Labs, then he must have known what he was doing when he killed his mother and grandmother a day later. But the doctors weren't buying: the defendant, they insisted, was in the throes of a drug-induced psychosis that was out of control. In the instance of the helicopter, he was trying to escape from danger of a sexual advance—his only focus of concern. As for the murders, he was defending himself or lashing out against an ominous threat, part of the delusion gripping him. The prosecutor and the witnesses became increasingly annoyed with one another, until Judge Kelso finally glanced at his watch and instead of declaring a lunch break, ordered a two-day recess because of other court business.

Everyone, Geoffrey noticed, rushed in relief for the doors.

31

NOVEMBER 1967

"Fix me a drink, will you dear?" Ruth asked her son, nodding toward a wall cabinet. She was already dressed for the day in an off-white silk dress and matching jacket with a single strand of pearls. She was calm, almost regally composed, and except for a smudge of darkness under her eyes hinting at fatigue from a long, sleepless night, there was no indication that only a few hours before, his mother had become a widow. During the night, King had driven off for a last ride up the coast. Police found his body slumped over the wheel. He had pulled off the road less than a mile from Camarillo State Hospital—the apparent victim of a coronary. Geoffrey handed her a bourbon on the rocks and made himself a gin and tonic. Ruth patted the cushion next to her in invitation and they sat together.

"Did he kill himself?"

"Of course," his mother said. "I finally got him to go to the doctor. His heart and liver were grossly enlarged and they wanted to put him in a hospital immediately. But he wouldn't hear of it. And that's that."

"I've got to tell you: I'm glad he's dead. I can breathe again."

"I'm sure," his mother agreed. "I called Dr. Whitten early this morning, and that's exactly what he said, too. He said, 'I'm sorry about Bob, but the news couldn't be better for your son. His only problem was his father. Now he can grow up in peace.'"

"Oh, Mother, I'm not so sure. I don't know what to think. I'm so confused about everything."

"Well, give it some time. I need you now, Geoffrey. I presume you're willing to come home immediately."

"I never wanted to be in there in the first place, so what do you think?" he replied with a scowl. "Mother, tell me honestly, why didn't you ever stick up for me? How could you go along with the things that man did to me?"

It was Ruth's turn to scowl. "Please, Geoffrey, don't ask me to account for my mistakes. I wouldn't know where to begin adding them up. Let's bury the past with him. God knows, we have enough problems right now."

"He came out to see me yesterday. He only stayed a few minutes; but dammit, if he knew he was dying, why couldn't he sit down with me and open up? Take me off the hook here."

"What would you have wanted him to say?" she asked.

"I don't know," he admitted with a sigh.

"Well, he probably didn't know either," his mother said. "I just went over all of his insurance policies, which total two hundred thousand dollars. Not bad, eh? The trouble is, he allowed most of them to lapse. I guess he just didn't have the money to pay the premiums. It's all very complicated, but Nick thinks that we may be able to salvage something."

Geoffrey snickered. "What a legacy! From start to finish."

"I've already burned our love letters. What happened between your father and me is our business. Believe me, there are dozens and dozens of chapters and verses in our story. But what difference does it make? The ending tells it all. Let's just put him to rest."

More than a dozen of Ruth's friends stayed well after midnight. Geoffrey drifted upstairs to his father's office, where Lowe and several King cronies were getting drunk and staging a rowdy replica of an Irish wake for the German Lutheran deceased. Nick knew the best stories, of course, and told how in Kansas City King had once negotiated a labor contract with such arrogance that the union rep became livid and threatened to kill him, then, repenting his impulsive outburst, had King followed by an armed posse of labor goons to make certain nobody else tried to assassinate him with the rep's threat on record. Or the time an employee requested permission from King to go home early to screw his wife. The guy was worried about impotence and had a sudden urge. King said, sure. The next day, the guy's wife sent King a chocolate cake. Lowe mentioned a cocktail party for a few old friends that King staged shortly after he and Ruth moved into this house. A stranger attended and the guy was hilarious, kept everyone in stitches, and when Lowe mentioned this to his brother-in-law, King grumbled, "Well, he should be funny. The bastard charged enough." Imagine, hiring a pro comic for a small cocktail party. But that was King. Broke and all, he left nothing to chance to make an impression. And that anniversary party . . . Geoffrey stood up unsteadily and put down his empty glass. "I could tell you a few stories about my father, too, but I doubt they'd make you laugh."

He staggered downstairs, but found he had to leave that house or burst, so he took the keys from a shelf and drove off in King's Falcon with its dented front bumper the only indication of what had happened in this car less than twenty-four hours before. He drove up to his father's favorite street in Brentwood, a street called La Mesa, lined with old eucalyptus trees and lovely homes. And he drove right into a police roadblock set up against neighbor complaints about hotrodding teenagers. He was drunk. He didn't own a license. The cops shone lights in his face and made him lean across the Falcon hood while they frisked him.

Geoffrey King got down on his knees to beg them not to arrest him. He told them what had happened in this car the night before and pleaded with them to have mercy on his grieving mother. They hesitated, not quite believing him, when suddenly a spark of an idea galvanized him. "Two policemen were sent to my house last night to tell my mother what happened. Radio in. Your logs will show it."

They did. They let him go. But with a warning.

32

On court days, prisoners at county jail boarded the prison bus at five-thirty in the morning. The bus made the rounds of two other downtown correctional facilities, loading on other court-bound prisoners, and depositing them all in the large holding cell in the courthouse basement by seven-forty-five. Geoffrey's trial was scheduled to resume at one in the afternoon, and by eleven that morning he and one other prisoner sat together in the furthest corner of the crowded, noisy holding cell, trying to become inconspicuous. By the vagaries of the court calendar, they were the only Caucasians present. Nervously Geoffrey took out a pack of cigarettes and offered a smoke to his companion, a thin, shy boy awaiting trial on armed robbery. The sight of a fresh pack of Marlboros drew a crowd.

"Hey, brother, give me a smoke," a thin, goateed inmate said. Other hands reached out, too, and in a moment the pack was empty. A group of eight closed in on him; Geoffrey's companion moved out of the way and disappeared while an Afroed inmate with a mean scar across the bridge of his nose leaned his body suggestively against the seated young prisoner and grinned.

"Say, baby, we got some time here before the man send for us." The prisoner unzipped his fly while his companions snickered.

The physical pain of his rape drove him to cry out, but it was so noisy and crowded in the large cell that those up front were unaware of what was happening at the back, in the center of a circle of eight men, purposely blocking the view from the guard's observation window. Geoffrey's nose was pressed against the concrete floor, his suit trousers around his ankles. They positioned his naked, upraised ass and took turns. If he moved or tried to obstruct them, he received a jabbing kick in the ribs, not damaging, but a reminder of what could be done if he resisted. Not much was said. The men encircling him smoked his cigarettes and flicked ashes on his back, and ragged at the one working him over. He cried out in hatred as in pain, hearing their comments about the pretty honky in his wool suit trying to impress the judge. They knew no matter what he had done, he wouldn't be going away as long as they would.

"What you do, boy, suck dick in a bus depot?" they jived down at him.

If they had known his crime, they might have killed him, aware that if any one of them had done such a thing to their own mothers and grandmothers, they would be en route to the gas chamber, while this pretty honky probably would be back on the street in a few years. Seven of them made him pay the price for the difference between them, before the audible rattle of a guard's keys unlocking the pen called a halt. They stood him up, buckled his pants, and leaned him against the bars. The guard called out his name, but he couldn't move. He was violently ill en route to the courtroom. Afraid to tell the guard what had happened because the rapists would surely kill him for squealing, once seated at the defense table, he told Leonard Stone, who blinked incredulously. "Christ, I'm sorry, Geoffrey," his lawyer said. "I'll speak to the judge about this at recess and we'll keep you out of that damned holding pen from now on."

His client, more dead than alive, slumped in his chair, and was only dimly aware of returning to the Queen Tank later that evening, where the news of his rape was already widely known. A note was waiting for him from the two mob brothers up the hall. "We'll take care of those guys," they promised.

When he next appeared at court a few days later, he was kept waiting in a private office with a sheriff's deputy as his personal bodyguard. He was relieved to be back in court, away, if only for a few hours, from the proximity of black inmates.

FEBRUARY 19, 1970

Reentering the courtroom three days later, Geoffrey suddenly realized that because of the rape, he had sat like a wilted vegetable, barely registering awareness of a momentous event in his trial. He remembered his lawyer shaking his shoulder with a broad grin. Dr. Bode, the psychiatrist who thought he had harbored malice, had been under cross-examination, and Stone won a vital concession when Bode admitted he meant a generalized malice as part of a drug-induced paranoia, rather than a specific malice directed toward Mrs. King. Bode was the final witness in the murder portion of the trial, and the three psychiatrists were now in agreement that the defendant had not harbored malice. Geoffrey had sat, oblivious of this promising development; nor was he aware of both lawyers summing up their cases, with Stone declaring that his client, operating under delusional malice, was guilty of voluntary manslaughter; while Prosecutor Bates, barely concealing frustration, insisted that the defendant's impairment of judgment warranted, at best, a reduction of the charge from first- to second-degree murder. But Judge Kelso disagreed.

"It is the court's finding that the necessary element of malice is not present in this case," he said. "Without going into detail, the court does find the defendant guilty of two counts of voluntary manslaughter."

At that point, Stone shook his client to life. "You just beat a murder rap," the lawyer said, and Geoffrey vaguely recalled glancing at his family. His uncle looked dour; Aunt Nora flashed him a quick smile.

Now back in the courtroom, where the sanity portion of the case was being tried, Geoffrey savored this almost forgotten event. He felt that society had vindicated him from any criminal intent, and he was glad for that much. Dr. Bode was recalled to the stand to testify on the sanity issue, and the defendant leaned forward with attentiveness. Bates badgered the psychiatrist about whether or not Geoffrey was aware of causing Ruth pain as he stabbed her, and the chunky psychiatrist glowered. "Counsel," he responded, "it's very difficult for someone in a psychotic condition to distinguish individual specifics of his or her behavior. And for me to then decide on the basis of an examination that occurs months later what his condition was at the exact moment, when he can't tell me about it because of his own confusion, creates enormous difficulties. Really, it is impossible. We just don't have the tools for that."

"In other words, Doctor, you are saying that it is impossible for you to form an opinion as to his state of mind at the time of the acts?"

Dr. Bode flushed. "No, I didn't say that at all. I said that it is not possible to know whether he was aware of causing his mother pain at the moment he stabbed her."

With Dr. Rose, Bates fared no better, asking the psychiatrist whether or not Geoffrey could have killed in the absence of LSD.

"In my opinion," Dr. Rose replied, "without the drug, this series of events probably would not have occurred. I think the lysergic acid aggravated a preexisting condition and led to the psychotic episode and a delusional system under which he was operating at the time of the killings."

The defendant nodded emphatic agreement.

By the end of a long day of testimony, the three psychiatrists concurred that Geoffrey King was legally insane when he killed. Both sides rested their cases. Bates summed up the prosecution's case by emphasizing the legal point that voluntary intoxication by a dangerous drug negated an insanity plea and was insufficient cause to absolve the defendant of his criminal act. Stone insisted that truth outweighed legalism and that the overwhelming truth in this case was that his client did not possess sanity when he killed his mother and grandmother, whether his drug intake was voluntary or not.

"This case," he declared, "turned all of our stomachs. It is the worst kind of crime, but also the most tragic I can recall." He urged the court to rule for insanity and send his client to Atascadero "until such time as he is able to meet society on equal terms, whether that be in a week, a month, or for the remainder of his life. There he would remain until three or more doctors conclude he would not do harm to himself or endanger others. Even then, he must be brought back for this court to pass final judgment. I hope that Your Honor has an opportunity in the future to be sitting and pass judgment on this young man, whether or not he is fit to live again in society."

Judge Kelso sighed and wearily shook his head. "We have before us a tragedy," he said. "Words cannot describe it. This court is convinced beyond any question that the defendant was criminally insane at the time of the incident and legally insane. If you study the psychiatric reports all the way through, these doctors were not describing the symptoms of diminished capacity. At the heart of the matter is this young man. He is, beyond reasonable doubt, legally insane. This court is further satisfied that he hasn't fully recovered his sanity.

"The defendant will be found not guilty by reason of insanity. He will be remanded to the custody of the sheriff, by him to be delivered to the Department of Mental Hygiene for commitment to a state hospital."

As Ruth King was so fond of saying, that was that.

Leonard Stone shook hands with his client. "Well, I wish you the best of luck," he said. "If you're smart, you'll do exactly what you are told up there and won't rock the boat. Maybe you will get out in five to seven, I just can't say. I'd suggest, however, that you never become a defendant again." Geoffrey asked his lawyer if the prosecutor might be tempted to appeal. "No way," Stone said. "If a higher court upheld Kelso, it would become state law, and any drug-zonked killer could plead insanity."

A guard stood between Geoffrey and Skip Harte, who tried to embrace him, "We'll visit you up there," Frank Estes said. As he was led away, he searched to see his family, but they had already left the now-empty courtroom.

33

An insanity verdict was as rare as a friendly guard, and when he returned to the Tank with the news, the girls gave him a standing ovation. "Oh, Gerrie, you're gonna love it there," they told him. "You'll meet some gorgeous Don Juan and everything will be peaches and cream." The mob brothers, Frank and Larry, somehow bypassed the strictest jail regulations and appeared in the Tank personally to congratulate him. They were disappointed to be going to prison without him, but predicted he would be out in three to five years.

"I'm figuring on seven," Geoffrey replied.

Only Costello, a thick-chested old trusty with a bad heart, who was confined in the Queen Tank for his own protection against the rougher elements on the lower floors, seemed to demur. Costello was expert on prison life and told him that Atascadero was a very dangerous place and definitely not a playground. "You've got to be very careful there, son," the old man said. "Walk on eggs and do what they tell you, or you'll never get out. And you can forget about sex. They watch you twenty-four hours a day." Costello was responsible for finding out his departure date, always kept secret from inmates to avoid suicide or escape attempts. The night before he left, a drag queen named Selma gave him a razor haircut, and a delegation led by Lisa presented him with a gift of spray deodorant and Old Spice shower soap wrapped in a blue ribbon. "Something borrowed, something blue." They grinned. And late that night, a kite was handed to him from the mob brothers containing two fifty-dollar bills. "Cigarette money. Happy landing," their note read.

On his last night in the old county jail, he wrote notes to his uncle, Skip Harte, and Frank Estes. "I'm glad to be going to a place where I can get help," he wrote. "I'm going to work hard to become well. I now have some hope." The guards fetched him at six in the morning.

"'Bye, Gerrie, have a good time," the girls called to him. "Please write. See you soon." He was very touched; and as he was escorted down the long prison corridor and passed the cell of Frank and Larry, the two brothers linked arms and saluted him. He burst into tears.

The prison bus held twenty inmates, half of them Atascadero-bound. Nobody said much, and a few prisoners broke out into tears during the four-hour ride. The institution was located halfway between Los Angeles and San Francisco, a few miles above San Luis Obispo. The bus took the faster, inland route rather than following the scenic coastline on U.S. 1; but twice on the trip, the shimmering Pacific flashed into view, moving Geoffrey to sadness, knowing it would be a long time before he saw the ocean again. With each mile, the enormity of being shipped to Atascadero grew in his mind. In later years, long after emotions faded, most of those persons intimately connected with his trial and sentencing—including the prosecutor, Bates—would admit that justice was served in this case. Geoffrey felt this was so at the time. Being sent to prison for murder would've indicated a criminal intent that he could

185

never admit to. The court psychiatrists had declared him free of malice, so it was only logical for the court to conclude that he was insane, and he did not doubt that he truly was.

But he could only guess at the malice buried deep inside himself. To know demanded the kind of courageous introspection that he did not yet possess. His malices were stored, chapter by chapter, in the brief but painful story of his life. He had been sentenced in ignorance by those who didn't know him at all, and if justice was served, it was purely by chance. His life stated different truths than those implied in Judge Kelso's courtroom.

It was the season of winter rain, and the air was thick with humidity. They took a back road into Atascadero, bouncing on macadam badly in need of repair. An electronic gate swung open and they drove through the back entrance into an enormous L-shaped compound. The bus braked in front of a delivery ramp where a few orderlies in white hospital uniforms stood waiting. Somewhere, probably only a few hundred yards away, was the front door to this grim place, and Geoffrey sensed that many years would pass before he strolled out that front door.

The bus door opened. Atascadero welcomed him.

II

I said, "Yet it must be hard for you with no eyes you can't even see what youre walking in to." He said, "No 1 can. Onlyes diffrents is them with eyes they *think* they can."

—Russell Hoban,
Riddley Walker

34

In 1967, the summer Geoffrey King was forced by his father to either stay with Nick Hopps in Arizona or return to a psychiatric ward, another teenager several hundred miles away stood uncertainly biting his lip at the entrance to California's most notorious mental institution, wondering whether to voluntarily commit himself. He was stocky and thick-necked, wearing jeans, cowboy boots, and a freshly laundered white T-shirt. He stood outside Atascadero, smoking and squinting behind aviator-style sunglasses as he pondered what to do. At issue that hot Saturday morning was his hair. He was nineteen, and his long hair meant a lot to him. Should he get a haircut? If he hadn't been hung-over, he would have decided before driving the thirty miles here. It made absolutely no sense walking in the place without a neat, regimental trim. But a haircut was a major bummer, a sacrifice for a job he might not even get. But with a baby on the way, he needed more money. He was earning eighty dollars a week assembling five-shelf office files—hard, back-breaking work, and no group hospitalization, either. He sighed. And finally he tossed his cigarette and drove off with a squeal in his six-year-old pickup, not quite knowing what he would do.

Ken Sprinkles drove no farther than to a tavern down the road. This was forlorn, remote hill country: only 100,000 people in the entire county. Most of them ranched cattle on sun-baked ranges. The town of Atascadero looked pitiful, but because of relatives and friends visiting inmates at the state hospital, the tiny hamlet boasted six motels. He entered the town's only tavern, ordered a beer; and when the owner learned why Ken was his first customer of the day, he tried to dissuade him.

"Oh, it's the goddamnedest zoo there is," he said, flushing with an angry grudge. "They pay good money, but they're always hiring—now, that tells you something, doesn't it? When that place opened in fifty-four, everyone in town got in line, but most of them quit in a day or two. You're in fear of your life every second on the inside, and plenty of people get hurt. Those nuts come back, too, after they let them out. Looking for revenge. The sheriff is always picking up former patients who come wandering back. Everyone working up there keeps un-listed phones; their families are scared shitless if a stranger knocks. Hell, they call it a hospital for the criminally insane, but they sure don't cure no one as far as I can tell. Awful place! Filled with murderers and sex maniacs. Don't know what they're thinking of, letting women work there. Some of those gals are mighty weird themselves. They turn on to madmen, and the next thing you know, one of them sneaks a gun inside to help her lover escape. Happened a couple of times already, but you don't read it in the papers. Anyway, you look like a smart young fella: what do you want to get involved in that mess for? Stay away! Take my advice."

Sprinkles listened through a couple of beers before finally flashing a smile. "Tell me," he asked, "is there a barbershop in town?"

He had been working since he was nine, and on his own by the time he was twelve, and now felt bored before his twentieth birthday, as if his life had been so clearly decided for him that he could accurately predict every moment for the next two decades. Nothing terrifically exciting awaited a high-school graduate with no particular skills trying to support wife and child. He was already drinking too much. Maybe working with criminally insane prisoners would be a needlepoint shower to invigorate his soul. He needed to shake awake his toughness and street-wise smarts, somehow atrophied since he became penned up and domesticated.

At the job interview, he made a good impression with his close-cropped Prussian haircut (he told the barber he might as well go all the way), and the interviewer asked him finally if he would like to take a look inside. He followed him out of the administrative wing into a sally-port complex manned by armed guards behind bullet-proof glass who operated a series of electronically controlled doors that opened and closed like air locks. At the last door, his hand received an ultraviolet stamp—a passport outside when the final door closed behind him.

Ken Sprinkles stood at the center of a dimly lit L-shaped hallway that in each direction stretched to infinity. Dun-colored concrete walls rose twenty feet to the ceiling. The hallways teemed with crazy men, many of them babbling and grotesque.

"God almighty," Sprinkles gasped.

"You'll get used to it," he was assured.

They gave him a white orderly's uniform and the prestigious title of "psychiatric technician," but he was a long way from being that. He was assigned to the security department, because on the inside, there were no guards or guns, just tough young muscle in white uniforms keeping law and order. They called themselves "The Flying Goons," racing like human squad cars down the hallways (each one-quarter mile long, they discovered), responding to the shrill alarm bell signaling a situation out of control. When that bell rang, everyone dropped what he was doing and ran to the scene. A phone left off the hook for more than ten seconds triggered a silent alarm, and all twenty-eight wards were bugged with listening devices fed into security operations. He spent much of his time sprinting . . . wrestling . . . dragging raving, incoherent men into lockup. If he had told his wife all that happened during one typical eight-hour shift, she would have miscarried. Often he undressed in the dark to hide his bruises, learning the hard way that psychiatric technicians walk in pairs for their own protection. In the wards and in hallways, there were assaultive patients who hit him for no reason. Older employees claimed to know the individual walks of most of the thirteen hundred inmates and could tell by the sound who was behind them. "It's your business to know . . . your own safety," they said. His first night on the job—hell, his first ten minutes—he was knocked down by a patient after greeting him with a friendly smile. "What are you looking at?" the patient snarled, and slugged him. Never make eye contact with assaultives, he was told. How do you know who's an assaultive? You'll learn by experience and instinct, he was told.

Dozens of times those first months, he thought about chucking the wild, often repulsive job, but his adrenaline surge was addictive. The inmates outnumbered the orderlies thirty to one, and everyone who worked inside the locked doors was scared to be there and developed a them-or-us mentality in which stress and fear overwhelmed compassion. For Sprinkles, the security detail was too fraught with peril to allow for much reflection. "Working here," they told each other, "is better than getting poked in the eye with a stick, but not much."

He knew nothing about mental disease, its cause, treatment, or cure, yet he witnessed treatments administered to patients that staggered his sensibilities and innate sense of fairness— horrors that no decent nineteen-year-old could imagine ever being authorized in the United States of America. Aversion therapy, for instance. Child molesters and rapists were strapped into a reclining chair, a metal ring placed around the penis, and electrodes attached to the testicles. Then they were shown sick pornographic films of rapes, of child-adult sex; when the ring indicated on meters that they were becoming sexually excited, their balls were shocked—shrieks of pain driving a wedge between their perverse pleasures. And God knew how many patients Ken forcefully brought to the brain-fry room, where electroshock-therapy treatments were administered by a rumpled old psychiatrist that everyone on the staff knew was daft. Ken was told that shock was a useful treatment for manic-depressives, destroying memory cells that stored sorrows and guilt. But most of the patients he carted inside, howling protests, were bad-asses causing the staff grief. "You asked for this, you son of a bitch," he heard senior staffers tell their victims. And when the juice was turned on, it was like watching an execution in the electric chair.

But even that was better than drawing duty in the injection room. Sprinkles had to steel himself not to run out the door. They injected patients with Anectine, a muscle relaxant, but administered in large doses, producing the horrifying sensation of a creeping, paralytic death, so that the patient struggled to draw breath, gasping with bugged eyes, experiencing all of the terror of drowning. Anectine was punishment for uncooperative and chronically assaultive patients. At the height of the patient's struggle against asphyxiation, the senior technician present recited a litany of complaints against the paralyzed victim and then told him how he could avoid such punishment in the future by cooperating and being pleasant. One hundred patients were punished this way, and Anectine became a maximum deterrent as frightening tales of its use swept the hallways. "How would you like to visit the injection room?" was a standard threat against unruly patients.

There were times when Ken ached to pound his fist into a patient's face. One of them almost bit off the nose of a fellow patient. They carried this raging beast to the disciplinary cells in Ward 14, hurled him onto a concrete floor, then beat him unconscious, stripped him, placed him in leather restraints, and locked him in a circus cage with a bed and chair bolted to the floor and a hole for elimination. Ken was becoming desensitized; the fact that this man was a desperately ill mental patient was obscured by Ken's revulsion at his attack and by the knowledge that he was a child rapist—a circumstance Ken would later shamefully acknowledge.

One night, his wife showed him an article about Atascadero. A Washington journalist named Nicholas Von Hoffman broke the story about the Anectine punishment, and Janice asked him if it was true. Ken scowled and denied it.

"Well, you haven't seen anyone die from it, have you?" his supervisor said. "This place is just a warehouse for human shit, and we've got to maintain discipline somehow." Sprinkles did not entirely disagree, but after a year in security, he transferred into the regular nursing service to become a real psychiatric technician.

Life was so regimented in the overcrowded wards, and the patients kept on such a short tether, that Sprinkles yawned incessantly with his mouth closed and struggled to stay alert as an overseer-housekeeper. The ward charge did not care what he or four other psych techs did during their eight-hour shift, as long as everything functioned smoothly: that patients received their medication dosages and were checked to be certain they swallowed it, ate without incident in the mess hall, and that all knives and forks were carefully accounted for before the ward was marched back for cleanup. Razor blades had to be counted in the razor room, floors swept, and so forth. Able patients were signed out to work in the machine shop or laundry. Except for group-therapy sessions in the dayroom and the notorious aversion therapies, there was no treatment program worthy of the name, therefore no accurate way to judge a patient's progress. Every patient had been sentenced by the courts to an indeterminate stay—for as long as it might take to become rational and no longer dangerous—and most of them were further stigmatized by automatically being diagnosed as schizophrenics, simply because any less-serious classification might enable them to get out within ninety days on a writ of habeas corpus. The majority of patients comprised the uneducated poor so typical of the prison population—a mix of criminals too mentally incompetent to stand trial for their crimes, and deranged sex offenders and violent murderers. To get out demanded not only hospital approval but also the concurrence of the offender's original sentencing court, and the open secret at Atascadero was that because of the heinousness of their crimes, many of these patients were being warehoused, possibly for the remainder of their lives—particularly those who had sexually molested children. Yet Ken didn't have to be Sigmund Freud to observe that the majority of these offenders were at least deceptively normal: shy, with low self-esteem, frightened of women, woefully insecure about sex, probably most in need of a satisfactory session with a professional prostitute to gain confidence in themselves. Much the same could be said about rapists.

Gradually Sprinkles began to interact with these patients instead of just observing them, struck by an awareness of the prejudicial surroundings that accentuated an air of mental illness simply by being locked into a ward at Atascadero. Patients *looked* crazy being confined seventy or more in a space designed for thirty or forty. Some were very disturbed, but not one of them was deranged continually. In fact, most of the time these men functioned rationally and acted up only under the stress of regimented confinement. There were patients, of course, who were dangerous human beings, incurably hostile and unrepentantly violent. But there were others like George, who was serving a minimum of five years for committing incest with a teenage daughter, a humorous and gentle man who was as normal as Ken's own next-door neighbor. One day Ken sat down with George and asked him point-blank why he had done such a terrible thing to his daughter and received an unsettling reply. George was from rural backwoods stock where such incidents were indigenous. He had done to his own daughter what he had witnessed his father doing to his sisters as a child. George wasn't the brightest man in the world, but he wasn't a sex pervert, either, and in this case the idea of his being forced to endure the hell of Atascadero for years seemed to Ken more criminal than the crime.

Atascadero overwhelmed the human spirit, but once these patients were no longer faceless, it was possible to separate them from their crimes and care about them as human beings. Ken was a good listener. He was tough and cocky, but most patients in the ward thought him to be fair and unusually concerned, in comparison to the other ward techs, who operated like stern jailers. At age twenty, Sprinkles began to feel as if he had a hold on a meaningful career. Atascadero was a hellhole, the worst imaginable place to try to get well in, but a young person like himself could really make a difference to men written off by everyone. Just by caring . . . listening . . . he could feel as fulfilled as a parish priest. What an opportunity for a twenty-year-old high-school grad! If he couldn't heal, he could sure as hell soothe and become the best practitioner of his trade. He enrolled in a night course in elementary psychology.

35

The doctor was elderly, with rumpled gray hair. He studied the new patient's file for several silent minutes. Then he closed the file and rubbed his eyes. "This is a hospital, not a prison," he said. "We want you to trust us and tell us about whatever is bothering you." The young patient being admitted nodded. "Oh, absolutely, Doctor," he said. "I have nothing to hide and I want to get well." The doctor asked him if his heart was causing him any trouble. "Well, sometimes I have chest pains and trouble breathing." Well, he was told, if your heart gives you any more trouble, be sure to let us know.

"You're a homosexual, aren't you?"

"Yes," Geoffrey King admitted.

"We don't care . . . but we do not allow homosexual activities to occur in this hospital. Is that clear?"

"Yes."

"I hope it really is, because you will be severely punished for it. Okay, that will be all for now."

He was passed along to the admitting psychiatrist, spent nearly two hours with him being questioned closely on his use of drugs and his sexual history. He admitted taking marijuana, LSD, Dexedrine, Dexamyl, Nembutal, Tuinal, Methedrine, and Eskatrol. The psychiatrist's written report concluded: "Insight is satisfactory. Judgment is not significantly impaired. There is no indication of delusions or ideas of reference or paranoid ideations or projective thinking or other abnormal mental mechanisms at this time. The patient claims he has strong guilt feelings about his crime and is quite remorseful over incident of killings, but actually he does not show any outward remorse or guilt. Patient undoubtedly suffered from psychosis due to LSD in past. His personality is schizoid in type."

The diagnosis: Schizophrenia, paranoid type, chronic. Drug dependence, hallucinogens (LSD) severe. Drug dependence, marijuana, severe.

In later years Geoffrey would dream about Atascadero in much the way that combat veterans moaned and thrashed revisiting battlefields in their sleep. It was a place stark and hopeless as no other. A steel door clanged shut behind him, separating him indefinitely from the known world. Overwhelmed, he stood transfixed in the identical spot where Ken Sprinkles had stood three years earlier and gaped at the enormous L-shaped hallways brimming with khaki-clad lunatics. He felt like a visitor. The psychiatric technician escorting him to the admitting ward saw him hesitate and tried to reassure him. "Do what you're told and you'll be okay," he said. Geoffrey

King nodded and lowered his eyes to avoid the passing stares of his fellow patients, his comrades in incarceration. "Holy shit," he whispered.

That first night, he was locked in his room next to the nursing station for close observation of suspected suicidal ideation. He sat up in bed staring at a slim shaving of moon through the thick shatterproof glass and began to sweat and shake uncontrollably ("the Atascadero twitch," patients called it) at the enormity of his confinement. Atascadero was the end of the line—the locked and guarded cage for those who made society's skin crawl—a place so forbidding that even the ghosts haunting his life refused to follow him inside. He tried to think of his dead family, his victims, but it was impossible. His remorse and guilt were overwhelmed by the oppressiveness of his surroundings, and dread compressed into one obsessive need: survive, somehow. That was all. No room for any other thought or emotion.

The admitting ward was like nothing he had ever seen in the relatively tranquil confines of Dr. Whitten's third-floor wing in the psychiatric hospital. Here, crowded together, were men with violent pasts, who exhibited hostile, often unfathomable behavior, the majority judged incompetent to stand trial for their crimes. The true schizophrenics among them, remote personalities with flat, dead voices, sought the furthest corners to put space between themselves and overcrowding. There was no privacy and no escape, and Geoffrey was afraid of accidentally bumping into a homicidal maniac who might react by lashing out violently. He moved among them as cautiously as if they were wired with high explosives. In self-defense, he withdrew into his nelliest Queen Tank posturings, although the other patients complained about being locked in with a flaming faggot and accused him of making advances if he glanced their way. Because he was gay, the orderlies watched him intently and made no attempt to hide their disgust. They called him "Queen" instead of "King," and made a point to escort him to the shower room after all the others were finished. What began as self-defense at first became defiance in the end, and a stubborn refusal to abandon his persona in the face of repressive regimentation. Yet, in the days that followed, he realized that surviving in the ward would not be easy. He was jumped by a patient and wrestled to the ground, offering no resistance in the hope that the ward techs would quickly intervene. (They did.) Another patient was attacked in the mess hall, his hand impaled on the table with a fork. Wardmates argued angrily with phantoms . . . while other patients wore crash helmets because they used their heads as battering rams against the doors and walls. Some men were forced to take so much Thorazine that they could barely move or speak, their peculiar shuffling footsteps echoing off the concrete hallways in what everyone called "the Thorazine shuffle." In comparison, Geoffrey felt he suffered a sniffle in the midst of terminal-cancer patients; yet the ward radiated too much psychosis not to feel touched with contagion—madness by association.

Everyone participated in group therapy and took turns describing their crimes. He was appalled hearing the details of crimes committed by child molesters and rapists. But it was *his* crime that seemed to shock everyone else the most.

"Christ, King, how could you kill your own granny?" a rapist remarked. "Your mother—well, okay—but your granny, man!"

From then on, he sat silently at group therapy, ignored as a kind of pariah by the others, and had to listen to grown men describe how they forced eight-year-olds to commit fellatio.

"When may I see a psychiatrist?" he asked the ward charge that first week, and was told that psychiatrists were not available to patients on an individual-treatment basis.

"Well, then, what treatment can I expect to receive?" he asked, and was told that group therapy was it.

"But that's geared to sex offenders," he protested. "Sex isn't my problem."

Group therapy was for everybody and all problems, the ward charge insisted, and at the end of Geoffrey's first month he wrote a progress report: "Patient has made a fairly adequate adjustment. He shows no overt signs of psychotic behavior at present and carries out his responsibilities maturely. But he feels quite lonely and seems to have especially strong needs for affection. He whines and complains for attention and has been observed of late striking up conversations with other patients. There is some concern that he is trying to instigate homosexual contacts. The patient will be moved into the dayroom for closer supervision."

*   *   *

Head down, Geoffrey sashayed through the hallways like a drag queen on parade. Although dressed in prison khaki and wearing the issued brown saddle shoes made and distributed in the California penal system, he tried to think of himself as a state employee on his way to work. And why not? He had been given a responsible job in the psychological-testing department run by a staff psychologist named Doris Leek, a perfectionist who by sheer will and terrible temper managed to make do with a staff of a few exceptionally bright functional patients and several state employees who impatiently awaited retirement. She selected Geoffrey because he scored 150 on his IQ test and particularly high in abstract reasoning, which meant he could quickly size up a situation and know what to do about it.

"It also means you're a good con artist and manipulator," she told him sternly, adding, "but not around me, sweetheart." Every patient, except for the wildly violent or delusional, was subjected to batteries of Doris Leek's tests, and her assistants at first assigned Geoffrey to administer them, which meant explaining the procedures, timing them, and making certain that patients did not attempt to copy answers from one another. One day Doris Leek entered the testing room and saw the patient-instructor explaining a test in a lisping soprano register, hand on hip. "Now, I want you to draw a picture, please, of a man and a woman . . ." The psychologist rushed from the class and tore into her assistant: "I don't want that faggot there, goddammit. Who could concentrate on a test with *that* giving instructions?" So Geoffrey was taught test scoring, particularly the complexities of the Minnesota Multi-Phasic Personality Inventory, a 550-question three-and-a-half-hour ordeal comprising the most comprehensive test of its kind. Scoring demanded intense concentration and skill, and within a month he had sufficiently impressed Doris Leek to be put in charge of the seven patients working in her department. He was one of the best and brightest workers she ever had and he convinced her to allow him to reorganize the messy testing labs, painting and polishing and reordering the files during a long holiday weekend, so that on Monday morning Doris assembled her entire staff to be briefed by patient King on the new procedures.

"Gawd," she muttered, "the queen on her throne."

The work was his life, his total obsession, and escape route to rationality in the midst of terrible chaos in the wards; and there were times when he almost forgot why he was an inmate at Atascadero. He would never be less than overwhelmed in this place, but by keeping busy, he could make peace with his predicament and save what remained of his sanity. Preoccupied by scoring and procedures in the lab, he would pass whole days without a conscious thought about his crime or his victims. Whatever ailed him was beyond Atascadero's skills to remedy, so he escaped into work, hoping that as the years passed his anguish would fade of itself, ignored in a highly structured daily regimen of work. At least he was functional. At night, in bed, he evolved grand designs for efficient seating arrangements in the test-scoring room, so that patient-test scorers could pass on their work to the person ahead, who would check on it and then add his scoring, and so forth, until the completed test arrived in Geoffrey's In box for his overall review. In his mind's eye he also evolved elaborate plans for a new filing system that would reduce by half the time now spent hunting for records. Occasionally, though, in the midst of a busy, stressful day, he would experience unpleasant reminders that his impersonation of a dedicated office worker was not wholly convincing. Under pressure, his hands began to shake and his temper exploded at the patients working under him.

Lying in the dark, usually sleeplessly, he strove to resist (rather effortlessly, at times) the kinds of recollections that would produce a night of anguish. Fantasies projected him into a baronial world closely approximating Skip Harte's, and he saw himself as a younger version of Picasso, who could deftly bolster sagging cash reserves with a few hours of feverish activity in his studio, and then turn over wet canvases to his eager agent-manager, Frank Estes. He boasted estates on the Continent and in Beverly Hills, entertained like a sultan, and rivaled Dali as a media celebrity. His mother lived with him in her own wing of the estate (he seldom allowed himself to actually visit with her), while his father appeared from time to time as an awed visitor torn between pride for and jealousy of his son's accomplishments. These fantasies were decidedly PG: the ward's repressive atmosphere quashed his libidinous imaginings; although he spent hours inventing flirtations and complex seductions, the scene always faded at the entrance to the bedroom. It was too painful and too futile to continue.

These fantasies were his only pleasure and escape, but they depressed him, revealing (he thought) how superficial he really was. He hated himself for that, and for the appetite for wealth and luxury instilled in him by his former life-style. He was a snob, a Beverly Hills brat at heart. "Happiness is not a Sony color TV," he told himself, only half-believing it. But knowing the tensions of the modern world, and doubting his ability to cope with them successfully, he drew on dreams of wealth and power to shield himself. King, he knew, operating on similar insecurity, had struggled to erect the same barricades. Geoffrey's fantasies reflected a family legacy of hiding from reality behind thick brocade draperies. It enraged him to realize that his fantasies were probably not much different from his father's.

Inside Atascadero, milestones seemed remote. But soon he would be twenty. He tried not to think about this particular birthday that would finally release him from what he thought were surely the most unhappy and destructive teenage years that any boy could experience. He had lived his entire life in hostility, but he had not really lived at all. He was imprisoned with the dregs of society, men who were unloved, unwanted, illiterate, and poverty-stricken—completely ignorant about the finer things in life. Yet he was as poor and uneducated as they were. In fact, most of them had gone further in high school than he. Worst of all, he shared with them the question: How could one hide the stigma of Atascadero from the outside world, presuming he would ever be released?

Ahead lay a thousand and one lonely nights in a locked ward. Although he struggled to block out family memories, these unwelcome visitations often interrupted his fantasies. The thought of his murdered mother reduced him to tears, while images of his dead father caused him to toss and turn in hatred. One memory in particular tortured him, filling him with hatred for both parents. It was the worst of all his childhood memories, proving to him how he had been manipulated.

The memory dealt with the time that Ruth had worked her will and forced him to spend a weekend alone with his father during the period they were separated from him in Kansas

City. "Do this for me," she had begged him in tears. When Geoffrey threw up in the toilet the moment they arrived at a lakeside cabin retreat, King acted as if he didn't hear, but his face seemed to darken. Until that moment, perhaps, he had not realized the damage he had inflicted on all of them. But he acted chipper and pushed his young son in the direction of a small dock and an outboard motorboat he had rented.

They sped around the lake, father turning over the wheel to his sullen son. "Come on, rev this sucker," he shouted above the roar and spray. The Great Manipulator knew what Geoffrey loved, but Geoffrey refused to smile so that his father could see, even as he stirred the still lake into a frenzy of waves that splashed against the shoreline. King grinned in satisfaction and pointed toward a sheltered cove. They anchored as the sun began lowering. King stood in the bow and slipped off his swimming trunks, scratching contentedly at his fleshy stomach. Geoffrey turned away in shock, as if his father had suddenly drawn a knife. The boat tipped from King's weight as King flipped off the side of the stern and dove into the water. He surfaced, sputtering with delight. "It's fantastic," he yelled. "What are you waiting for? Come on. Get that suit off and jump in. It's only us boys. Swimming bare-assed is one of life's great joys."

Geoffrey hesitated. He thought about starting the engines and speeding off across the lake, but visions of his mother intervened.

King's voice was mocking, insistent. "Come on. I won't look."

The bastard! What right did he have to demand such an intimacy, camaraderie? King taunted him about being shy when he turned his back, peeled off his trunks, and plunged into the cold lake. He dove to the bottom, wondering how long he could stay under and swim to escape. The water was murky, and he searched in vain for large boulders in which he could wedge a foot that would hold him under until he drowned. Ultimate revenge! He envisioned his frantic father diving repeatedly to try to find him, then giving up and racing across the lake to get the police. Maybe, because of the strained circumstances, King might be held in suspicion of murdering his son. Wouldn't that be fabulous! No boulders. And no remaining air in his lungs. His body shot to the surface, ignoring his will.

"Bravo!" King laughed from not far away. Geoffrey ignored him and swam back to the boat. He climbed aboard and put on his trunks, glowering down at his floating father.

"I want to leave—now!" he said.

King looked up, surprised. "We just got here," he protested.

"I don't care. I want to go back immediately. If you won't take me, I'll hitchhike."

"What are you talking about?"

"I don't want to spend another minute with you. I never want to see you ever again. I hate your goddamn guts."

King silently hoisted himself aboard, then plopped soaked and defeated onto the backseat, shaking the water out of his ears while Geoffrey started the engines.

His father's arrogance and insensitivity enraged Geoffrey. King had trapped his son into sharing an unearned intimacy, devoid of either closeness or trust, that resulted in Geoffrey feeling empty and sick. He could never relive that scene on the lake without remembering when there was still time to save his soul and his mother's, too. She came to him, shortly after King died, to disclose her plan for a new life to share. Probably this secret dream had sustained her through the long, unhappy years before King's death. She showed him a brochure and Polaroids sent to her from a realtor back east who had found for her a Swiss-style chalet in Vermont ski country. The two of them would help run a small gift shop and restaurant and hire a manager to run the rooms. The asking price was reasonable, and the lure of escape from California and its bitter memories was irresistible. She would do the cooking for the restaurant, and the notion of being self-sufficient and prospering on her own bolstered her determination to take the risks. Crisp mountain air and rosy cheeks . . . she could smell soup bubbling on the kitchen stove to satisfy the ravenous appetites of the skiers. "Oh, Geoffrey, I just know this is the right move for us to make. We can be whole again. Don't you see? This is a fresh start that makes sense. Just imagine! Close your eyes. Come on, I mean it. Close your eyes. Can't you *feel* how right it is?"

Maybe he could, but he would never admit it. "Oh, Mother, go feed your hungry skiers if you must, but leave me alone. I won't allow you to uproot me ever again. L.A. is where I'm staying, and that's that." He had old scores to settle, too many to ever forgive and forget. Yet his destructiveness (because that's what it was) depressed him even more than it did his mother. He had become the engine of his family's final defeat, a role which they had instigated for him. One day, alone on the beach, he threw down his school satchel, pulled off his shoes and socks, and began walking out into the ocean until a breaker slapped him down on the seat of his pants, bouncing him backward to the shore, where he sat in the wet sand and cried. That night he told his mother he was finished with school—for the present. He just couldn't handle it. She gave in. What choice did she have? It made no sense to go on. None of what followed during his brief, pathetic foray into the world made much sense. He had doomed them. He alone. He.

These memories dominated his thoughts and he finally begged the ward night staff to give him tranquilizers. Clearly he was working too hard at the psychology lab, and a decision was made to give him a week's rest from work. He seemed depressed, ate little, and complained of severe chest pains. He was sent to the infirmary and examined. "You have a systolic murmur and a ventricular septical defect," a doctor told him. "In six months or so, it could cause serious problems." He needed surgical repair in a hospital within the state's department of mental hygiene. He asked them how serious it was. "Not unserious," they admitted, and he was surprised to feel pinched by anxiety. Dying was what he thought he yearned for.

On his six-month anniversary at Atascadero, the psychiatric technician filed his daily report: "Patient King crying. Says he can't stand the thoughts about people he has hurt and the two murders he committed. He sees no hope for worthwhile future and states were he on the outside now, he would take a large dose of Seconal."

He was now under close watch and supervision. His hall pass was taken away.

36

A dream perhaps? A fantasy? No, but after the grimness of one year inside Atascadero, it could have been. Geoffrey sat on a sun-drenched patio on a perfect day in May, holding the hand of his girlfriend, his usually pale face flushed from laughter and champagne. Oh, his mood was rollicking and the laughs of his three dearest friends echoed amid the glass and concrete of what appeared to be a luxury hotel in the Westwood section of Los Angeles. His story was perhaps a bit cruel, but the champagne plunged him onward as he described a patient who rolled down the long hallways of Atascadero—*rolled* the way kids roll themselves down a hill because he was convinced it was the only way to "equalize gravity pressures on the body that can kill you." Frank Estes chuckled. Skip Harte wiped tears from his eyes, which always happened when he laughed. Annette, who sat with one arm around the storyteller while squeezing his palm with her free hand, grinned at the artful way her wonderful Geoffrey told the story. That was why it was funny—the *poor* man, of course—but Geoffrey's description was deliciously funny after too much champagne in the warm sun. She kissed his neck and hugged him. "More bubbly?" Skip Harte asked. He had brought three bottles of good domestic and they had already finished two.

Was it a dream when Harte and Estes raised their glasses to toast Geoffrey and Annette, who had just announced their engagement? If that was a dream, it was a good one, and he needed good dreams at this point. Who could believe in the reality of the past two weeks? Here was Geoffrey King, an inmate of California's maximum-security mental institution, unguarded and alone, enjoying the companionship of his friends on the grounds of the UCLA Medical Center, where he was recovering from open heart surgery. A psychiatric technician had driven him down from central California and then departed. He had his own private room in the hospital, but no guards, no security of any sort. A two-week interval—"on leave from hell" is the way he described it. Was there ever a stranger, more dreamlike interlude? Of course, he thought about escaping. Annette, in particular, urged him to run off with her into the back country of Mexico, where they would marry and start a new life. "You've suffered enough," she sighed. But the Atascadero administrators told him that if he behaved himself and caused no problems during the two weeks, he would probably be rewarded by a transfer to a minimum-security institution—a major step toward release. Tears shone in his eyes as he raised his glass to his friends and toasted them, "I have hope now," he told them, "I really do. I'm going to feed off this day for a long time. You can't imagine what it means to me, knowing that you are willing to forgive me for what I've done and let me back into your lives. If I ever do get out of that damned place, I'm gonna need all the help I can get from each of you." It was his final day of freedom. His next lunch would be in the dining hall at Atascadero.

"Geoffrey, a bottom-line question," Estes asked. "Do you think you need to be there?"

"I need to be in a real hospital like Camarillo, where I can receive professional care. There's nothing they can do for me at Atascadero. It's really a prison, not a hospital. I have serious problems, Frank, that I haven't yet faced. I'm not ready to come out, but God, I'm not ready to go back to that place."

Negotiations between Atascadero and UCLA concerning his operation evolved over six months and eventually produced letters and memos a quarter-inch thick in his permanent file. But as his general condition deteriorated (fatigue, palpitations, difficulty breathing) and various tests revealed the need for surgery more complex than a state hospital could safely manage, it was the patient who suggested UCLA, never dreaming it would become a reality. And in the midst of his travails, he had received an unexpected and amazing letter from Annette, who had only recently learned of the tragedy by a chance encounter with Geoffrey's friend Bud, and admitted never having lost her intense feelings for him. "Geoffrey," she wrote, "I was blown away the day you told me you had taken a male lover. I was blown away when Bud told me what happened to you. I guess you think I just feel sorry for you now, but I have searched my heart and I know now that what I feel toward you I never have or will feel toward any other person. You are the special person in my life. I love you." He wept. And he responded immediately with a passionate letter in reply. She visited him twice and wrote every day. God, he needed her in his life. That's all he knew.

The night before his operation, he was convinced that he would not survive and picked up the phone in his hospital room and called his Uncle Raymond, who had been advised by Atascadero about the surgery. His nephew emotionally sought to be forgiven, and when Aunt Nora came on the line, he asked her to pray for him. Then he called for a duty nurse and asked her to fetch him a Catholic priest. The resident Catholic chaplain, an elderly gentleman, came to his room and found the patient sobbing inconsolably. "I'm not Catholic," Geoffrey said, "but I need to make confession and beg forgiveness for the terrible things I've done." The elderly priest heard him confess his crimes of murder and then told him, "Our Lord forgives you as He forgives all His children who seek His divine grace." Geoffrey chose to believe him, and even as the orderlies arrived to give him a preparatory enema, he felt as if he had already been cleansed.

The surgeons were amazed at the damage, but managed to suture closed about ninety-eight percent of the hole in his heart. "You'll be fine," they assured him. When he arrived back at his room from intensive care, he found Annette waiting, and she seldom left his side for the next two weeks. The doctors and nurses looked the other way when she sneaked in pizza and beer and sat with him watching TV long after visiting hours ended. Oh, she hadn't changed much: lanky and tall and boyish. She was now a junior at UCLA and studied in his room. One night he impulsively proposed to her.

"I have no right tying you up this way," he said. "Who knows when I'll ever be free to marry? Promise me you'll see other people. I really want you to." But she would not promise that at all, instead declared that after they married, she expected him to remain faithful. "I don't want to share you with anyone else . . . especially not with some man." She laughed sadly at his tight look and slapped at her forehead. "Good ole Annette really knows how to score points, doesn't she? Well, I'll bite the bullet. Half of you is better than none."

Everyone cried the day he departed, but not even the most

sensitive of his friends could comprehend what it meant to him to surrender after two weeks of glorious freedom, to return to the horrors of Atascadero and be locked again behind its walls. Even the psychiatric technician who arrived to fetch him seemed apologetic about his task. "Oh, Geoffrey, this is so inhuman," his fiancée cried, hugging him.

He kissed her. "Look at the bright side," he told her. "At least now maybe they'll transfer me so I can get some help."

He drove back as depressed as he had ever been in his life. When he returned, he discovered that they had transferred him to Atascadero's toughest ward, housing a freeway sniper, a mad bomber of airports, and assorted other murderers and madmen, a ward infamous for its maximum control and security. The staff called it "Murderers' Row."

Uncle John, the ward charge, raised turkeys. Everyone called him Uncle John, even though he was an unavuncular old curmudgeon who had spent his life in the California penal system, mostly as a jailer. He enjoyed his reputation for relishing the company of the most vicious criminals housed at Atascadero in much the same way as a lion tamer covets the fierce reputation of his beasts. Uncle John always received the worst ones, and in return, had his pick of two or three of the most cooperative and intelligent patients to bolster his staff, which wasn't why the King boy was sent to him. "You're here because no one knows how being on the outside for a couple of weeks affected you. Now, just relax and make yourself at home," Uncle John told him, not pleased at having Geoffrey in his ward. He detested queers. "Give me an ax murderer any day," he muttered. And he meant it.

Geoffrey's outrage was smothered by fear. In one corner of the dayroom the freeway sniper sat on his bed all day, stalking everyone with murderous eyes. Two beds away, the mad bomber lay muttering about the insult of being so near a fucking homo. "Keep away, you prick," he snarled at Geoffrey King. Next bed was a Hell's Angel, built like an iron boiler, who arrived in the ward with four strings attached to his foreskin for reasons unexplained, and he refused to remove them. Then there was an assaultive, hallucinatory character who called himself "The Captain" and ordered everyone else to, also. He thought he was in a military barracks, and if a ward-mate forgot to address him as "sir," the captain's fists were brought into play. (Geoffrey would later learn that the Captain became delusional under pressure of the ward's regimented life.)

That was his homecoming.

"Hey, you, come here."

He looked up and saw a young psychiatric technician beckoning to him. They went down the hall, where the tech stuck his head in a patient's room. "Fred, take a hike. I want to talk to this guy for a few minutes." The patient left and the tech closed the door.

"Sit down," he said. He was young and very arrogant, short and stocky. A blond with close-cropped hair.

"Now, listen," he said, "we're gonna have to change this or you won't survive two days in here."

Geoffrey's puzzled expression seemed to anger him.

"I'm talking about this limp-wrist, nellie shit. You're flaunting, sweetheart, to the point of obnoxiousness, and it's gonna get you hurt."

Geoffrey hadn't acted that way during his two weeks in L.A., but the moment he reentered Atascadero, he stepped back into his Queen Tank role.

"I don't know what your problem is," the tech continued, "whether you're on a punishment trip to degrade yourself or what, but I'm telling you for your own good—cut it out. One of those jokers inside is gonna cut your throat. Look, is this how you really want to come across? I find you very offensive, and I want to be on your side. But that queen stuff is a real barrier. It makes me damned uncomfortable, and I'm not alone."

Geoffrey sighed and nodded. "You have a point," he admitted.

"A point!" Sprinkles replied, flashing an angry smile. "I have more than that, friend: you're fucking outrageous. If you're smart, you'll change it immediately. If not . . ." He just shrugged and began to head toward the door.

"Well, I have some complaints about how I've been treated, too," Geoffrey said.

"At this point, who cares?" Sprinkles replied, and left.

Dear Judge Kelso:
   My name is Geoffrey King. You may remember my trial.
I killed my mother and grandmother while under an LSD
psychosis and you sentenced me to Atascadero for as long
as it takes to have my sanity restored. I am writing to report
to you on my progress. I have been here one year and two
months and have not yet received one minute of professional psychiatric counseling. I want to get well and know
that I will need years of intensive psychotherapy. But I've
been told by the staff that such treatment is beyond the
scope . . .

Dearest Annette,
   Please don't worry. I should never have sent that heavy
letter the night I got back. I wasn't in the best mood, believe me. I'm slowly adjusting to this new ward, and I was
very shocked and hurt by the sneaky way they transferred
me. I requested the administration to hold a staffing on my
case as soon as possible so I can remind them of their
promise that if I behaved myself at ULCA, I would be
considered for transfer to Camarillo or some other hospital where I can be helped. Annette, I'm so afraid that I will
run out of time before I receive the help I desperately
need. There's so much bottled up inside that must come
out, and I live in fear of suffering a major breakdown that
could make me a permanent psychotic. I don't want to
worry you, and honest to God, I don't think this will really
happen, but it is on my mind as a price I might have to pay
for the criminal neglect in my case. There are times when I
just . . .

Dear Frank,
   I have a rather strange request which I hope you won't
find too inconvenient. I've been trying to recall all of the
events in my life for that crazy year that led up to the
murders, but I find I was going off in so many different
directions all at once that much of it is a confused blob. I
could use your sharp, clear eye on this to kind of put me
into perspective. What was I like, Frank? Did you think I
was crazy? (At times, I know you did, but at other times, I

know you were damned proud of how I behaved with people like Laurence Harvey and Skip.) What did you think was right and wrong with me? I remember we had long soul talks, but I can't recall a word. Can you? Write me up, Frank. You probably have better insight than any of those so-called shrinks, who can't see the woods for the trees. Would you do this for me, Frank? Am I asking too much? If so, just let me know how . . .

Dear Geoffrey King,
    Don't you think it is high time to stop playing games? You received good advice, so take it before you get yourself maimed or killed by these lunatics around here. Really, I'm disappointed in you. Masks, always masks. How many have you worn? Do you even know your own face anymore? I doubt it. I doubt you ever will. Don't you realize how much harm . . .

Only a madman would write a letter to himself or save dozens that he started and never completed to a score of others.

In tears, Geoffrey complained to Doris Leek that he had been refused his request for a staff meeting to discuss his transfer to another hospital. "I'm not asking to be set free," he argued; "I need real help, real psychiatrists and psychotherapy. They agreed, but said there aren't any psychiatrists available for that sort of thing. God, this is Catch-22. Here I am in a mental hospital . . . they've got me at the table, but they won't let me eat."
    Doris was only mildly sympathetic. "This isn't Menninger's, kiddo," she remarked. "This is a state hospital for the criminally insane, and we're underbudgeted and woefully staffed— so you're going to have to be patient and make the best of a lousy situation. Keep cool and play the game, because there's just nothing we can do for you at this point."
    "Why can't I be transferred?"
    "You haven't been here long enough."
    "Doris, that makes no sense, and you know it."
    Ken Sprinkles found him lying on his bed after refusing to attend the dinner meal.

"Not hungry, huh? Uncle John wasn't too happy. From now on, try to go to chow, even if you only poke at your food. No sense getting everyone down on you. By the way, I've been assigned as your sponsor, like it or not. If you need anything— fine. If not, I don't have time to waste."

"Oh, swell," the patient said. "Today's been my lucky day."

Each patient was assigned a sponsor from among the three shifts of psychiatric technicians monitoring daily activities in the ward: a person he could turn to for special problems or needs. Sprinkles would've been his last choice. So cocky and callous, looking exactly like what he had once been: a member of the security goon squad. Probably kept a blackjack in his back pocket, that swaggering, immature twenty-two-year old who acted like King Shit.

Sprinkles worked the three-to-eleven-P.M. shift, describing his job as a Coast Guard cutter cruising in trouble waters. He was assigned eight patients, including Geoffrey King, to ob- serve for mood and behavior, filing daily, weekly, and monthly reports to the Atascadero bureaucracy. Because of his previous membership in the hospital's goon squad, he earned the grudg- ing respect of some of the sinister characters on Murderers' Row, and most patients considered him tough, fair, and, unlike most techs, a sympathetic listener to their problems. The day- room was the center of ward life, where patients played chess and Ping-Pong and watched television. Sprinkles was an avid chess player, although no match for a fifty-year-old rapist who beat him insultingly, watching TV between moves. The game was constantly interrupted by unexpected turbulence—argu- ments, fights, seizures. The ward was so overcrowded that nine- teen patients slept in the center of the dayroom. Geoffrey's bed was in the center of the first row, where he could be watched closely as a homosexual with a suicidal history. "Keep your eye on that queen," Sprinkles was instructed by the ward charge. "He's sneaky. He'll pull a fast one if we let him." Sprinkles was appalled at the crude jokes about Geoffrey he overheard in the nursing station. They called him "Queen King" and "The Killer Faggot" and treated him with crude contempt. How, he won- dered, could his colleagues make jokes about someone who had suffered such a tragedy? Whoever transferred this shattered young kid to Murderers' Row should be fired. He felt drawn to

Geoffrey, mostly because of his own youth: Geoffrey was two years younger than Ken, but he acted like an old man whose life was already extinguished. In truth, Ken felt as threatened by overt homosexual flauntings as the others, but he volunteered to become Geoffrey's sponsor knowing that this patient would not survive this tough ward without friendship and protection. After nearly four years at Atascadero, Sprinkles thought it was time to save a patient's soul, and the faggot everyone harassed seemed a perfect candidate.

So he read him the riot act on his nelliness and then sat back and waited to see if he would moderate his behavior. A few nights after this initial encounter, the patient asked him if they could talk together privately. Ken got the keys to a small office used by the psychiatric social worker.

"What's up?" he asked.

"I was really pissed at you," Geoffrey admitted, "but I've been thinking about what you said. I think you're right. Acting like a flaming queen is the only way I know to protect myself in this ward. But I guess I'm making things worse for myself."

He sighed dejectedly. "Look, I really need someone to talk to . . . a friend I can trust. You're the only person here who ever showed any real interest in me at all. Will you give me your time?"

Sprinkles nodded. "That's what I'm here for," he replied.

He told the ward charge that he wanted to try one-on-one therapy with Geoffrey King.

"What for?" Uncle John asked.

"To try to get him more masculine," Ken partially lied.

"Well, don't waste too much time at it," his boss said.

Geoffrey needed to talk or he'd explode. "I've got to deal with my feelings about the murders," he told Ken. "It's eating me up, but I don't know if I can handle it. I'm afraid I'll crack."

"We'll take it real slow," Ken promised. "One good thing about this place: we've got all the time in the world."

And so a twenty-two-year-old former factory worker became therapist to a twenty-year-old conscience-stricken murderer. "I wasn't about to play Freud or God," Ken would recall years later. "We both knew I had no professional answers to offer, but I was very strong and cocky and I felt I could give him my strength. I just said to him, 'Tell me your story, right from the

beginning.' I felt as long as I kept him talking, he'd be okay. My
fear was I'd arrive at work one day and be told he'd killed
himself. Suicide was never far from his thoughts; you could
sniff it on him. He was so repressed and depressed, holding in a
lifetime of accumulated crap, so we began from ground zero.
The guy was in horrible shape—his thoughts disorganized,
blocked, confused, wandering all over the place. He'd say, 'Oh,
I just thought of something really important to tell you.' The
very next moment, he forgot what it was. We met every night in
that little office. I remember being very uptight, wondering if I
wasn't getting in way over my head, but the first few times, I
just held him in my arms. He cried for hours. All those stored
feelings came gushing out. Looking back, I remember his feelings more than anything he actually said. Some nights, the
windows steamed, believe me. He'd be telling about things his
parents did to him, turning beet red, pacing, kicking at the
walls, frothing at the mouth. 'Those fuckers,' he screamed,
'what right did they have to do these things to me?' I remember
being shocked at how livid he'd become talking about childhood grievances. I thought I was the only freak on the block
who still slammed walls remembering my drunken old man
beating my ass when I was ten or eleven.

"That little office was close quarters. I remember feeling
strange being behind closed doors with a queer and reaching
out to hold and comfort him. But that was very early in our
sessions. There was no room for bullshit or neutrality in that
close space. Either I was totally involved or he'd turn off and
walk out—the end of the ball game. A guy as sick as Geoffrey
could spot a twitch of disapproval at twenty paces, but it wasn't
hard for me to cry with him or bleed with him: here was a guy
born with every advantage, only to be systematically destroyed
by a destructive family life. I was raised in the shadow of Palos
Verdes, on the blue-collar side of the peninsula, and I hated
those rich bitches on the hill. But our lives connected in so
many ways; so many of his hurts I knew all too well. You bet I
bled with him; there were nights when I staggered out the door
and needed six beers before I could think about going to bed. I
had wanted to achieve real intimacy with a patient—well, I got
it. I began by feeling sorry for him, gradually came to really like
him, and we ended up as close as brothers. I loved the guy. I

did things for him that could've got me fired. I didn't care. I was determined that I wasn't gonna lose him. If it meant giving him more than one hundred percent—a hundred and fifty and up—I just wasn't gonna lose him. Many times I wished there was a decent psychiatrist I could trust to consult, because we were dealing with very raw emotions and I watched him staggering around. Where he got the strength to keep going, night after night, I'll never know. I couldn't have done it. But he was so motivated to get well—that's what touched me most of all. And he was such a sensitive kid. I remember urging him to get exercise—Atascadero had a decent gym. He told me he loved to swim but he was ashamed of the scars on his chest and what others might think. Teenage vanity I guess. I told him, 'Forget the scars. The beauty of Geoffrey will shine through.' I meant it. One night he said something that really knocked me out. He said, 'You know how I feel about my life? I feel like a pope who died, went to heaven, and discovered that God is a Buddhist.'

"Man, I related to that! I remember saying, 'Geoffrey, if I had your brainpower, I could rule the goddamn world.' And he said, 'Aw, Sprinkles, cut the shit. Whatever I've got, you wouldn't trade places with me for a minute.' What could I say? He was right on. Aside from all his other problems, Atascadero had him tied in knots. The psychiatrist here who admitted him gave him the usual diagnosis of schizophrenic, and because of his drug-related crime, added to it by claiming he was drug-dependent. That blew Geoffrey away. That stigma would be attached to him for the rest of his life, even though he was acquitted for his crime. He had so much to deal with, we could have talked for years. We talked for months before we got around to the murders. He was in no rush. I left it up to him."

"You didn't kill in a vacuum," Sprinkles insisted. They spent a lot of time exploring the months leading to the murders, a period of time when, finally free of his father, Geoffrey hit the streets on the run and ultimately became lost in a drug-shrouded fog.

"Images, Ken, I was trying to invent dozens of new ones simultaneously. But I was a totally split personality, because the other part of me was desperate to prove to my mother how much I could accomplish on my own.

"Ken," he said, "you just can't imagine the unreality of the life I was living." As Skip Harte's lover, wrapped in a flowing kimono, being served an aprés-sex glass of champagne from a sterling-silver bucket . . . existing inside the veils of a dream that matched, item for exquisite priceless item, his own gilt-edged fantasies. Marvelous dinner parties . . . weekends at Palm Springs . . . screenings at Harvey's mansion, sitting next to Bette Davis.

But then, always home to the pumpkin—back to the shoddy Palos Verdes tomb and his towering resentment of his dismal, drunken mother.

"How disgusting she seemed after a day with the beautiful people in Beverly Hills. I know I should feel ashamed for thinking that way, and I was, just a little. You see, Ken, what a snob and bastard I am?"

"An unlucky bastard," Sprinkles remarked. "A kid like you running wild in the sixties never had a chance."

One day Sprinkles arrived in the ward with a gift for his friend from a weekend at Disneyland and handed over a black felt cap with two round ears—compliments of Mickey Mouse. G-E-O-F-F was stitched in gold lettering across the front. "God, he was delighted with that hat," Sprinkles later recalled. "He wore it in the hallways and got a lot of laughs. He wore it to our session that night, feeling really high and good. We had been at it now for about three months, and I said to him, 'What do you think, pal, should we go for it?' And he said, 'Sure, I'm ready.' And for the next couple of hours he relived the murders in all their gory detail, almost moment by moment. When he was finished, we were both in tears. The awful part was him not knowing whether he was actually aware of killing his mother and his grandmother. Bad enough to have killed, but to wrestle with that for the rest of his life . . .

"He told me:

"'When Mother fetched me from jail, I didn't really want to go home with her. I wanted a doctor or a hospital. I was in torment from hallucinations, and how the police could release me in such a state, I'll never understand. I was in obvious emotional turmoil, and she drove me home to take a nap! Well, that's a pretty good indication of how willing she was to invest time and energy in helping me, isn't it? What overwhelms me now is how, under any circumstances, I was capable of picking up a knife and killing two people. We can rationalize about LSD forever, but that's only a lame excuse.'"

Ken continued: "Well, I took acid several times and knew that was B.S. I told him the truth. I said the critical point was when he came down to the living room and got worked up talking to his grandmother. That was just before Ruth came back to the house. Goddammit, there's no human being on earth who can control a temper tantrum under acid. That's a fact, pure and simple. I said, 'You weren't psychotic. You were delusional and in a rage over all the grief and depression in your life. Anyone walking in that door—me, Frank Estes, the pope—was gonna catch that knife in the back. Unfortunately, it was your mother. And unfortunately, your grandmother stumbled in while you were still delusional. Now, that's the truth of it, or as close as we'll ever get to it. Anything else is wheel-spinning that will tear you to pieces.'

"Geoffrey began to sob. 'Oh, God, it's too awful. I never meant to hurt them. I miss my mother. I think about her every day. I loved her. In spite of everything, I really loved her.'"

Ken agreed that he did. And he probably missed her, too. "Especially," he added, "inside this place. It would be great having a mother who could visit you, bake cookies, cheer you up, and root for you. But how would you feel about her if you were back outside? Geoffrey, my hunch is that you'd be damned sorry she was still around."

The patient hid his face in his hands. "That's the worst," he gasped. "I'm sorry I killed her, but I'm glad she's gone. And I can't live with it. I'm so guilty."

Sprinkles peeled his hands away from his face. "Listen to me," he insisted. "You can't help how you feel. Just face up to what your feelings really are. Let go and feel them."

"Don't you understand?" Geoffrey said, hunched in his chair. "When I woke up at the hospital and realized what I had done, I felt . . . relieved. That's when I ripped those tubes out of my nose and mouth. I can't live with that, Ken. It proves I got away with murder."

"No, it doesn't," the tech insisted. "It proves only that she was a weight around your neck. Hell, you told me that dozens of times."

"Aren't you listening?" Geoffrey shouted. "I'm telling you I'm glad I killed my own mother."

"No, you're not," Sprinkles shouted back. "You're telling me you're horrified you killed her, but you're glad to be rid of a pain in the ass. That's slightly different, you asshole!"

They were close to the heart of the matter, but could go on no further. Geoffrey was too upset and overwhelmed by guilt. But at least he did not crack. Not immediately. Sprinkles watched him closely over the next days and weeks, and the patient showed no overt ill effects from the ordeal of reliving his crime. They went on to talk about other matters. Yet, unpredictability is synonymous with mental illness, and toward the six-month mark in their nightly encounters, Geoffrey took a sudden nose dive for no apparent reason, plunging into a steep depression and staying submerged to the point where Ken began to fear that he had really lost him. "Acute depression," he recalled, "where he couldn't eat or sleep and barely had the ability to speak. He lay in bed almost comatose, and nothing we could do shook him out of it. I'd seen patients like that slip into psychosis. I really panicked."

WARD OBSERVATIONS

10-31-71. Patient is presently on psychotropic medication (Mellaril, 200 mgs). This past week he appears to be very withdrawn and upset, afraid of the ward patients. Very depressed. Quit his job at the research lab claiming he cannot cope and asked that his hall card privileges be withdrawn. Skips meals saying he is too nervous to eat and complains constantly about "terrible chest pains." Has been to infirmary practically daily. Case discussed by staff and sponsor and agreed to allow patient plenty of bed rest while on self-imposed ward restriction. Hopefully, this period of crisis will soon be over and a good rest is probably what he needs most of all. Patient had been doing well this past month but has now slipped back. K. Sprinkles, P.T.

11-2-71. Mr. King approached ward charge tearfully, saying he was extremely upset and frightened. Appeared upset—pacing, high rate of respiration, general attitude. Patient requested that he be placed in seclusion for his own protection, feeling he was "about to explode." He was placed in a stripped room and not official seclusion. He seemed satisfied. John Simmons, ward charge.

12-7-71. Patient asked me to call his fiancée and tell her not to visit this week because "I can't handle it." Period of extreme emotional distress continues. Behavior is rather erratic; sometimes he is logical and understanding, at other times very emotional, suspicious, and frightened of himself and others. K. Sprinkles, P.T.

12-21-71. Care plan reviewed, no changes made. Patient presently is in a highly emotional state: this could possibly be due to holiday season, also could be he has been propositioned by other homosexuals in ward. John Simmons, ward charge.

12-25-71. Patient spent day lying in bed in fetal position, got up twice to go to latrine to smoke cigarettes. Refused breakfast but did take brief shower before lunch. Complains of pains in chest. C. Brooks, P.T.

37

1972

January—no change.

February—Patient seems to be eating and sleeping better but is very withdrawn and easily upset.

Uncle John, the ward charge, was clearly displeased. "Now, Kenny, enough babying. Time to shake the tree. We've got thirty-seven other patients to think about in this ward. That boy is demoralizing the entire ward and taking too much time and attention." Sooner than later, Uncle John would recommend shock therapy, and Geoffrey would be carted off to the brain-fry room. Before that happened, Sprinkles tried to shake the tree alive.

"Look, you've had a setback. You've got to expect that, because we were making real progress. You're repressing hostility. You vented a lot of feelings that are damned tough to accept. We opened a can of worms, I think, but you can't help your feelings. I've told you that, Geoff. You're not responsible for feeling as you do. They did stupid, rotten things. They were assholes, and you've got to stop punishing yourself for coming to grips with that particular truth. Come on, pal, let me help. Don't shut me out. Work with me. Reach down, babe, reach down inside. There's plenty of strength left. Reach down. You'll find it."

Geoffrey turned his face to the wall.

"I made a basket case out of a highly motivated guy who trusted me," Ken told his wife. "I should be fired. Hell, I should be arrested. I had no right to tamper. God damn me."

One Monday morning he came to work and found that Geoffrey was gone.

"We transferred him yesterday," the ward charge told him. "We all needed a change."

As angry and hurt as Sprinkles was, he knew that was true.

"They sent him to an advanced-treatment ward," Sprinkles would recall, "which in those days meant a ward only slightly less repressive than Murderers' Row. I was under strict orders to keep away from him. In a way, I was relieved, because I was obsessed with his condition—drinking heavily and losing ten pounds myself. I must've pushed him too hard to face problems he obviously was not ready to cope with, but a part of me was disappointed. I thought I really knew this guy. Geoffrey King was much tougher than anyone suspected, and fading away wasn't his style. Geoff was an all-or-nothing man: up and out or down in flames. And, by God, he proved me right. He got out of bed about a week after the transfer, madder than hell at the sneaky way he'd been transferred on my day off. They put him to work in the industrial laundry and I peeked in one day to see how he was getting along. He told me, 'You'd better steer clear of me from now on, because I'm going to war, and those fuckers have never seen the ruthless Geoffrey in action. They did me a big favor. They gave me my strength back. I've been living off hate all my life. Listen, I'm getting my ass out of here.'

"It was great seeing him so steamed. By the time he was finished, even his worst enemies in this place had to admit that he was the most memorable son of a bitch who ever walked through those steel doors."

A few weeks before Geoffrey's two-year anniversary at Atascadero, he was summoned to an annual staff review of his progress. He entered a small conference room and was greeted by the chief of the medical staff; James Burke, his new ward charge; his old boss, Doris Leek; and a psychiatric social worker. The doctor told him to be seated and asked him how he was doing.

"As well as anyone else around here, I guess," he replied.

"Fine," the doctor said. "Okay, we'll talk to you again next year."

He flushed with anger. "Now, you just hold on here, Doctor. I think it's about time we got something clear. I was told that if I behaved myself when I was alone at UCLA having open heart surgery, consideration would be given to transferring me to a minimum-security hospital where I can receive real help. Now, what about it?"

The doctor shook his head. "There are facts of life which I would have expected you to figure out by now, Mr. King. Society expects us to keep you here for a certain length of time, whether you feel you're being helped or not. I think it would be unrealistic for you to expect transfer or release before at least five years."

"Oh, really?" Geoffrey exclaimed. "How interesting! And what am I supposed to do for the next three years?"

"Be positive and cooperate in the treatment programs."

"Doctor, I'm through cooperating in something so worthless. This is a very serious matter. I'm a mental patient who is being denied beneficial treatment. Do you realize that I was acquitted for my crime? I was committed here two years ago to receive treatment that has been systematically denied to me."

The doctor fussed in his chair impatiently. "For whatever reasons—good or bad—we are expected to hold you here for a certain length of time. That's our obligation to the citizens of California. Now, whether or not you accept this fact, a fact it is . . . and it won't change. Now, you've got three more years with us. You can do them nicely or not so nicely, but you've been here long enough to know the consequences of not so nicely. Mr. King, you're excused. We'll talk again next year."

The doctor glanced at his watch.

"That's it?" the patient exclaimed incredulously. "Well, I have no choice except to take legal action against all of you. Three more years here will ruin me. You'll all be hearing from my attorney."

Burke, the ward charge, almost laughed. "Make sure you get yourself a law student who's at least old enough to shave." He grinned and winked.

"My attorney," the patient replied, "is Mr. Melvin Belli of San Francisco. You may have heard of him, Mr. Burke. Mr. Belli is an old family friend. My father ran Rexall Drug Company. So you're not dealing with the usual poor, dumb patient you love to push around. I'm well-connected, I assure you, and I know my rights. I won't need a law student, Mr. Burke, but you may use one before I'm through. I just can't wait to see Mr. Belli make all of you sweat in court."

"Are you finished, Mr. King?" the doctor asked testily.

"Am I ever!" the patient exclaimed. "I'm finished with all of you, once and for all."

He left. Outside in the hall, his hands shook and he felt frighteningly diminished—aware of his high, shrill voice and his still-beardless face. He had been possessed, had spoken without thinking, concocting nonsense about Melvin Belli, whom he knew only by reading tabloid accounts of his famous trials. Angry, he had lapsed into an old childhood habit of using almost fey formal speech that used to drive King to the edge of hives. He was now living beyond Ken Sprinkles' help and protection . . . beyond anybody's. Doris Leek caught up with him, her face dark with dismay. "What possessed you?" she whispered. "No patient ever spoke that way at a staffing. You've done it now—you've burned your last bridge, Geoffrey. You're on your own, kiddo." He knew that was true.

Doris hurried away.

*   *   *

No patient got away with such insulting behavior. Overnight, he became infamous, as word of his threat of a lawsuit against the institution swept its hallways. The malevolent potential of Atascadero intimidated everyone, on the payroll or not, and no one told him what he didn't already know—that trouble-makers were not tolerated and paid a painful price for re-bellion. Ken Sprinkles found him working in the laundry and was so upset he almost punched him. "You're going to write a letter of apology immediately," he declared, calling him "a fucking lunatic." Geoffrey replied that he didn't care what they did to him, that he was fed up and was going to the mat with these bastards, sink or swim. Of course it was a lie. No one locked inside Atascadero who still maintained a sliver of ra-tionality could claim not to care what they did to him. The threat of the punishment cells or the brain-fry room was suffi-cient to make even a Hell's Angel sadist bite his knuckles in apprehension. Ken warned him that unless he apologized im-mediately, they would make an example of his insurrection. "They can't tolerate such behavior, and you know it," he ar-gued. "If they let you get away with it, every psycho in the joint will be writing to a lawyer."

Geoffrey managed to grin. "Good," he said. "They deserve it."

Ken begged him. "I'm afraid for you," he said. "This is *very* serious."

Geoffrey's blood ran cold. He needed advice and went to see Dr. Michael Serber.

Dr. Serber was a young psychiatrist in charge of the research department. He worked down the hall from Doris Leek's psy-chology lab, and at one point Doris had volunteered Geoffrey's services to aid the psychiatrist in a research project. Geoffrey brought him hundreds of case files of former patients. Serber was engaging and seemed to be genuinely interested in Geof-frey's case, questioning him about his crime, his sentence, his treatment in the ward, and so forth. Serber asked him if he would write his impressions of life in Atascadero on a con-fidential basis. Geoffrey agreed. He wrote:

The biggest problem we prisoners face is that we are constantly under the scrutiny of the nursing-service staff.

Each patient is assigned to a staff member who "charts" his progress, and we live under a microscope twenty-four hours a day. With no privacy, no room for self-expression, we are in a constant state of paranoia.

The psychiatric technicians run our lives. Some may seem friendly when actually they are secretly hostile to a patient because of his crime or his personality. You never know who is really a friend or an enemy. They watch you constantly for signs of unacceptable behavior, especially displays of anger or hostility to other patients, or, especially, to other staff members. Yet they verbally encourage us to "Deal with your hostilities." So patients are always confused. Even a minor depression (being sleepy or grumpy) can cause the staff to come down on a patient and tell him, "Hey, buddy, check your attitude." Those of us who are still coherent are expected to be optimistic always—a bit difficult under the circumstances. If not, this change is considered to be a sign of mental instability.

Most of the patients here are sex offenders, yet any sexual activity is strictly forbidden. As a homosexual, I have been treated with special hatred by the staff and kept under very close watch. Strange that in a place treating men with sex problems there is neither room for any sexual contact nor programs to help prisoners become more self-assured. Atascadero knows nothing about sex or homosexual life. It is not a hospital. It is a prison with hospital beds.

Serber read this document without comment. "This is just between us," he had said.

Now Geoffrey went to him simply because he needed a sympathetic and intelligent ear. He told Serber all he had said during the staffing and was disappointed to see the psychiatrist stiffen.

"What prompted you to be so bold . . . at this particular time?" he asked.

"Just desperation, Doctor," Geoffrey replied honestly.

Serber nodded. "Well, don't worry too much about it. I really don't think anything dire will happen to you."

He suggested that Geoffrey go ahead and write a letter to attorney Melvin Belli. State his case. "You never know," Serber said. "He might take it. And even if he doesn't, he will reply. Everyone will know you are corresponding, and it's no one's business what's inside the envelope. For all they know, Melvin is writing to inform you about a trial date."

"But all patient mail is censored and read."

"Not patient-lawyer mail. Not even here in Atascadero would they violate that right."

He asked Serber if he would read the letter to Belli after he drafted it.

"Sure," the psychiatrist said. "And just keep in mind that things are not so bleak as they might seem."

Serber closed his eyes, looked mysterious, and put his finger to his lips.

That night Geoffrey began drafting the most important letter of his life. A neighbor in the next bed saw what he was doing and whispered, "Don't write in pencil or use notebook paper. Every con and psycho in the world writes letters that way." Good advice. He wrote out a draft in longhand and then used the typewriter in the hospital library. He laid out his case succinctly and spoke from the heart—human being to human being—in the hope that Melvin Belli would be moved sufficiently to take him on. In the end, his desperate plea was no different from thousands of others received by famous attorneys from prison inmates. But if Mr. Belli read through to the last page, he might be impressed by an unusual hooker: the names of fourteen Atascadero employees against whom the patient was prepared to file individual malpractice suits. "Mr. Belli," he concluded, "I plan to ask one million dollars in each of these suits and I have a real case here. I have been systematically deprived of my rights to adequate medical and psychiatric care. You would be amply rewarded by representing me, because I can prove all of my allegations. Please, Mr. Belli, give me a chance to prove to you that the information contained in this letter is factual. I can guarantee you complete satisfaction. I give you my word as a human being."

He took the letter to show to Dr. Serber, who was the person who had encouraged this bluff, but discovered that the psychiatrist's office was locked. A secretary he knew across the hall told him that the director of research had had his hospital pass withdrawn so suddenly that he had not even been allowed to clear off his desk. Very strange. Geoffrey ambled down the hall to drop in on Mrs. Appleby, Doris Leek's gossipy assistant, who liked him and kept her ears pressed to the walls. He asked her about Dr. Serber and she became very guarded. "Just pray," she whispered, "that no one remembers you helped him in his research." Serber was a fink. He had gone through thousands of old hospital records gathering evidence of mistreatment. The hospital had discovered Serber's treachery too late. The research director was already in Sacramento, blowing the whistle. Heads would roll. A major scandal was brewing—an avalanche that would bury a lot of people. Geoffrey didn't know whether to slit his throat or dance a jig of joy. "Hush, now, Geoff," she whispered. "You didn't hear any of this from me."

38

From his first day as a patient, Geoffrey had courted and charmed certain staff personnel—the Protestant chaplain, for one; a psychologist in the aversion-therapy program, for another. Atascadero, for all its awesome madness, was an insular small town that could not keep secrets. Rumors insisted that Serber had been feeding his revelations to Sacramento for months, and a team of investigators had swooped down on the administrators like a furious wolf pack, questioning everyone. There would be dozens fired and several criminal indictments. The staff was caught off balance in panic and fear. Geoffrey planned to use this evolving strategy to intimidate the staff into transferring him out of Atascadero, getting rid of a hot potato, a pain in the ass. Sink or swim, he told himself. Either they'll transfer me or crush me; and really, even the dire alternative seemed preferable to wasting away for years on end, neglected, until finally slipping into a permanent psychosis. No question, the Serber business created the kind of atmosphere of insecurity that made a pest like Geoffrey King intolerable. They might move quickly to get rid of him. But it was also a terrifically dangerous moment to make waves. He knew too well the brutality of frightened people lashing out. He really didn't know what his next move should be, whether he should even mail his letter to Melvin Belli. He needed time to think. But James Burke, his irascible ward charge, forced his hand.

Geoffrey wrote his letter to Belli on Tuesday; the following day, Burke burst onto the ward and ordered the door locked and all eighty-six patients confined to quarters—a punishment unheard of even at Atascadero. The place was a pigsty, he screamed; and Geoffrey wondered whether this hostile venting wasn't the result of stress at the Serber rumors—Burke was the type who would be thigh-deep in abusive conduct toward patients.

"How you behave in here is how you behave on the outside," Burke told the ward. He ordered everyone to remake the beds with hospital corners and blankets stretched so tightly that coins could be bounced off them. The techs were ordered to keep ripping up beds until they were perfectly made. Then everyone would assemble in the dayroom for a marathon encounter session to discuss their poor attitudes. Burke's encounter sessions were notorious for stripping away a patient's last remnants of self-esteem. He encouraged bloodletting. "Don't let this fellow off the hook," he'd command other patients. "He's rationalizing. There's no way he'll ever see the light unless you stomp on him. We're here to help him change, not be entertained." He called the tactic "gang-tackling," and not until a rapist or child molester squirmed in tears did he seem to be satisfied.

On his first day in encounter, Geoffrey refused to say a word.

"What's the matter, King?" Burke had challenged him. "Don't you like therapy?"

"I don't like *you*," the patient impetuously replied. "If this is what passes for an advanced-treatment ward, God help us."

Now, assembled in the dayroom with the other restricted patients, he saw Burke fix him with a hateful stare.

"King, you're one of the culprits around here, dragging down everyone else with your poor attitude. This will change immediately or it is up to the disciplinary cells for you. Now, what do you have to say about that?"

Geoffrey stood up. "Mr. Burke," he said, forcing strength

227

into his voice, "I must ask to be excused for a few minutes. I have a very important letter that must be mailed to my attorney before the postal clerk goes home today."

The ward charge seemed incredulous. "Are you deaf, King? Nobody leaves this ward for any reason whatsoever."

The patient flushed. "You can't deprive me of my constitutional rights. I must mail this letter to my lawyer . . . Mr. Melvin Belli of San Francisco. This is a vital letter about my legal rights. You have no right to stop me. It's against the law and you know it."

"King, sit down and shut up," Burke replied.

"I want everyone here to witness that you are purposely keeping me from mailing a letter to charge you and many others with malpractice against me. You're trying to obstruct justice, and you can go to jail for that."

"Yeah, I'm all shook up." Burke glowered. "Sit down, or I'm sending you straight up to discipline."

To Geoffrey's amazement, the other patients began spontaneously to boo and catcall. Burke looked as surprised as everyone else. There was palpable tension in the dayroom, and several of the more excitable patients were grimacing ominously at the ward charge.

"Mr. Burke," Geoffrey called out over the noise, "there's a psychiatric technician in this hospital who will contact my lawyer immediately if I'm sent to the cells. And believe me, there's nothing you can do to me that Mr. Belli won't do to you when he gets you on that stand in court. You'll never work in this industry again."

Burke mimicked panic by gnawing at his fingernails and then dismissed Geoffrey with a disgusted shake of his head. But the patient leaped ahead.

"And you won't be the only one," he shouted. "Listen, everyone, there's going to be a real shake-up around here. I worked for Dr. Serber in the research department, and he has blown the whistle on all of them. He's filing a formal complaint against the administration, and heads will roll. Do you know why? Serber found that thousands of our hospital records have been changed by the staff to keep patients warehoused here forever. The people who did it are all going to jail. Mr. Burke knows all about it, I'm sure. He knows I'm telling the truth."

Burke was in no mood either to confirm or to deny. Instead, he turned to a psychiatric technician at his side and told him to take King's letter and mail it.

"Oh, no," the patient protested. "This goes certified mail. I've got to sign for it myself."

Again Burke and the tech conferred in whispers. "Okay, King," the ward charge finally said. "You'll need an escort to get through the sally port to the administrative wing." The tech stood to escort him, but was this a ruse to get him out and into the disciplinary cells without triggering a riot?

The technician unlocked the ward door and Geoffrey followed him into the hallway. His face was ashen.

"Are we really going to mail my letter?" he asked.

The tech surveyed him with a tight look. "What do you think we're gonna do?" he replied.

Burke unlocked the doors to his ward the next day, and his patients were awash in a surge of excitement that had engulfed the institution for the past day. Atascadero was on the front page of the state's major newspapers. Dr. Serber had carefully documented his charges that medical records on twelve hundred patients had been altered by the staff to keep them warehoused or to help the prosecution in cases where men were being held in the institution as incompetents awaiting trial. Governor Ronald Reagan was appointing a commission to investigate and clean up the mess, promising that heads would roll. Ironically, a few thoughtful staffers believed that Reagan's administration had facilitated the abuses by severely cutting back on mental-health funding and by being so hard-line against crime and criminals, encouraging a belief (perhaps misplaced) that harsh treatment of offenders would draw a blind eye in Sacramento. Clearly Atascadero had gone too far: the hallways buzzed with rumors that nearly everyone in authority—including most of the ward charges—would quickly be replaced. The patients grinned at their solemn keepers. On Burke's ward, several of them congratulated Geoffrey King, as if he had personally marched on Sacramento.

Geoffrey exhaled. The Serber publicity might help to save him from angry retaliation; he had been allowed to mail his letter to Melvin Belli, but he would feel safe only if the famous lawyer agreed to take his case and personally came to Atascadero to meet with him. He was now beyond being considered a mere troublemaker: he was an insurrectionist, a bomb-thrower, and he knew it was only a matter of time before he would be severely punished. Ward discipline and keeper authority demanded harsh retaliation. He could not be allowed to get away with his rash, belligerent outbursts. Even he realized that. He was very frightened and prayed for a quick, positive response from Belli, imagining Mr. Burke's angry frustration at the arrival of a safe-conduct pass. Yet he also could not help sensing that he was riding a crest of unaccustomed good fortune, that events were breaking his way. Thus far his instincts had proved infallible, but there was no room to falter. He was attempting a colossal scam that normally would be ignored or brutally quashed by arrogant keepers; now, vulnerable and insecure, the administration might be tempted to transfer him out—either that or break him on the rack. One mistake would be the end of him.

In the ward, the mood was angry insurrection. The patients defied Burke and again booed him when he stood up to speak at a ward meeting. The ward charge was so incensed that he again ordered the door locked only one day after it was opened. It was a tense, serious situation and Geoffrey knew who was blamed for it. Once more the patients were cut off from the rest of the institution, marched out only to meals and deprived of TV, cards and other recreation. Only the mail was allowed to be delivered (apparently it was against the law not to). Geoffrey was barely able to swallow while letters and packages were handed out.

He received a reply from Belli on the fifth working day after mailing his letter. Taking it into the john, he closed himself into a stall and tore open the envelope. The letter was from one of Belli's legal assistants. "Please be advised," he read, "that we have fully considered your letter at a recent office meeting. Unfortunately, we have concluded that we could not successfully pursue any action in your behalf. I am sincerely sorry, as I wish there was something we could do to help you."

He stuffed the letter into a back pocket and buried his face in his hands.

Managing a brave smile, he returned to the ward and sought out one of Burke's pets, a patient everyone knew was a snitch.

"My lawyer thinks the Serber business will make me rich. He wants to go for an early trial date," Geoffrey told him.

Cause and effect? Who could tell? A psychiatric technician on the night shift came for him just before lights-out and told him to pack his things.

"You're being transferred," he said.

Geoffrey began to tremble. "Where to?" he asked.

"I'm under instructions not to tell you," the tech replied, "but if you have a brain in your head, you'll go quietly and without any fuss. Now, pack up, and be quick."

He threw his belongings into a suitcase and followed the tech down the long hallway, sweating profusely, and not merely from the exertion of carrying a heavy suitcase. His legs felt leaden as they approached the corridor leading to the disciplinary cells, but they kept walking straight, down the entire quarter-mile stretch of Atascadero hallway that arrived at the ward housing the victims of the brain-fry room. The ward was in the ministrations of a rumpled, quirky old psychiatrist named A. J. Plough, rumored to be dangerously senile and known to all as "Dr. Feel Worse."

"Oh, shit," Geoffrey exclaimed at the entrance to this ward.

"Geoffrey, don't make any trouble," the escorting tech told him. "You asshole, you're going to get what you want."

It was a strange, ominous ward, divided between shock-therapy zombies and others who were minimal-security risks and apparently in full command of rationality. The most unforgettable patient was Big Ernie, a giant black man who stalked the dayroom with a handkerchief on top of his bald head, emptying ashtrays while wearing a permanent blank grin. He had endured dozens of shock sessions until it was finally discovered that Ernie's incoherent behavior was the result of a brain ravaged by syphilis. Even Big Ernie had heard about Geoffrey King's exploits. "You been a bad boy . . . mighty bad," he said, grinning at the new arrival. Indeed, most of the rational patients greeted him like a conquering hero. His multimillion-dollar malpractice suit against Atascadero was bigger news in the wards than the Serber-led investigations. He was kept isolated—no work, no participation in daily group-therapy sessions, and no hint from his new keepers about his eventual fate. Their indifference inspired paranoia: he sat alone in his room, tense and expectant. After three days of such benign neglect, he was ready to explode, and impulsively took a daring risk by asking a fellow patient to deliver a note to Ken Sprinkles. The note was brief and succinct: "I'm in the brain-fry ward. Help!" If the patient showed the note to any of the staff, he was doomed. But Geoffrey was desperate, and the patient seemed reliable. He was a former actor on TV commercials who had gone berserk on drugs and smashed the windshields of a dozen parked cars in his neighborhood. He promised to get the note to Sprinkles.

But what could Ken do? What could anyone do to help him now? Once old A. J. Plough fired the voltage . . .

They came for him on his fourth day in the new ward. He was led through connecting doors into what seemed to be a staff wing that undoubtedly housed the shock-therapy apparatus, straight to an office to confront an old man seated behind a desk. His hair was the color of virgin snow and he sat staring at the top of his desk as if in a trance. Geoffrey's heart raced; his file was open to the elderly doctor's rheumy gaze. He sat down in front of the desk, but only after several minutes of dead silence did the old man finally look up.

"What does it mean to you that a rolling stone gathers no moss?" the doctor asked.

"You're Dr. Plough, aren't you?" Geoffrey asked.

Plough nodded.

"Well, Dr. Plough, I really don't care what it means. What does it mean to you?"

Plough rubbed his nose. "Very well," he said.

"That's all." He dismissed the patient with a wave of his hand. Geoffrey knew he had blundered in antagonizing that old bastard, but his defiance was a matter of pride: at least he had not groveled, or found himself too frightened to find his voice, the way thousands of other patients probably had in coming face to face with Dr. Feel Worse and his electrical chamber of horrors. Anyway, he figured that at this point it probably made little difference what he did. He seemed fated to an appointment in the leather reclining chair and its electrodes.

Late that afternoon the ward charge, a stout, balding man named Horn, came into his room and closed the door.

"How do you feel?" Horn asked.

Geoffrey shrugged, not knowing what to say.

"Well, I have news that might cheer you up. They've approved your transfer out of here. You're going to be sent to the state hospital at Camarillo."

He had won!

Only later, in retrospect, did he realize that his risky scam—because that's exactly what it was—was probably unnecessary. In a matter of months, Atascadero would undergo a thorough housekeeping, and in the new spirit of reform, Dr. Michael Serber would be appointed by Governor Reagan as the hospital administrator. Surely one of Serber's first actions would have been to transfer out a young patient he had actually mentioned at his Sacramento news conference. Ken Sprinkles showed Geoffrey the clipping:

As an example of the way that Atascadero warehouses mental patients, Dr. Serber cited the case of a nineteen-year-old boy who killed his mother and grandmother while under the influence of LSD. "He was deranged by the drug," Serber declared, "but once the effects wore off, he was neither psychotic nor unbalanced in any way, yet he has spent two years inside Atascadero and faces three to five more years until he will be allowed release."

Geoffrey was the youngest patient in the hospital, and Ken said the staff would have moved heaven and earth to get him out, even if he had done nothing, once the scandals broke. "Serber mentioning you was your ticket out," he insisted.

Geoffrey didn't care. What mattered to him was that he had finally won a major battle in his life. The taste of victory was sweet nectar. Luck was finally an ally, and unexpected events swept him on like a fortuitous tail wind. Omens perhaps that his karma was finally in synch with the fates. Ken told him, "Geoffrey, after all you have gone through, the rest of your life will be a cakewalk." Yes! For the first time ever, Geoffrey began to believe that this could be true.

The administrative paperwork involving his transfer took forever, so that it was late summer before he was escorted to the sally-port complex for the last time, walked through the arrangement of steel doors, and emerged into the lobby of the administrative wing. He opened the glass doors and entered a station wagon parked at the curb. The car drove off, and he didn't glance back.

39

To Ken Sprinkles:

Camarillo State Hospital
August 23, 1972

Dearest friend,

Well, I'm here! After two years, five months, and sixteen days at dear Atascadero, they came for me at six this morning to tell me I could leave immediately with a deputy driving down a prisoner to L.A. or wait forty-eight more hours for the scheduled plane ride. Ken, I feel so awful not being able to say good-bye to you, but I wasn't about to wait one second longer, baby! I took the station wagon and it was so poignant sharing the ride with a young man named Michael, who traveled in chains. I felt guilty being so happy while poor Michael was in tears. He was in Trotter's Ward for six months till his mind cleared, and now he's going to stand trial for killing his wife. Ken, he murdered her under LSD! He said he freaked out on a bad acid trip and stabbed her while their little daughter watched! He loved his wife so much that he just can't bear it, and hopes they execute him for the crime. I told him it was senseless to keep tormenting himself and that he had to be objective and realize that he was still alive, still a father, still had responsibilities and things to contribute. Boy, I heard you whispering to me a dozen times: "Are you listening to yourself, pal?" Of course, I know that what's true for Michael is true for me, too. Now I know three people who killed under LSD. Michael said he met another guy at

Atascadero who killed his girlfriend, stabbing her fifty times thinking she was the devil. And to think I used to take acid as if it was a pep pill!

Ken, I never felt better and worse in my life than when that station wagon drove off with Michael and deposited me here. This hospital is fabulous! Walks, gardens, Mediterranean style, only forty minutes away from downtown L.A. Much less supervision, but the wards are not too different, except for a lot of mental retards and nervous-breakdown cases. First thing, I met my staff psychiatrist, named Dr. Milton Strawn, who read through all my charts and records from Atascadero. At first I thought: Oh, boy, here we go again—because Dr. Strawn seemed very stern and hostile. But that is just his way. Actually he is a very bright and sympathetic doctor. Ken, the first thing he said to me is that the diagnosis I received at Atascadero is "sheer poppycock." He said I obviously was not a paranoid schizophrenic and would be rediagnosed in due course. I could have kissed him except I'm not sure how they feel about fags here! Anyway, he told me that it was *extremely* unusual for them to accept patients from Atascadero and that I was *very* lucky. He said I could expect some hostility and apprehension against me from a few staff members, but to remember that their attitudes are more prejudiced against Atascadero's horrible reputation and the fact it holds dangerous, violent patients than against me personally. Then he said that his first impression of me is that I'm not legally insane by any definition, but obviously need extensive therapeutic help. He asked me how I felt about starting therapy immediately, and I told him I spent most of the summer doing nothing but waiting for the chance. He said fine, we'll get started right away. I asked him how long I'd be here, and he said he would be extremely disappointed if I was still a patient one year from now!

The only unpleasant moment was when Dr. Strawn turned me over to the psychiatric social worker (a young woman in her thirties), who refused to close her office door talking to me. I could tell she was petrified. I'm just going to have to learn to live with this kind of reaction. She won't be the first or last.

I need advice, Ken. What should I do about my dear uncle? I haven't heard from him in more than a year. Does Atascadero automatically inform him about my transfer, or should I? What do you think?

Do you know what would be perfect? If you got yourself transferred down here, too, and became my sponsor.

As ever,
Geoffrey

P.S. Do you know this poor guy Michael?

September 1, 1972

Dear King Geoffrey,

I'm going to have your letter framed to hang over my bed. I wonder what my frau would think of that move? I cheered reading it and honestly it is all so great for you that I don't have any words at all to spring at you to tell how I really feel about it. I miss my old pal. The Big A just doesn't have that many high-class loonies in storage anymore. Just the usual riffraff. Have you heard that six docs and staffers left last week, including your friends Dr. Plough and the one and only Burke the Turk? Uncle John was transferred to the administrative wing and ain't too happy. But the biggest news of all is that Dr. Serber takes over the hospital next month. Now, I can *really* live with that!

Geoff, about your uncle. Do be careful. I've known too many patients whose lives were wrecked by their families. From what you've told me, he doesn't sound like the kind of guy who will ever do much for you when you get out, but if you are not real careful, he can cause you grief. Especially he can try to block you from ever getting out. I checked and found out that Atascadero will notify him as your listed next of kin about the transfer. I think you should write to him in about a month or so. Be upbeat and tell him how good you feel, etc. Don't ever try to call him. Hearing your voice will blow him away and he'll probably freak out and think you're in a phone booth around the corner, coming to get him. Be careful, careful, careful dealing with that guy.

No, I don't know that guy Michael, but I'm not surprised. LSD really sucks, and Tim Leary should get a life sentence for promoting that dangerous poison.

No thanks on the transfer. I'm a happy masochist here.

Best,
Ken

October 8, 1972

Dear Ken,

Sorry for not having written for so long, but I have been very busy. First I want to tell you that Annette and I broke up. She waited till I was out of Atascadero before writing to me that she has found another. I know the guy from around Santa Monica and he is a real stud! Believe me! To tell you the truth, I am greatly relieved. The poor girl was going to explode from sexual frustration. Let's face it, she was a pipe dream for me, but a very wonderful one, and aside from you, there is nobody else in the world that I owe so much for saving me from the lowest moments of my life. Anyway, we are still great friends and she came up last weekend with her new boyfriend and we had a great visit.

Ken, a real miracle is happening here. I don't mean I've been cured of my neurosis. I don't really know how to explain it except that until now I never realized what stress does to a human being. I am absolutely convinced that someday they will find that stress is a major cause of cancer as well as every other serious disease. In the month since I've left Atascadero, I have become a different person. My stress level is less than half of what it was, and the result is a miracle. My thinking especially. I constantly amaze myself by my ability to think so clearly and powerfully. I really feel as if I'm thinking like a mature man, and this has nothing to do with my emotional problems or my therapy. I'm talking about lying back and thinking about life and human values and issues important to me. It's as if a light bulb was turned on inside my skull. I'm coming alive again. The best sign is I am *very, very* horny. I doubt I ever thought about sex in Atascadero, or if I did, I repressed it because it was so hopeless. But there is a *gorgeous* guy in my ward who excites me greatly. I'm letting my hair grow and I took my state clothing-allowance money and went shopping last

237

week with my sponsor and bought the tightest pair of designer jeans I could find and a pair of flamer boots with three-inch-high heels. My ward charge was not pleased! He said to me, "Is this the way you want to appear?" I told him if I didn't I would not have purchased these clothes and shoes. He said, "Well, frankly, I think it stinks!" I said, that's your problem, not mine. And boy, did I mean it! I feel very masculine-aggressive being feminine. Do you know what I mean? It is how I want to look, and if anybody freaks out, I couldn't care less.

Did I tell you I have a job working as a lifeguard in the hospital's outdoor pool? Not really much to do except keep a close eye on the retarded kids who swim before lunch every day.

In case you think this is a hotel, I should say that I am deep into psychotherapy. Dr. Strawn, quite brilliantly I think, assigned me to a woman psychiatrist, Dr. Marie Dowling, in her last year of residency here and who plans to open her practice in L.A. next year. She is *wonderful*, a tiny, almost shy woman in her late thirties (divorced, with an eleven-year-old daughter) and extremely sensitive and gentle. But she also has a fabulous mind—a real intellectual who knew me intimately the moment I sat down. I'm positive that eighty percent of successful therapy involves the ability of a shrink to be a sympathetic listener. You were terrific, and so is she. And by the way, I am amazed to hear her say so many of the same things you told me. She also thinks that our goal should be to eventually turn me around from being stuck inside my unhappy childhood so I can face a future as a responsible adult. She agrees with you that the reason I'm so stuck in there is that I have never worked out these unhappy experiences and problems. Oh, but it is so painful, Ken. I really would love to duck this entirely and just get out of here and begin living. But it must be done—suffering and all—if I'm to have a chance at happiness. And anyway, I'm not so brave about the future. I'm scared. I am all alone in this world. But with friends like you and the doctors here, I think I will make it. Do you agree?

My love to you, dear *Friend*,
Geoffrey

October 11, 1972

Dear Geoff,
    You bet your ass I agree!

Ken

October 23, 1972

Dear Uncle Ray and Aunt Nora,
    I haven't written in ages because I really wasn't sure you wanted to hear from me and I felt hesitant not knowing how you felt about my transfer to Camarillo. I am very aware that I've caused you so much pain and grief already that the last thing I want to do is cause you any more. I just want both of you to know that I love you and wish I could somehow repair the terrible damage I've done to your lives. It has taken me a long while to realize that maybe the only thing I can do is become the kind of human being that you, Gram, and Mother would be proud of. Actions speak louder than words, I know. But my hope is that by my actions I will be able to regain your trust and love.
    I am at present making excellent progress with an extremely capable psychiatrist, Dr. Marie Dowling. I am tremendously lucky that she has been assigned to my case, and I see her twice a week. I also participate in group therapy and meet with Dr. Strawn, who is in overall charge of my case, once a week to discuss my overall progress. The care here is *excellent*. I am extremely fortunate to be out of Atascadero, where I could easily have been warehoused forever.
    I have real hope for my future. I am determined to get well and live up to all my potentials. I want very much to get back to school. Being a dropout in my frosh year at high school does not make me feel proud, believe me. The librarian here is feeding me books to read: *Grapes of Wrath*, *Pickwick Papers*, *Moby Dick*. I have so much to do and catch up on. It's scary but it's also darned exciting.
    Please take care and drop me a line one of these days.

Love,
Geoffrey

October 28, 1972

Dear Geoffrey,

Thanks for your letter. We both appreciated it very much and think it made a lot of sense.

I admit being surprised at receiving word of your transfer. I know you appreciate how lucky you are. You could easily have been sent to a hard-core prison to be brutalized or even killed; you could have continued to be warehoused at Atascadero for another ten or fifteen years; instead, by whatever means, you have been given a chance to be *reborn*. In short, within a relatively brief time you will have a chance to use your God-given talents in some meaningful, self-fulfilling way.

How you use this gift of freedom will go a long way toward earning the trust and confidence of members of your family and former friends. Actions, as you say, are louder than words. What you do with your life *on your own* will make the big difference.

All the best from both of us,
Ray

Dr. Marie Dowling reminded him of a tiny woodlands creature—an alert and busy gatherer, full of kindness. She liked him, felt sorry for him, and her manner was almost coddling, although he was intimidated by her sharp intelligence, a reassuring indication of her credentials. At times he played mind games with her, anxious to impress her with his own thoughtfulness and emerging maturity. They met two times weekly in her messy basement office piled high with books and medical journals, belying her scrupulous attention to his case. She was thorough and took copious notes but never lost eye contact with him, as if her scribbling right hand functioned by some independent mechanism. At times when she thought he was being harshly judgmental with himself, she had him switch chairs and move into her seat behind her metal desk and then she read back to him some of his statements while he, acting as shrink, questioned her about them. It was a slick trick: it forced him to see "what a Nazi I can be" (his words). Her preliminary diagnosis was that he suffered from a severe depressive neurosis that she suspected might be chronic. He wasn't at all psychotic, but she worried about his recurrent suicidal ideation and his low tolerance in handling tension and stress.

Dr. Dowling's careful notes reveal both Geoffrey's progression and tense complexities during six months of psychotherapy:

"Before we start, I must know: are you afraid of me?" Geoffrey asked.

"I considered the possibility but I chose not to be."

"I tend to manipulate instead of work. I hope you call me on that. I may tend to give up."

"I don't give up."

"If you have to, beat my head against a wall. I feel this is my last chance. I'm so afraid they will send me back to Atascadero as criminally insane. So I'm tempted to be very political with you and try to seem better than I really am. But I'm eager to get well. I'm afraid of being chronic, in and out of institutions for the remainder of my life. I need to trust you. I'm willing to work hard."

"Give me a chance and I'll help you."

"I've had disappointing experiences with shrinks since childhood. I don't trust doctors. I hope you will be as depersonalized as possible. There's a lot to unload here, but I'm very fearful. So much to risk. Afraid of being disappointed, failing. Afraid of being sent back to hell."

10-3-72

"I got away with murder. Actually, I killed three people. I put my father in an early grave. Feel less guilty about that. He asked for everything he got.

"Wonder what it really was I wanted from those people. They gave me a lot more than most kids had—materially. Never clicked with my parents; never felt part of their lives. Terrible emptiness inside. Rejection and anger.

"Killed my family. Deserve gas chamber. Fact of killing impossible to deal with. Overwhelming: how could I do such a thing? Can't really grasp the outrageousness of it. I committed crime of century: double matricide. Sometimes I feel sorry for myself. I'm all alone in the world. But whose fault? I took knife and orphaned myself.

"Inherited parents' trembling fear of life. They were scared that the world would turn against them and it did. Built a fortress to protect selves, hid behind big show of power, authority, being in control of their destiny. I have same fears, same need. Truth is, my life is over. I get the shakes when I think about the day I'm released from here. What to do? Stigmatized, all alone, no money, no education, no skills really. Overwhelming. Don't think I'm being neurotic or depressed. I should feel as I do. If I felt confident and eager to go out and face life now, I really would be insane. Feel like slinking off, hiding. Anyone finds out what I did will hate me nearly as much as I hate myself. How explain it to them? Can't explain to myself. Got to make damned sure I won't kill again. How can I guarantee that?"

11-14-72

"Child—very private. No one else a part of me. Tremendous fantasy life. Cocoon—now gone. Don't like it in there. Stay too long, hard to come out. Want to feel sane. Hurts that relatives and friends afraid of me. Frighten others who know my history. They back off and think I might be violent again."

"I'm not afraid of you," Dr. Dowling replied.

"I'm afraid of *you*."

"I'm not formidable."

"You're a meek person, helpless, your office so untidy and disarranged, wonder how you made it through medical school. Hope you're not offended."

"I'm complimented by your honesty."

"You remind me of Ruth. You're sort of weak. She always had other people making decisions for her. I feel uptight with you. You're so cool and professional: I'm not used to that. Think I'm holding back with you. Feel vulnerable. Afraid of being shafted and sent back to Atascadero. My track record is I'm always shafted in the end. Always."

"You're afraid to trust me?"

"You. Anyone. Sprinkles helped me when he could, but I took matters in my own hands—lied, cheated, conned, and risked life to get out of Atascadero. Put all my cards out on the table—me against them, no one doing it for me—and I made it. I'll kill myself if I'm ever forced to go back."

"These anxieties similar to childhood?"

"Very. Remember amazement when Father had his heart attack in St. Paul. Afraid of him, but he took care of me and I thought he was gone. Felt betrayed. When parents separated, I had enormous hostility to Father. I'd fantasize killing him and mistress. If he were still alive today, I would still dream about killing him. Father didn't know how to love or share feeelings. Very lonely. He and I said very wounding things to one another. I can't defend my behavior; tore my guts out having bloody brawls with him.

"I love and hate intensely. Have to learn to live with it. Feel more comfortable hating my parents than loving them because then less guilty for things I did. Think they felt more comfortable hostile to my behavior than trying to understand causes. Feel I left all of my feelings back in childhood because I was so traumatized. I've got to recover my ability to love, to trust, to care about myself and others. I was a trusting little boy at one point. So eager to give of myself. Feel such a longing to rediscover those feelings. So hard for me to step out of my childhood, climb a wall, and jump down into adult territory. All my unfinished business is back there in the past. Maybe the answer I really want is, why do I hate with such a passion?"

1-5-73

"Realize I'm copping out, blaming parents for all that's wrong in my life. There's real evil in me. Enormous capacity for destructiveness. Created most of my problems myself. Retaliated against parents' neglect. Disrupted their home and marriage by driving a wedge into their relationship whenever possible. Knew King would blame Mother if I acted out aggressions. He was afraid of confrontations, hated them, expected her to discipline me. Couldn't face fact that his kid had serious problems. Probably I was too close to where he was living. I dramatize my illness the same way I dramatized everything to get parental attention. Their neglect distorted me: made me a flamboyant little pest capable of doing anything to be noticed. Still that way. People don't change very much. They think they do. But they don't.

"I get letters all the time from friends I met in the psychiatric hospital, telling me to keep my chin up. People who are hurting and vulnerable themselves reach out. Doctors reach out. But I'm gonna need tremendous support on the outside if I'm gonna make it— and it just isn't there. If only my family would be supportive. I understand their feelings, but it really hurts.

"I spend time with Mother every day. Just talk to her in my mind. I feel the emptiness and loss of her death. She loved me. In her own way, she cared. I wanted much, much more than she gave, but that doesn't mean she failed to give. Just before the murders, she came and begged me to sit down and talk to her. I said: 'Mother, you've had your fucking year-long sabbatical from reality, now leave me alone. I'm having mine.' And she said, 'That year off almost destroyed me. Geoffrey, don't be afraid to fail. You're still so young. You have every right to make mistakes. You're pushing your life too hard and fast.'

"I've got to let up on myself or I'll repeat the same mistakes when I get out of here. Because of my father, I rebel against authority or criticism. My big battle has always been to be free. Well, when you people set me free, I'll be as free as I've ever been in my life. The idea of being on my own so completely scares the shit out of me."

3-12-73

"Feeling low. Asked for Valium last night and felt ashamed needing a crutch. Very upset by confrontation with patient (Kantor) during group therapy. She said, 'After what you've done, you should never get out. Not everyone who took drugs killed their mother and grandmother. In fact, there are very few murders recorded by LSD users.'

"I told her 'the drug didn't kill. The drug brought to the surface feelings buried in my subconscious. LSD doesn't put anything into the vat that isn't already there. Just stirs things up. In my case, it brought anger to the boil.'

"She said, 'You were old enough to be responsible for actions. Danger of drugs is well-known; kids act as if they were caught by surprise doing violent things under drugs.' (She is a middle-aged L.A. housewife; very hostile.)

"I said, 'Reason kids take drugs is because they need a friend. They feel lonely, alienated, confused.' I said, 'You heard the expression: kid who's angry at the world?' That's who I was. Kids don't have the answers; they just know what they don't want: which is to be like their parents. Told Mrs. Kantor about my friend Vi. She went to San Francisco for weekend and OD'd in Haight-Ashbury crash pad. I went to her house to get word about her. Vi's mother threw Vi out a year or two earlier, wanted nothing more to do with her. I was very upset, unraveling myself (this was two weeks before murders), and Vi's mother looked daggers at me, as if my fault her daughter strayed from all the middle-class virtues.

"Finally, I began to cry, and I asked: 'What are we all doing to each other? Why are we this way?'

"She looked as if she wanted to slap me. 'How in hell should I know?' she said, and slammed door in my face.

"I told Mrs. Kantor it's easier to stay in jail than deal on outside with people like that. People are so trapped, ugly, frightened."

"Mrs. Kantor: 'No matter what happened to you, no license to kill. No excuse.'

"Impossible to rationally discuss, hold dialogue. A real hopelessness and existential despair thinking of having to deal with so many Mrs. Kantors in the future.

"But I refuse to lose my idealism. Believe life can be better than that. My parents never had a serious thought or discussion; neither did their friends. Get drunk, get a raise, plan a vacation. And that's it! Not enough for my generation.

"Sometimes I think when I lashed out against Mother, I lashed out as much against inhuman society we've created."

3-14-73

Dream: Fetched from ward, told he has a visitor. Enters lounge and finds Mother there. She's wrapped in silver-fox furs, looking happy and radiant.

Orderly whispers to him, "Here, you'll need this." Hands him a butcher knife. Mother beckons to him with outspread arms and happy smile. He rushes to her, overjoyed seeing her again. They embrace.

"Why, what's this?" Mother says, noticing knife clutched in his hand. He's confused, doesn't know what to say or remember why he's holding knife. Puts it down in large silver lounge ashtray.

Orderly comes running over, retrieves it, and wrapping knife

245

in wax paper, tells him, "Don't lose this. You're going to need it." Geoffrey angry. Very angry. Orderly has upset Mother. She turns away from him, adjusts furs, and rushes out of the lounge. Gone. He hears her car drive off.

Orderly tells him, "Don't worry. A woman like that always comes back." Orderly tucks knife into belt, and it is then Geoffrey recognizes him as his father.

40

I hath slain
And upon myself
I hath slain

Unto my people
I hath slain
Unto myself.

The poem was written from the bowels of depression during Geoffrey's incarceration at Atascadero, perhaps the best of his despairing, obtuse poetry that clearly revealed a troubled mind and conscience. Nevertheless, his poems represented a record of experience and he gathered them in a folder, typed them, and supplied several abstract watercolors as illustrations. He had begun dabbling in art. Four uneven months in Camarillo. His hair now reached his shoulders and he was deeply tanned from lifeguarding every day. Next to the pool was a small office used for pool chemicals and first aid. He unlocked the window and climbed inside at night to be alone, writing letters or sketching. "Privacy," he wrote to Ken Sprinkles, " is more important to me right now than freedom. I'm so tired of being watched and observed."

He also confided to Dr. Dowling that in his daydreaming about the future, his most comforting vision was seeing himself as the stay-at-home mate of a rich young businessman-stud who bought them a house at the beach and complimented Geoffrey on his gourmet meals and the spotlessness of his housekeeping. He also talked openly of finding himself a cabin up in the Sierras, surrounding himself with a few chickens and goats, and painting up there in total solitude. He was not eager to embrace the world again.

In a separate notebook he began jotting "Recipes for Living." He spent hours trying to compose his own Ten Commandments:

1. Love thyself to be able to receive love from others. To give and receive love is man's most precious gift.

2. Realistic goals lead to healthy ego. To accept myself and others (family, friends, everyone) as they really are— as I really am—is the key to my eventual happiness. Too often my idealism leads to destructiveness—my hope for what I want myself to be and others to be in the fantasy world I erect always leads to bitter disappointments. Avoid at all costs. Remember—accepting half a loaf and doing it gratefully leads to compassion and eliminates destructive tendencies in myself and others.

3. To find happiness, the ego must be controlled. Self-centeredness blocks sharing. To allow into my life someone who matters to me beyond my own self is the rarest of marvelous human relationships. I hunger to experience this gift of giving, to share, to care, to put my beloved's needs ahead of my own. The key: trust and courage. Courage, courage, and more courage.

4. Keep checking your values, buddy. Values vs. desires. What matters most to human beings is unchanged since the beginning of time. A man wants a family, good friends, to enjoy love, affection, appreciation, warmth, laughter, and be comforted in sadness and soothed in love. To live in the center of a circle of loving friends and relations is what every human being yearns for. (Paul McCartney's lyric about looking at all the lonely people.)

5. The heart vs. the mind. Be true to thine own instincts in order to . . .

That was as far as he got before showing his recipes to his

psychiatrist. Marie Dowling smiled, handing him back his spiral notebook. "You have the rest of your life to fill in the others," she told him. He doted on Dr. Dowling's every word, sometimes sending her long, flowery notes of appreciation while in an upbeat mood, or painful, depth-plumbings of six or seven felt-tip-penned pages in between sessions when he felt himself sinking like a torpedoed ocean liner. There were plenty of bad days with plenty of tears—progress came in fits and starts, only to be sabotaged by hopelessness and retreat. Yet he agreed with Marie that he was making progress and that a mature version of the old Geoffrey was being created in her untidy basement office.

He began to feel restless, as if sensing that fewer days remained for him at Camarillo than the time he had already spent. He was now living in a self-care ward, receiving minimum supervision. Dr. Strawn refused to be pinned down on a possible release date. "Just keep up the good work and you'll be out of here before you know it," he said. Strawn's specialty was counseling youthful drug addicts, and once a week Geoffrey submitted to tape-recorded interviews with the psychiatrist in conjunction with a book he was writing. One day, Strawn took him and three other young drug patients for a beach outing, and Geoffrey was moved to tears discovering that the ocean now intimidated him. Strawn noticed his hesitancy to plunge in. When Geoffrey explained that after more than two years of not seeing the Pacific, he felt overwhelmed by the breakers, it broke the ice between the brawny middle-aged shrink and the youthful patient.

But there were times when Geoffrey felt as if his psychoanalysis was a mere charade of empty words that neither penetrated nor conveyed the self within his self. Marie's notes were now as thick as the L.A. Yellow Pages, but most of this was mere blatherings, shadows rather than substance. The bedrock self was still virgin, untouched, a mysterious phantom deep inside, known to him by its continual whisperings in his ear, a soundless voice that was him, but which seemed to abandon him the moment he opened his mouth to speak. Oh, at times he knew he spoke with real insight and conviction, impressing himself as much as he did Marie, but his feelings were often impacted— powerful forces inside himself like building thunderheads that unexpectedly stormed in upon him just when the sun seemed to be shining brightly. So many of these feelings and emotions were uncharted territory, and no words could define or explain them. He mentioned his quandary to Dr. Dowling and one day she presented him with a framed motto that hung over her work desk at home:

> Thinking brings forth only thought,
> But feeling is with living fraught.

The author was the German poet Goethe, whom he had never heard of, but then, there was so much he didn't know. Once, his friend Frank Estes frowned at him and said, "It makes me sad to think that you young barbarians will probably go to your graves without hearing a Beethoven symphony or reading a Shakespearean sonnet. Right now, all of you are so colorful and intense and charming, but when you get older, you'll be as interesting to talk to as a box boy at Safeway." No question, he was raw, unformed, uneducated, with so much to catch up on when he got out.

Frank Estes finally came up for a visit one weekend and took him to lunch. They got tipsy on wine and Frank told him he knew someone who was looking for a decorator for luxury homes he was constructing in Bermuda. If Geoffrey would be released within the next three or four months, the builder might be maneuvered into waiting. Geoffrey was ecstatic and told everyone at the hospital about the new job awaiting him. When he told Dr. Strawn, the psychiatrist startled him by suggesting that it was perhaps time for his uncle to come to Camarillo and pay a visit.

"He's not a friend." Geoffrey scowled. "I don't want him nosing around in my life."

"He must be dealt with," Dr. Strawn insisted. "When the time comes, I'll do the dealing and you'll sit and keep your mouth shut."

"Does this mean you're getting ready to release me?" he asked the psychiatrist.

"How do you feel about that possibility?"

"Well, I'm trying to fit together all the pieces. I want to leave here knowing who I am and what I'm all about."

Strawn chuckled. "You're twenty-one," he said. "That exercise will carry you into your thirties. By then you may begin to make some sense out of it all."

Dear Mr. Lowe,
Your nephew, Geoffrey King, is now a self-care patient at this state hospital and has made significant progress in our treatment program over the past half-year. The staff is pleased with his determination and cooperation in our therapy programs. Geoffrey has worked hard and well with his doctors and at this stage in his treatment I think you might find it beneficial to meet with me, at your convenience, to discuss his case and his future more throughly. As the psychiatrist in overall charge of his case and future disposition, I am most eager to receive the benefit of your thoughts and feelings, as well as those of other family members. Hopefully, such a meeting will help those of us responsible for Geoffrey's welfare to weigh the external factors involved in his eventual release and rehabilitation into society.
Sincerely,
Milton Strawn, M.D.

Dear Geoff,
What fabulous news! If your friend Dr. Strawn thinks the best route for you is to file a writ of habeas corpus, I would not second-guess him. As he explained to you, and I figure you've given me an accurate account in your letter, Camarillo would welcome having you file a writ and getting out that way because it takes the staff off the hook. All they have to do is support your writ rather than biting the bullet and recommending your release themselves. Because of your history and having been in Big A, I'm sure you can get out faster on the writ than waiting around for them to get up courage. I asked around and found out the following about writs: you file with the court in Camarillo. The court appoints a public defender for you. The writ is then sent directly to the D.A. who prosecuted your case. He confers with your trial judge, assuming the guy is still on the bench. They have exactly two weeks to comment

back to Camarillo court. They could request your appeal be denied and that you be sent back to the original sentencing court for final disposition. If they have no objection, they simply don't reply. And on the fifteenth day, or after, your writ goes to the court and you appear before the judge in a hearing. I assume your shrinks will vouch for you. The judge will then decide (for sure, favorably) and issue an order freeing you. As simple and terrific as that, babe.

As for your uncle coming up, remember what I once told you about him—he can't help, but he sure can hurt. Do what your doctor tells you and keep quiet, act nice, and smile a lot. You don't want to get the old boy pissed at this point. If he raises hell about your release, it could *really* complicate your life. So go along, count to ten or a thousand if necessary, and *be a good boy* around him.

Promise you'll call collect anytime if you need help or advice or anything. I'm pulling for you, baby. Seems to me you're finally on your way, getting the breaks you deserve.

Best,
Ken

41

Ray Lowe had aged dramatically, his nephew thought, recalling that the last time he had seen his uncle was during a brief visit early in his incarceration at Atascadero. Lowe smiled and offered his hand, then stepped aside while his wife embraced her nephew. "Oh, Geoffrey," Nora said, "you look just fine." They all sat down in Dr. Strawn's office and the psychiatrist introduced them to Mrs. Wurst, the psychiatric social worker assigned to Geoffrey's case, who, from the beginning, refused to deal with him unless the office door was open. The patient was perturbed, wondering why Marie Dowling wasn't present, and only as the meeting progressed did he realize that Strawn was the better personality to confront his uncle, certainly physically superior to a tiny, soft-voiced psychiatrist in her final year of residency. Dr. Strawn laid out Geoffrey's case brilliantly, the patient thought.

"Your nephew," he said, "was not psychotic when he arrived here and is certainly not psychotic now." He spoke at length about the patient's progress, noting that he had been crippled by guilt and remorse for the tragedy and was now in the process of finding self-worth and discovering realistic goals. "Geoffrey has realized that the past cannot be undone and is learning to live with terrible memories," Strawn insisted. "His great strength is his determination to get well—he's one of the more highly motivated patients here. He's not on any medications and, I must say, he's dealt very bravely with bouts of depression. He's been through hell and has emerged much stronger from the ordeal. He's a different Geoffrey than the boy you knew. He's rapidly becoming a man."

Ray Lowe listened intently, occasionally cocking a cynical eyebrow, but said nothing. Dr. Strawn spoke for several minutes before turning the meeting over to Mrs. Wurst, who explained that the hospital always was concerned about the kind of family support awaiting a patient discharged, particularly so in Geoffrey's case. "Would you, for example, Mr. Lowe, consider the possibility of having your nephew move in with you for a time? Family emotional support is the best antidote against the rough spots surrounding adjustment to a normal life again."

A sardonic smile spread across Lowe's careworn face.

"Assuming," he replied, "and at this point it is a very major assumption, that Geoffrey is no longer a threat to himself or to others . . . assuming for the moment that that is so . . . I don't think that's possible. We have no room. And frankly, his presence in our home would upset most of our friends and relations, not out of vitriol, understand, but out of fear for their safety. Which goes right back to my original point: what proof can you offer that my nephew is no longer a threat?"

Dr Strawn replied, "There are no guarantees in this business, of course. But it is our judgment that in the absence of LSD, which induced his violence and psychosis, Geoffrey poses no threat to anyone."

"Now, Doctor, whose judgment are you speaking of?" Lowe asked, his expression contemptuous.

"My judgment. The judgment of other colleagues who have examined him and dealt with him professionally."

Geoffrey's uncle nodded. "That's what I thought," he muttered, then shifted in his chair and recrossed his legs. "Well, I'm only a layman, and for all I know, you may be right. But this boy wasn't sent to Atascadero because he stole a trunk or was rowdy in the classroom. He killed two innocent people, and I want proof he won't do it again."

Dr. Strawn shook his head. "Mr. Lowe, you're an obviously intelligent man—"

"Oh, yes," Lowe interrupted, "I'm intelligent. I know my nephew far too well. I know he can charm the birds off the trees to get his way. I know that for a fact. I have a feeling he may have conned you a bit. I remind you of the terrible things he's done: he wiped out his family and destroyed the lives of the rest of us, and now here you are, a doctor in a state hospital, telling me he is no longer a threat. I wouldn't accept that verdict from Sigmund Freud."

"How may we satisfy you on this score, Mr. Lowe?" Strawn asked smoothly, without the slightest note of irritation in his voice.

"Only one way. I want to hear from a panel of four to six psychiatrists, all of them experts in criminal behavior. Now, if each of these experts examined him thoroughly and reached a unanimous conclusion . . . I'd accept that. I won't accept less. It seems to me that those who stand in danger of this release deserve consideration and protection from the system and the courts."

"Unfortunately, Mr. Lowe, there is no such machinery," Strawn stated.

"I'm not so sure," Lowe said. "I'll look into it, believe me. I must say I'm shocked, Doctor. I think you are moving much too quickly here. My nephew has been a patient all of six months. He claims not to have received any treatment at all at Atascadero. Considering that boy's problems, six months is a drop in the bucket."

"Oh, we don't claim he's cured of all that ails him," Strawn replied. "Geoffrey would benefit from years of treatment. The fundamental point is not whether he's manipulative or a con artist or whether he needs many years on the couch . . . but whether he still needs to be hospitalized. Our judgment is that

253

he has made progress sufficient to warrant consideration of release."

"Well"—Ray Lowe shrugged—"that's your opinion. I don't buy."

Geoffrey could no longer contain himself. "What do you know about it, Uncle Ray? It would be different if you showed any interest at all. You could've come up anytime and sat in with me in encounter sessions and seen for yourself how I was doing. If you're upset now, that's just—"

"Geoffrey, please hush," Dr. Strawn said, frowning severely.

"Doesn't matter." Lowe stood up. "I've said my piece. You people have had the wool pulled over your eyes. That's clear. I'm going on record right now and in front of witnesses: if Geoffrey ever shows up on my doorstep without an invitation, I will immediately call the police and have him arrested for trespass. That's all."

And he huffed out the door. Geoffrey walked with his aunt down the hallway to the parking lot. "Darling," she sighed, "what can I say? Ray is very hostile these days. Not only toward you, but everything. Life has chewed him up. I think he'll come around, but it won't be anytime soon. Try to be patient and understanding with him, Geoffrey. He doesn't mean to do you any harm, honestly."

Her nephew flashed a small smile. "You sound just like Mother making excuses for Dad."

Nora Lowe shrugged. "Well," she said, "people who are trapped sometimes deserve excuses. Don't they, dear?"

The meeting with his uncle enraged Geoffrey, who asked Dr. Strawn about his uncle's insistence on a psychiatric panel. The doctor laughed and said, "He'd probably be stuck with six different opinions. Mental illness isn't as simple as a gall bladder, you know. We react to our patients more subjectively than we'd ever dare admit to the lay public or sometimes to ourselves." But he clapped Geoffrey on the back and told him not to worry. "You're not a security risk to him or anyone else." Because of his uncle's hostility, Strawn felt they should proceed quickly in filing a writ of habeas corpus and "get you out of here before he can stir up the dust back in L.A."

During a group-encounter session in the ward, one of the patients tearfully remarked that "being a schizo is forever," and her words slapped hard because Geoffrey knew the same could be said about a murderer. He was doomed to carry the horrible weight of that baggage through his life, struggling to hide it, terrified of its discovery in the hall closet where skeletons were kept. People would leap out of reach of his leprous touch. He had already concocted an explanation for remote acquaintances about where he had been for the past three years. "In Paris," he'd say, "working for an antique dealer." In moments of gloomy contemplation he saw only isolation and alienation for all the years ahead, and sagged dispiritedly, realizing how hopeless was his dream for a fresh start. Broke. Friendless. "But remember," Marie told him, "all of your destructiveness has not defeated you. You are a remarkable survivor, Geoffrey. Never forget that fact." Yes, but a survivor to do what? To hide and lie and squirm with guilt for the rest of his life?

"Do you have any money?" Dr. Strawn asked him. "Any family money? If so, I'd like to have it on the record when we go to court. A judge might feel different about sending a young man with no family support back into the world if he had a nest egg at least."

Geoffrey laughed bitterly. But he thought that the proceeds from the furnishings in the Palos Verdes duplex might have netted a considerable sum. "We had several valuable paintings and very expensive silver." He also dimly recalled that his mother had made a modest investment in a mutual fund.

"Can I still collect?" he wondered.

Correspondence between the hospital administrator and Nick Hopps indicated that he could collect an estimated fifteen thousand dollars, mostly in mutual-fund stocks from Ruth King's modest trust fund for her son.

A legal brief, prepared by a young Los Angeles attorney hired by Ruth to help reclaim some of Bob King's lapsed insurance policies, indicated that since Geoffrey was acquitted of his crime by reason of insanity, he could claim his portion of the estate if a court should find him to be legally sane. In the midst of his correspondence, Geoffrey received an unexpected letter from his family's lawyer, Nick Hopps:

255

Dear Geoff,

The last few years have produced great amounts of pain, anguish, frustration, and unhappiness in all directions. You are going to have all you can do to put your head back where it belongs and keep it glued there. I hope that you do not permit yourself to be infected by a cancerous bitterness. Decide what your position is from the standpoint of all the considerations of the last few years. Do not let anyone else influence your decision as to what you may want to do. Then, Geoff, go out and do it. You can.

Nick

MR. FRANK ESTES
SANTA MONICA, CA.
WRIT GOING FORWARD. RECEIVING SUBSTANTIAL MONEY FROM FAMILY INHERITANCE. PLAN TO STAY WITH YOU AFTER RELEASE TILL FIND OWN PLACE. WILL KEEP YOU POSTED BUT PLAN WILD NIGHT WHEN SEE YOU AGAIN. WILL HANDLE EVERYTHING. YOU JUST HANDLE SICK LIVER.

GEOFFREY

Dr. Strawn was annoyed. Several colleagues told him privately that they opposed the hospital's sanction of a writ for Geoffrey King at this time. They promised to remain silent when the issue was raised at the weekly administrative staff meeting, but they urged him to reconsider the matter. Geoffrey's ability to handle stress was suspect. He had scored dismally taking a battery of psychological tests, a worrisome indication of this patient's wilting under pressure. Even worse, he was in and out of the infirmary for treatment of tachycardia, his heart racing at two hundred beats a minute—anxiety attacks in anticipation of his sanity hearing. He now required mood elevators and antianxiety medication.

"How would he react if he was pushed into a corner and thought himself in a trapped, desperate situation?" Strawn was asked.

"Milt, if his offense wasn't so serious, I'd be inclined to support you on this. But this is a case where we should err on the side of caution—don't you think? A few more months of therapy wouldn't hurt at all."

But Strawn was adamant. "He should have been on an outpatient basis here after his first six weeks . . . not six months. He's ready to leave."

Marie Dowling supported his view, and no one knew the patient better. Strawn was Marie's supervisor and mentor and credited her with a brilliant performance in handling a suspicious, skittish, hostile, quixotic young patient, establishing with him a degree of rapport and trust that Strawn had never thought possible. Monitoring her work closely, Strawn at first suspected that Geoffrey's manipulativeness had diminished Marie's effectiveness by appealing to her maternal, sympathetic instincts, so that she was pampering and overprotective. But she proved to be a tough-minded woman who somehow managed to balance a soothing sympathy with a disciplined objectivity. Marie was convinced that Geoffrey was ready for release.

On March 2, 1973, Strawn obtained administrative approval for Geoffrey King to file his writ of habeas corpus. A panel of three psychiatrists and administrators signed a statement supporting the patient's action. The hospital administration concurred: Geoffrey was the first and last Atascadero transferee they would ever accept. He was under their care because of a loophole in the hospital regulations that had been immediately changed. Atascadero had never before transferred a patient to a minimum-security hospital, and Camarillo had been caught unaware.

Years later, Raymond Lowe would admit he panicked at the idea of his nephew's release. He called Judge Tom Hemmings, who was in the process of retiring from the bench, but the old family friend refused to get involved. "Justice is being done in this case, Ray, and I'm staying out of it." Lowe wrote to Judge Herman Kelso, the trial judge, but received no reply. He tried to make an appointment to meet personally with the judge, but the clerk dispatched him almost rudely.

"I was so frustrated, I just sat and cried," Lowe confessed. "I felt they were making a terrible blunder releasing that kid so soon."

Geoffrey King seemed unusually quiet seated with a lawyer from the public defender's office. He hesitated with a pen in his hand and then quickly signed his name to a legal document, scrawling it so that his signature was almost illegible. The document was an application for a writ. It read: "I was transferred to Camarillo State Hospital from Atascadero State Hospital on August 23, 1972, after having been committed to Atascadero as a 1026 Penal Code from Los Angeles County. I was found Not Guilty by Reason of Insanity for the deaths of my mother and grandmother. I hereby request a hearing to determine my present sanity in this County of Ventura, California."

The document was dated March 27, 1973.

Geoffrey cried in Marie's office. "You have so much faith in me, and I'm so scared I'm going to let you down. I'll never make it outside—never. Oh, Marie, I'll be so lost out there. I'm afraid of what I might do." She tried to be reassuring by stating the obvious. "You have every right to feel scared; it shows you're being realistic." He knew that was so, but he couldn't eat or sleep. Yet, as days passed, he seemed to rally in spurts. His ward sponsor took him on shopping trips to downtown Camarillo, and watched with wry bemusement as the patient zipped through the clothing racks in search of "a spring wardrobe." At night, though, he complained about his heart and his nerves and demanded tranquilizers.

"Geoffrey," Marie finally told him, "I'll be leaving here at the end of May and opening an office in L.A. Meanwhile, if you need help, I'm only a phone call away." These words seemed to calm him somewhat.

The Superior Court in Camarillo forwarded his written application to the Los Angeles district attorney's office on April 2. April 16 was circled on Dr. Strawn's desk calendar, the deadline for the D.A. to contest the writ request.

At the end of business on April 16, the public defender phoned Dr. Strawn to inform him that no reply had been received from the Los Angeles district attorney's office. "We are clear for a court hearing," he said. The attorney called the following day to report that a hearing was scheduled the very next day—April 18.

258

Dear Marie,

I'm sitting in bed writing to you at two in the morning on what I hope willl be the last night I will ever spend in a psychiatric hospital. There's so much I want to say to you, Marie, but I don't know where to begin. I'm just numb, maybe because I'm on Librium, but my mind feels paralyzed, which is just as well, because I'm trying not to think about tomorrow. Marie, I owe you my life. If you do nothing more than what you have already done for me, your career as a great psychiatrist will already be fulfilled. I am the most fortunate human being alive to have had you as my doctor. Your compassion, understanding, patience, and kindness pulled me through a terrible ordeal and brought me to the point where I can finally hope to start a new life and succeed on my own.

Marie, you know how frightened I am of all that lies ahead. But I want you to know that deep in my heart I know I will be the kind of person I am capable of becoming—a mature human being who has much to offer humanity. I will not be defeated by the tragedies of my life. I owe to myself, and to my mother and grandmother as well, the fulfillment of all my potentials. I am a creative person. I am a loving person. I am a generous person. You have shown me these positive attributes that will carry me over the obstacles that are certain to confront me in the future.

I'm sure I will have bad moments. We both know that. You may receive late-night phone calls from me. But, Marie, no matter what happens in the future, I want you to know how much I love you and how appreciative I am of your warm friendship. Just know, Marie, that I will never stop trying and never give up hoping that my life will justify your belief in me.

Thank you, Marie. That is all I can say.

My love always,
Geoffrey

42

He stood in the driveway wearing sedate gray slacks, a blue shirt open at the throat, and dark loafers, his cold, clammy hands stuffed into his back pockets, watching Dr. Strawn berate two Ventura County sheriff's deputies who had arrived to transport him in a prisoner's van. "I'm sorry, Dr. Strawn, but it's the law," the senior deputy replied. Geoffrey also had to be handcuffed while en route to the court hearing. "Outrageous," Strawn insisted, "to treat a patient in this manner." But to the deputies, he was merely another murderer with a court date. They helped him into the back of the van, closed the door, and locked it. Dr. Strawn drove behind them in his own car, and by the time he parked and entered the hearing room, Geoffrey was already seated at the defense table with his public defender at his side. Across the aisle, a young prosecutor was studying some legal documents. There were no spectators and no witnesses scheduled other than Milton Strawn. The elderly judge entered and everyone rose. Writs were unheard of at Camarillo—it wasn't that kind of institution—and the judge frankly stated his confusion. "I am not sure as to the burden of going forward with evidence," he admitted, and turned to the prosecutor. "Mr. Lyle, would you care to assume that burden?" The prosecutor nodded. "Yes, your Honor, it is properly with the patient and I am ready. I call Dr. Strawn and ask to have him sworn."

Strawn testified briefly and stated his opinion that Geoffrey King was now in full possession of his mental faculties and no longer posed a danger to himself or others. Under questioning, he declared this to be his own professional opinion as well as the opinion of a panel of physicians, psychologists, and doctors who rendered their judgment before the patient filed his writ to the court.

The judge interrupted. "It was the opinion of all of them that the patient had recovered his sanity to the extent he is no longer a danger to himself and others?"

"Yes, your Honor," Strawn replied. "It was a unanimous opinion."

There were no further questions.

The judge seemed to hesitate, and turned again to the prosecutor. "What exactly would be the formal order of the court?"

The prosecutor said, "Your Honor, the order of the court as outlined in the Superior Court bench book is that—I will quote it: 'If your finding is that the defendant's sanity has been restored, you must order his release.' So, I would ask the court to make an order forthwith that he be released."

The judge nodded. "I do find within the meaning of the law as expressed in Section 1026a that the sanity of the petitioner has been restored and his immediate release is ordered."

Geoffrey and the psychiatrist joyfully embraced. "I need to borrow a dime," Geoffrey said, and dashed to a phone in the corridor. Strawn stood near the booth watching him laughing and bouncing up and down in excitement. When he left the booth, there were tears in his eyes. He handed back the dime. "That was my friend Ken Sprinkles. He made me promise to call collect the moment this was over."

Dr. Strawn drove him back to the hospital. They were both too emotional to say much. Geoffrey was going to stay with Frank Estes in Santa Monica until he collected his inheritance money and could find his own place. "I think I'd like to take a small trip, maybe to Mexico, and rest for a while," he said. Strawn nodded. "Sounds like a good idea. If you need me or Marie, we're right here. Just remember that." They pulled up to Geoffrey's ward, where an enormous gray Mercedes 600 limousine was parked. Strawn gaped. "Looks like we've admitted some sultan," he observed, but the former patient in the passenger's seat began to chuckle.

"Now, Dr. Strawn, don't you know Geoffrey by now? You didn't think I'd leave here by *bus*, did you?"

By this time next week, he could be in Mexico or the Bahamas or Tahiti . . . maybe on a deserted tropical beach. Who knows? He was free to go anywhere and do anything. At this very moment, his aunt and uncle were probably having lunch, and if he wanted to, he could drive directly to their apartment. That would be the last thing he wanted, but the point was, he could do it. *He was free!*

He had dreams, barely formed, dreams of splendor and wealth. He might well become a caricature of his late father—a more flamboyant, exotic creature yet. "You don't change that much," he told himself. "I'm still who I was up on Sunset Plaza. Still infatuated with beautiful things." But of course, he was different, too.

People had reached out for him in the dark and touched his life, and he had touched theirs: Ken, Marie, Dr. Strawn. They had held him up from drowning and saved him. He felt love for them and he knew that Ken and Marie loved him, too. But they didn't really know him. How could they? He didn't know himself. Three years under the closest observation, and he had shown them only bits and pieces of what he wanted them to see. He was a mystery of expectations, hungers, wants, and needs. But they would come, the answers. As he lived, the questions would answer themselves. "You are what you live."

At this moment, he felt resurrected, a living miracle. He would celebrate this miracle for the remainder of this day. . . far into the night.

The enormous Mercedes drew a curious crowd. Patients peered out windows, speculating to whom it belonged. The uniformed chauffeur smiled and tipped his visored cap as Geoffrey approached. "Mr. King, it's a pleasure to see you again." His name was John, a ruddy middle-aged man who had driven the late Robert Luther King on dozens of occasions during the Rexall years. He was now Hugh Hefner's personal chauffeur and this was the *Playboy* owner's personal limousine. Geoffrey called the Playboy limousine service and insisted on a Mercedes 600 to fetch him, the largest in the fleet. The only one available was Hefner's, who was out of town; since John knew Geoffrey's father he had volunteered to take the job.

John followed Geoffrey inside and emerged carrying accumulated luggage and belongings, then waited while the now former patient changed his clothes. "I think we are ready." Geoffrey smiled, emerging. John opened the back door.

Marie Dowling had a patient and was not on hand to say good-bye. But nearly everyone else at Camarillo State Hospital seemed to be peering out windows or ogling in doorways as the stately Mercedes swung toward the front gate. There was a stocked bar in the backseat and a color television set. One flick of a switch rolled open a sunroof.

Geoffrey stood up, holding a Coke and bourbon, and pushed his head through the sunroof, hoisting his drink aloft in a final toast of farewell. . . .

Epilogue

Geoffrey's old friends welcomed him warmly and seemed as relieved as he was that he was finally out. But to do what? He had no idea, and planned to take his time deciding. Although he was a high-school dropout with limited finances, he knew that the central issue confronting him was guilt. Once he allowed himself to put the tragedy behind him, the future would link into place and largely decide itself. First, he had to feel worthy of achieving happiness and success. "I was acquitted of my crime," he told Frank Estes, "but somehow I'm going to have to acquit myself."

Skip Harte had moved to London. Frank Estes would soon be relocating in Hawaii. The wild sixties were definitely over and after a decade-long binge, Geoffrey's circle had sobered and were seeking a place at the middle-class trough. Hard drugs were out; white wine was in. There was no one around to offer any clear notion of how to put together a coherent life. "Just do it, Geoffrey," Estes advised him. "Get yourself a job and a lover and you'll be on your way."

Geoffrey rented a small, tidy apartment, but soon the isolation got to him. He didn't seem to belong—his remaining friends were preoccupied with their own lives and careers. At night he wandered the streets hoping to meet someone special who might change his life by sharing it. He always returned home alone. His dreams were terrible, so bad that he forced himself to stay awake. Yet he also prayed for sleep as a release from his tensions and depression.

Marie Dowling, now in private practice, often found him slumped in a waiting-room chair looking pale and drawn. He confessed to her that he was drinking heavily.

Marie urged patience. "You're going through a difficult period of adjustment. Hold on and give yourself a chance," she said. She suggested he take a job—anything, even working at a car wash—to get out of the house and take his mind off himself.

Former prisoners or mental patients seldom lack for mail. He spent a lot of time writing letters to friends still incarcerated or, like himself, recently released. Only these friends could fully appreciate his suffering. To one of them he addressed a long bitter letter. "There are those in my family circle who resent that I'm still alive and expect to read about me any day. I'm sick and tired of being judged only for the harm I might do myself or to others. The pressure I feel trying to prove myself is tearing me apart." He posted the letter only a few days short of his first anniversary on his own. His correspondent, a former schoolteacher whom he had met at Camarillo, appeared soon thereafter at his door. "Pack your bags," she commanded. "You're in no shape to be alone." Her name was Margo Ritter. She had been committed to Camarillo for attempting suicide following a nasty divorce, and what touched Geoffrey most was that Margo's new husband helped to carry his bags down to the car and patted his back reassuringly. They put him up in a small guest room built over the garage, where he had privacy and could come and go as he pleased.

Being far from Los Angeles and finally being part of a family life triggered a tonic effect that was immediate. Within days Geoffrey began to smile. He took a job working in a small antique shop in the local shopping mall. One day a customer asked his advice about a living room she was redecorating and Geoffrey volunteered to assist her. Soon his phone was ringing with others seeking his help. His love for this work was unabated, and taking a gamble, he quit his job and had business cards printed. Within a few months he opened a small office. Several clients became social friends, inviting him to dinner parties, where his circle of acquaintances grew. The style and pace of his new surroundings were distinctly slower and more relaxed than in L.A. He felt productive, although happiness and a real sense of belonging somewhere continued to elude him.

Only one or two close friends in town knew about his past. The scars on his chest were now barely noticeable, but the emotional scars remained vivid. He was more stable, able to function, but his ability to withstand stress and tension were suspect. On a bad day his hands shook and he had to get out from where he was and head for the hills. He had still not known contentment. "I've plenty of lovers," he told a friend. "But I've never been in love." His compensation was his work—twelve to fourteen hours a day. For a brief moment he regretted that his father wasn't alive to see him seated behind the mahogany desk. He hired a bookkeeper to post his bills.

On the eve of his twenty-eighth birthday, Geoffrey took a long and leisurely vacation in Mexico, and returned home tanned and smiling, accompanied by a handsome man a few years younger. They lived together for more than a year, the happiest period of Geoffrey's life. When it ended, Geoffrey fell hard. He needed to get away, and borrowed the keys to a friend's summer cottage in the high mountains. It was late September when Geoffrey drove off for a few days. He was still gone when the first autumn blizzards began to howl at the higher elevations.

Wrapping himself in blankets, he huddled in front of a stone fireplace. The snow blew through the chinks of the flimsy wooden door. He had only to remove his clothes and stumble outside into the subzero cold to end it all—and he could argue more reasons for doing it than not. By now he realized there would be no miracle cure for his myriad problems—that progress would be measured in painful fits and starts, probably for the remainder of his life. There was nothing more psychiatrists could do for him: squeezed between guilt and gnawing loneliness, he was grinding himself into a circular trench. Still, he hadn't hurt anyone and no longer worried about any homicidal tendencies, and he had proved himself to be a keen businessman. Until now he had demonstrated admirable fortitude facing his private ordeals. But he was almost drained of stamina—a mystery to himself, a stranger he would never understand.

One night he waded into snowdrifts to call Dr. Dowling from

a pay phone. He told her he was at the end of his rope and asked her to get him into a good private hospital. They talked for a long time. His psychiatrist hinted at what he already knew: another hospital stay was a crutch that would cure or solve nothing. "Why don't you try writing a letter to yourself?" Marie suggested. "See if you can put your thoughts and feelings into perspective." The idea was strangely appealing; there was so much he needed to learn about himself and the world. Maybe with pencil in hand he could compose his thoughts into fresh insights.

Much of what he managed to write, he discarded, but a few strong convictions emerged: the acceptance he sought from his estranged family was hopeless; he never would have made it this far if it weren't for the loyalty of a few friends who stuck with him; and he had trapped himself inside an unhappy child-hood. "It's time to put the past to rest and get on with my life," he said to himself.

He was ready to come down from the mountain.

On October 10, 1981, Geoffrey King celebrated his birthday with a few close friends. Eight years of freedom had added thirty-five pounds, mostly in his chest and shoulders, to what was once a spare and sinewy frame. Shorter than his father by several inches, he appeared strapping rather than physically imposing, a fleshy maturity broadening his features below a receding hairline. He had moved since his mountain pilgrimage, made a fresh start, and held a good job. His friends said they had never seen him appear more confident or in better spirits. Geoffrey was still uniquely Geoffrey, by turns a delightful, warmhearted companion and an outspoken pain in the ass—startling friends with unexpected impulsiveness or intuitive prescience. He had emerged from his mountain ordeal with an expanded awareness of himself and his family. "I feel compassion for myself and for them," he said, "where previously there was only angry recrimination." Friends who know him best agree that he works too hard, needs more exercise, is constantly thwarted by an unbalanced budget, and is comically insistent on crash diets. On reaching thirty, Geoffrey had begun to resemble the rest of us.